CHARLES WESLEY
MAN WITH THE
DANCING HEART

CHARLES WESLEY
MAN WITH THE DANCING HEART

T. CRICHTON MITCHELL

Beacon Hill Press of Kansas City
Kansas City, Missouri

Copyright 1994
By Beacon Hill Press of Kansas City

ISBN 083-411-4496

Printed in the
United States of America

Cover Design: Crandall Vail

10   9   8   7   6   5   4   3   2

For Elizabeth

Companion and sweetheart of my youth
Companion and coworker in my calling
Wife, and mother of our children
Spouse of 53 years
Fellow laborer in the gospel of God
Companion of my senior years

> She was called to commitment to Christ with me many years ago and has patiently borne the burdens and shared the blessings of the highest and most satisfying calling in the world, that of being coworkers together with God.

> *Till all the seas gang dry my dear,*
> *An' rocks melt wi' the sun:*
> *And I will love you still my dear*
> *'Til travelling days are done.*

Contents

FOREWORD

There is more here than first meets the eye. Beneath the surface of a biography of a man whose name is familiar, perhaps only from headings in hymnals, are layers and layers of depth and subtlety.

Charles Wesley lived in a century of religious awakening. He was a principal leader of that awakening and at the same time its chronicler and its hymnist. He was a man of the 18th century, but he brought to it, and to us, all the Christian centuries. He drew on his massive knowledge of the Old and New Testament Scriptures. He could read them in their own languages, and he quoted them almost constantly and spontaneously in the stately words of the King James Version. But he was more than a "restorationist," jumping from Scripture to his own century as if nothing had intervened. He knew Christian history. His Christian identity was clearly that of one who stood in the historic stream of faith, with its accumulated wisdom, its confessions of faith, and its deeply rooted forms of worship. More particularly, he was an informed, self-consciously loyal follower of the English Reformation.

He was a vastly complex person, embodying the tension between the free spirit of the Evangelical Revival and the liturgical traditions of the English church. To the free spirit he brought biblical and theological order. To the liturgical tradition he brought what this biography calls a "dancing heart."

For the reader, the biography of such a man is an education, a true "instruction in faith" (to use a term from John Calvin, whom Charles Wesley did not always appreciate). The gospel is taught in this book.

There is yet another layer, the author of this book himself. Dr. T. Crichton Mitchell has spent a lifetime with his Christian brother Charles Wesley. He, too, lives and breathes Scripture. Charles Wesley's life and hymns are for Mitchell a prime expression of their common love for Christ and Scripture. Mitchell's love for Wesley is not uncritical adulation, for he knows Wesley well enough to make judgments that are critical as well as affectionate. In this complexity of layers, with the counterpoint of past and present, the reader is invited to join all who love Jesus Christ with singing hearts.

—CARL BANGS
Professor Emeritus of Historical Theology
Saint Paul School of Theology
Kansas City

INTRODUCTION

"Charles Wesley, Methodist hymn writer (1707-88)" is how the books introduce him. But Charles Wesley was more than a Methodist, and he did much more than write hymns.

Charles Wesley was the Methodist music man, the youngest of the most remarkable trio of blood brothers in Christian history, and the younger of the most famous and revolutionary pair of siblings in the history of Christian evangelism.

It seems that many writers believe Charles Wesley to have been predestined to remain under the shadow of his famous brother John both in life and in death. It is part of the objective of this book to deny and to correct this approach to one of the formative figures in the history of the modern church. The writer desires to coax Charles out from that shadow insofar as the records allow.

Probably Charles must blame himself for such a state of affairs. Had he been half as diligent as John in keeping a journal, preserving his letters, and exposing his personal and domestic life, the shadow would not have been so heavy.

The life and thought of John Wesley is preserved for us in scores of volumes; it is analyzed and assessed and applied in scores more; and it is presented romantically, critically, and affectionately, in many, many biographies. As Frank Baker says, "The main reason for the neglect of Charles Wesley is, of course, John Wesley"[1]; and yet the history of Christianity, although embracing the records of many pairs of blood brothers, knows of no other partnership like that of John and Charles Wesley, the sons of an obscure Church of England pastor. They are absolutely unique. This the elder brother John knew to be so. He once remarked to Charles that no two men in Europe were doing a similar work. Maldwyn Edwards writes:

> But in saying so, he was being unduly modest both in reference to geography and time. In all the history of the church there is not even a remote parallel to the story of what these two brothers accomplished for the kingdom of God, sustaining each other by invincible affection, providing a foil for each other, and by their gifts each supplementing what the other could do.[2]

John had a flair for scribbling. He jotted down descriptions, impressions, assessments, actions, reactions, and analyses of people, places, and events; he recorded, often in his own brand of shorthand, his goings, doings, and feelings; and he did it constantly and conscientiously for half a century (1735-84). The result is a masterpiece conglomeration of memories, observation, book digests, reviews, editorials, prefaces, letters to editors, letters to critics and friends, sermons, psalms, etc. He took in everything, from criticism of the British museum to home-brewed medicine, from not-so-plain "plain accounts" to interviews with philosophers and bishops. John Wesley's *Letters* and *Journal* give us a verbal microfilm of the passing show of 18th-century England.

Charles, however, shares our infirmities, and we love him the more for it. He gets closer to us because he has many of those failings common to humanity. Many of his own letters are undated, and many that he received he mislaid. He made sincere but spasmodic attempts at keeping a journal. Many of his poems and hymns he scribbled on scraps of paper, and some of them he alone could read, so covered with corrections and changes were they; at times he had to make special note of which version he preferred. Just to add perplexity to mystification, even what remained of his *Journal* got lost, a presumed fatality of domestic turmoil. Eventually it turned up among the garbage of a furniture depository in London in which his family had stored its goods. But however fragmentary and intermittent its record, we do have it; and together with some of his sermons, letters, and thousands of psalms and hymns, many of which are autobiographical, we are able to procure and present a moderately complete biography of Charles Wesley, the Methodist music man.

A number of factors assist us in the task of rescuing Charles Wesley from his brother's shadow. John Wesley is probably one of the very few men whom most Christian people know about—in the same way they know about Augustine, Martin Luther, John Calvin—even if what they know is little and not too important. The man John Wesley is probably much more widely known than his writings. The reverse, however, is true about Charles; his writings are more widely known than their author. For every person who reads through just one John Wesley sermon, letter, or treatise a year, there are actually thousands who sing at least one Charles Wesley hymn each week and use his words constantly in their prayer and devotional life. He is still by far the most popular and most widely used hymnist of the Christian Church. The Methodist music man is warmly welcomed by just about every branch of Christendom. Charles Wesley is an ecumenical man in spite of himself.

Yet there are probably 40 or 50 major biographical studies of John for every one of Charles.

For another thing, there was something about Charles that made people feel more at ease with him than with John. John sometimes seemed almost aloof and apart; he was usually so serene, even-tempered, and self-sufficient in relation to the work of the Evangelical Revival. Also, he always seemed aware of his own powers and of his freedom to use them; in him self-reverence and self-respect blended with a godly humility; he was a kind of benevolent dictator who even yet seems a bit austere and distant from his warmest disciples. Of course, there is much evidence that John was really a most congenial and companionable person; nevertheless, no one but Charles ever got very close to him.

Charles was modest. He can be loved for his weaknesses in a way that John cannot; he was a loving and lovable "human," a person of many moods with whom we, with the Methodists of his day, feel at home. He was a family man who shares with us the smiles and tears of family life in a way not open to John. This all helps to attract to Charles many people whom John overawes a little.

F. Luke Wiseman, Methodist scholar and saint of the first half of the present century, who studied the Wesleys closely and constantly, wrote:

> So far from shining with reflected glory, Charles Wesley's fame is dimmed rather than enhanced by his relation to his renowned brother. Too often he is regarded as moon to its planet, traversing the same orbit as his powerful and brilliant brother, but only by revolving around him. Actually, however, their relation to the firmament of the Evangelical Revival is better represented by Castor and Pollux in the constellation of the Twins. . . . Each with the other did rare exploits; neither without the other could have accomplished the mighty work which was wrought.[3]

Charles Wesley cannot be cut out of the history of the Evangelical Revival nor divorced from contemporary Christian worship and evangelism. He is much more a part of our Christian worship than John. Charles Wesley did much more than write hymns. Indeed, his brother declared that "his least talent was his talent for poetry." If that gift, which many have regarded as his greatest, was in fact his least, what were his others? And how are we to read them?

His gifts were different from John's but were every bit as impressive and in some situations more immediately effective. He was the first Methodist, the real founder of the Holy Club, the first of the brothers to be converted, the first to get into field preaching, and the first to break with the Church of England in the matter of celebrating Communion in an "unconsecrated building." The spread of the Revival owed as much to Charles as to John. Our purpose, however, is not to set each man over against the other. That would be like making the right hand fight the left. Our intention is rather to show them as the most gifted and complementary duo in the history of the Church, and thereby to "praise God who gives such gifts to men." The Wesleys were real and true brothers, in the flesh and in the Spirit. They were also "inalienable friends," "partners in distress," "comrades in battle," "fellow travelers," and "workers together with God" (see 1 Cor. 3:9; 2 Cor. 6:1) who labored abundantly in the Lord.

* * *

My special thanks go to Dr. Carl Bangs and Dr. William M. Greathouse, who provided the initial impetus and ongoing encouragement in the writing of this book. I also thank the editorial staff of the Church of the Nazarene's Communications Division and the Nazarene Publishing House, including Jonathan Wright, who did extensive work in preparing my manuscript for production.

=1

The Christmas Baby

A Baby for Christmas

The 18th child of Susanna and Samuel Wesley became the 9th to survive infancy. For about three weeks the matter was in doubt, but in the providence of the Lord, the baby made it.

Christmas 1707 was slightly less lacking in life's necessities than some previous Christmas seasons had been. For one thing, father Samuel was not in jail! Lincoln debtors' prison had been graced by the rector's presence as a prisoner before now, but this Christmas he is at home. And for another thing, none of the cattle had been stabbed in a month or two. To help things a little, even his savage parishioners seemed less barbaric—even distantly friendly to the rectory family. To top it off, young Samuel was in the top form at Westminster School, London, and had been elevated to king's scholar that very year, thus lifting some of the financial load from old father Samuel's shoulders. All in all, it had been one of the better periods for the Epworth Wesleys, and Christmas looked quite promising.

True, wife Susanna was not well, but then she was in her eighth month of yet another pregnancy. Since the baby was not due until mid-January, however, the Wesleys would have a good Christmas—at least as good as could be expected.

It was neither planned nor expected that Susanna's new baby would arrive for Christmas, but he did! He came almost a month prematurely, and although most welcome—a boy to company John, the only boy then at home among a half-dozen girls—he cast a damper over that particular Christmas, for the little newcomer was weak as well as small. He lay so still, just like a corpse, that the normally lively girls and the precocious John tiptoed around the upper floor, especially when near the parental bedroom.

Had you been able to peep into that bedroom late on December 18, 1707, carol singing would not have occurred to you, although the baby lying there will one day give you "Hark! the Herald Angels

Sing." You would have seen a pale but lovely lady lying in bed, her fine, slightly auburn hair wisping across the pillow, and a worried look in her tired eyes as they focused intently and appealingly on the bundle of soft wool in the cot at her bedside.

No cries from the crib. There is little movement, only that caused by the shallow breathing of the infant. No one has yet seen his eyes. Thus lay Charles Wesley until mid-January 1708, when—as Whitehead puts it—about "the time when he should have been born according to the usual course of nature," he opened eyes and mouth simultaneously (was there something prophetic there?), gave a whimper that heralded a cry, and wholly arrived on his contemporary scene.

When Charles Wesley was born, Samuel, Jr., was already 17, Emilia ("Emily") was 15, Susanna, Jr., was 12, Mary was 11, Mehetabel ("Hetty") was 10, Anne was 5, John was 4, and Martha was 1. Kezziah ("Kezzy") came after Charles, and there were nine little bodies in the churchyard. Therefore, since Samuel was already at Westminster School, London, when Charles was born, and John had left for Charterhouse School, London, when Charles was about 4, the third of the boys was surrounded by girls at Epworth.

A Rectory Heritage

Charles came into a home environment and atmosphere that shaped his whole mental, emotional, and religious temperament. His father was a lifelong and painstaking student and interpreter of the Scriptures. Old Samuel loved the biblical languages and spent long hours every day in his book-lined study. There were books everywhere, even in Susanna's cupboards. He had dictionaries, grammars, and exegetical writings in Hebrew, Chaldee, Syriac, Arabic, Greek, and Latin. His special loves were Greek and Latin.

The rector was also a bit of a poet. He wrote a *Life in Christ* in verse and a three-volume *History of the Old and New Testaments,* also in verse; while his commentary on Job—which some have regarded as a further affliction visited on the patriarch—was piloted through the press by John and presented to Queen Caroline, a famous episode.

It is clear that the rector's passionate love and diligent study of Scripture also became the hallmark of Charles's life. The same must be said of the rector's versifying, although only one of his hymns has retained its place in the hymnbook:

> *Behold the Savior of mankind,*
>   *Nail'd to the shameful tree!*
> *How vast the love that Him inclined,*
>   *To bleed and die for thee!*[1]

Charles Wesley's lifelong loyalty to the Church of England was likewise a heritage of his Epworth home and parents, with their undeviating and often hazardous attendance at all the public services and means of grace, their devotion to the Anglican economy, and their continuing use of the Prayer Book in church and home. No doubt also his father's strictly orthodox and evangelical interpretation of the gospel by sermon, teaching, and prayers was a major molding factor on the heart and mind of young Charles. It should also be borne in mind that the Epworth rector and his wife had a strong partiality toward world missions and evangelism that could not but impact their numerous brood and certainly did affect John and Charles powerfully. Samuel, Sr., had once offered himself as a missionary candidate to the Society for the Propagation of the Gospel and was all of his life an earnest advocate of the Church's worldwide commission. This can be grasped easily by reading his hymn in the light of the Lord's standing orders to His Church in the Olivet communique.

Susanna, too, was mission-minded. One of the peaks of her life was the decision of her boys John and Charles to be missionaries in Georgia, and her earlier sensitivity to the mission of the Church may be seen in her stout insistence on the right of the Epworth villagers to hear the gospel and celebrate the means of grace, even in the absence of the rector and in spite of the opposition of his assignment.

The world was in and on the heart of the Wesley parents even before grace fired the hearts of the boys. John's words, "The world is my parish,"[2] and Charles's words, "O for a trumpet voice / On all the world to call!"[3] may represent the matured convictions of the Wesley duo, but the main tributary rises in Epworth.

Another decisive factor in the early life of Charles Wesley was the theological persuasion and emphases in his parents' opinions. Both Samuel and Susanna were firmly of the Arminian persuasion, Anglican-Puritan brand, which was evangelical, rather than of the brand of the Cambridge Platonists. Susanna's Arminianism was strongly corrective and supportive of both John and Charles, as is manifest in her letters.

On a breezy night in February 1709, a famous fire broke out at the Epworth rectory. Susanna's letter to Samuel, Jr., provides the basic story:

> I suppose you have already heard of the firing of our house, by what accident we cannot imagine; but the fire broke out about eleven or twelve o'clock at night, we being all in bed, nor did we perceive it till the roof of the com chamber was burnt through and the fire fell upon your sister Hetty's bed. She awakened and imme-

diately ran to call your father, who lay in the red chamber; for I being ill, he was forced to lie from me . . . We had not time to take our clothes, but ran all naked.[4]

John's dramatic rescue is well known. Charles, however, not yet two, was grabbed and shielded by a servant girl who carried him to safety out of the inferno. Susanna, strangely enough, was forgotten in the rush. Presumably she was expected to escape unaided. But she, being pregnant, moved with some difficulty and was caught behind a door, wading in flames. When released after some frantic despairing minutes by the rector, she was unrecognizable, her face blackened by smoke and soot.

The house was totally destroyed. "Everything was consumed," wrote the rector to Duke of Buckingham, "for the fire was stronger than a furnace, the violent wind beating it down upon the house."

John was five and Charles not yet 18 months old when the fire occurred. John remembered the fire, but not Charles, other than subconsciously. On the other hand, his most frequent metaphors are fire and wind.

> See how great a flame aspires,
> Kindled by a spark of grace![5]

As for the rector, he hurled defiance at ill fortune: "Let the house go; I am rich enough: All is lost. God be praised."[6]

But upon Susanna fell the real hardships resulting from the fire. The fire blocked the family's resources for years. In 1722, 13 years after the fire, she wrote to her brother:

> Mr. Wesley rebuilt the house in less than a year but nearly 13 years have elapsed since it was burned, yet it is not half-finished, nor are his wife and children clothed to this day.[7]

The firing of their home and the heavy expense involved in caring for the scattered family and at the same time trying to recompose their deeply loving home brought the Wesleys on very hard times. Things were especially difficult for the girls of the family, for it was very much a man's world; but with their remarkable home background and their immense abilities, the boys could reasonably be expected to do well in the world. They did, all three of them, but the expense of their education was one of the main reasons for the poverty persisting in the Epworth household.

It was different for the girls. They were almost all as promising and had as much ability as the boys. Looking after gardens at Epworth and at the rector's other charge in nearby Wroote, acting as baby-sitters-domestic to the frequent new arrivals, and numbers of household chores required of them even when a maid was employed, kept life very busy and a bit of a drudgery. But they were a gifted and generally happy bunch. Hetty, probably the most gifted, who has impressed many writers and has been the subject of a classic romantic biography by Quiller-Couch, could read the Greek Testament when she was eight and had the ingrained aptitude for verse that was characteristic of the Wesleys.

The inside story of the tough times at Epworth comes from Susanna herself and from her eldest daughter, Emily. Susanna writes:

> My dear Emily, who in my present exigencies would exceedingly comfort me, is compelled to go to service in Lincoln where she is teaching in a boarding school. My second daughter, Suky, a pretty woman and worthy a better fate, rashly threw herself away upon a man that is not only her plague, but a constant affliction to the family. The other children, though wanting neither industry nor capacity for business, we cannot put to any, by reason we have neither money nor friends to assist us in doing so . . . so that they must stay at home while they have a home.[8]

Emily the schoolmistress also wrote about those hard times at Epworth:

> After the fire, when I was 17 years old, I was left alone with my mother and lived easy for one year—but after we were gotten into our house, and all the family settled, in about a year's time, I began to find out that we were ruined . . . then I learned what it was to seek money for bread . . . and we of the female part of the family be left to get our own bread or starve as we see fit.[9]

Mary, often called "Molly," married the rector's curate, John Whitelamb. The marriage promised well, but in less than a year she was dead. Kezzy never married, and it would probably had been better for some of the others had they remained single.

Hetty, the brilliant girl, lively and sprightly, being thwarted by her father from marrying an able and respectable gentleman, threw herself away on a local no-good described as "low and rude in address, and much inferior to her in understanding." He proved to be a rough but not unkind husband, and Hetty's poem addressed to him concludes after about a hundred lines with:

> Till life, on terms severe as these
> Shall ebbing leave my heart at ease;
> To thee thy liberty restore,
> To laugh when Hetty is no more.[10]

But at length, Hetty received peace in Christ and became what Charles Wesley described as "my sister Wright, a gracious, tender, trembling soul; a bruised reed which the Lord will not break." Charles preached her funeral sermon, taking for his text Isa. 60:20.

Through male chauvinism, the spirit of the times, or whatever you call it, the rector saw to it that things began differently for his sons, and they were clever enough to take advantage of their running start.

Samuel Wesley, Jr., may not have been the most handsome man in London town, but he was among the most courageous and kindly. He was "a scholar and a gentleman," a brother indeed to Charles, and a son extraordinary to his Epworth parents.

Samuel left home when John was but a few months old and long before Charles was born. He entered Westminster School, London, in 1704, becoming, as we have noted, a king's scholar in 1707. Entering Oxford University's Christ Church in 1711, he took his degree and returned to his old school as assistant teacher. In this capacity he was a success and moved to Tiverton in 1732 as headmaster or principal of the grammar school there.

Samuel was, we are told, a wit and a poet. When Samuel was able to help the Epworth family, he did so splendidly. He divided his income between himself and the Epworth family, thus further easing the almost intolerable situation there. He was a sincerely spiritual man and had a genuine concern for social reform in England. He opened the first free dispensary in England, an institution that developed into St. George's Hospital.

It is, however, as his brothers' brother that Samuel Wesley, Jr., has come to be best known. The rector himself stated it well in 1732, in a letter to his eldest son:

> You have been a father to your brothers and sisters, especially the former who have cost you great sums in their education, both before and since they went to the University. Neither have you stopped there, but have shewn your pity to your mother and me in a very liberal manner, wherein your wife joined with you, when you did not overmuch abound yourself.[11]

Samuel Wesley exerted a gentle but firm influence over his two younger brothers. John left Epworth for London in 1714, not yet 11 years of age, and Samuel took up residence at Westminster in 1715. Thus for a while they were fairly near to each other. The academic influence of Samuel over John may be reflected in their similar university courses. The moral and domestic influence is seen in the correspondence passing between them, especially from John's side. Next to seeing his mother, he wants to get back to Samuel at Westminster.

They had their differences. Domestically, they were divided over the Hetty scandal, John defending her against the rector, and Samuel supporting the rector against Hetty. They differed religiously, in that the conversion of John and Charles was to Samuel one confusing mystery; and ecclesiastically, in that Samuel could see neither good sense nor good churchmanship in the evangelical doctrines of these two brothers of his. Especially did the emphasis on the working and the witness of the Holy Spirit perplex him, particularly the profession of assurance by new converts. In vain did John beseech Samuel to consider the existential evidence: "Saw you him that was liar till then and is now a lamb; him that was a drunkard, but now exemplarily sober; the whoremonger that was, who now abhors the very lusts of the flesh?" But Samuel was not persuaded and continued the mild and loving brother but stolidly orthodox Anglican priest to the end of his life. For his part, John went on his crusading way, returning his brother's unfeigned love and admiration with deep respect for Samuel's opinion but, I doubt not, still praying for that strange warming of heart for Samuel that he had himself experienced. But Samuel died prematurely in 1739.

The Westminster Captain

Charles Wesley tersely capsulizes his early education in a letter written when he was almost 70 years of age:

> At eight years old, in 1716, I was sent by my father, Rector of Epworth, to Westminster School, and placed under the care of my eldest brother Samuel, a strict churchman, who brought me up in his own principles. My brother John, five years older than me, was then at Charterhouse. In 1727 I was elected Student of Christ Church. My brother John was then Fellow of Lincoln.[12]

It must have been a traumatic experience for a lad of eight summers to exchange the primitive rural life of the Epworth village for a crowded city, and to some a modern Nineveh. The transition, too, from Susanna's kitchen college, with its female scholars, to a large school of boys under the tutelage of masters with little of the patience that characterized Susanna was indeed like a baptism into hard facts for the child Charles.

Rector Samuel would not have had to wonder at the Westminster teachers in the same manner as he wondered at Susanna. Her patience never seemed to flag.

> "I wonder at your patience," said the Rector once to his wife, "you have told that child twenty times the same thing." "Had I satisfied myself by saying the matter only nineteen times," answered

Susanna, "I should have lost all my labor. You see, it was the 20th time that crowned the whole."[13]

Efficient though the Westminster teachers were, they were radically different from Susanna, who, while a firm believer in reasonable discipline and by no means an indulgent parent, had nevertheless that dual motivation. She might well have quoted Paul, who was "among you, even as a nurse cherisheth her children" (1 Thess. 2:7).

Charles had been accustomed from earliest days to a well-ordered life. The careful use of time, regularity for meals, family devotions morning and evening, the expectation of his parents that he would pause frequently throughout the day to think of things spiritual, appointed times for counsel—to all this he was accustomed, probably more than any other eight-year-old boy in England.

But Westminster School was different. Here were 430 boys, not two or three girls, and here, too, was a system of slavery that Susanna would have squelched at its first appearing. Here, too, was noise, noise, noise in the dormitory shared with 50 others, while Charles so often dreamed of the quiet little bedroom in the village rectory. Instead of the soughing wind over the fenland and the brushing of the rushes, there was the incessant rattle of iron-rimmed wheels on the cobblestone streets. Even in the lone watches of the night, the boom of the Westminster clock seemed like a threat, whereas the gentle ring of the Epworth church clock had been so friendly. At Epworth, time seemed to stand still, but here in the heart of London and under the shadow of Westminster Abbey, Charles seemed to be both pressured by history and caught up in the making of it.

But Charles had come to Westminster at an opportune hour in its history, and in his. The school was of Benedictine origin and boasted a long line of notable headmasters.

At 5:15 in the morning the loud voice of a senior scholar, usually one of the privileged group of king's scholars, roused the sleeping boys and bade them first of all kneel at their bedsides to unite in reciting the responses of the morning collect. Next, each boy made his own bed and took his turn in sweeping the dormitory before lining up to wash hands and face at the old cloister pump—all under the eye of the king's scholar.

Six in the morning, and time for prayers, followed by classes in Greek and Latin, followed in turn by prayers. Feeling no doubt that mouth and stomach had parted company, the boys were now called to the first meal of the day! Filing into the dining hall like Noah's passengers, the boys flanked the tables in two rows during grace and then consumed the plain fare to the accompaniment of the reading of a

Latin manuscript. This was intended for their amusement and education.

Thus began the schoolboy's day. The curriculum majored in the classical languages. Prayers were said in Latin. The monitors were expected to "keep them strictly to the speaking of Latin." Latin grammar was, predictably, the first class-subject of the day. Charles came to love the classical Latin poets. He quoted them profusely in his poems and frequently borrowed their ideas, transposing them into English, converting them to a Christian use, and employing them in his hymns.

At this point in his studies, be began to prove another benefit of his parentage. At Epworth he had studied both Latin and Greek under the guidance of the rector, who was a classical moth, and Susanna, who continued to read especially the Greek she had learned in girlhood and youth. At Epworth, too, the unfortunate Hetty had learned to read Greek before she was eight. And Samuel, Jr., who presently kept his loving eye on Charles, was himself a brilliant classical scholar intent on making both of his younger brothers equally proficient in the ancient languages. He succeeded, in consort with other teachers, to the extent that at Oxford the amazing duo conversed in Latin.

Westminster Abbey stood squat, tall, and strong, like a turreted sentinel watching over the city! Its long black shadow, circling with the sun, was cast over the school in more ways than one. The Abbey served the school as college chapel. The Anglican liturgy, so familiar to Charles, gave him some feeling of rootage and security. Matins, evensong, and Sunday worship provided a familiar framework for his religious life.

Charles apparently fulfilled traditional expectations in the area of schoolboy correspondence, for few letters arrived at Epworth from Westminster. The more surprising fact is that few parental letters arrived from Epworth, and such as Charles received were from Susanna, whose hands were certainly full enough at home.

Charles Wesley's letters have not been collected with anything distantly approaching the assiduity and tenacity shown by the devotees of John, and yet it was none other than renowned letter writer John who declared, "I am very sensible that, writing letters is my brother's talent rather than mine."

Commenting on this fact, Frank Baker, chief champion of Charles, writes:

> This is certainly high praise, for John's own letters are among the clearest, the most terse and direct in the world. Yet their very strength is also their weakness, for they usually lack color and warmth. Whilst Charles Wesley can be just as concise as his brother,

and even more aphoristic, his letters are usually more rounded off; there are more touches of humor and of tenderness, more passages of description and exhortation, more variety. Charles was primarily a poet, not a logician, and his letters undoubtedly reveal a greater sense of the rhyme and melody of words than do those of this brother. They are a worthy contribution to literature, as well as to biography and history.[14]

Charles Wesley's earliest extant letter was written in January 1728, on his mother's birthday. It was not written to her but to John, who was by then curate at Wroote, near Epworth. The letter inadvertently makes reference to two aspects of Charles's life that shed oblique light on his school days at Westminster. He says that he now finds at Oxford a freer and sharper air (was he being a bit smothered at Westminster?), and that he is as much in need of cash as ever, a familiar student wail.

Although the least pugilistic of males, Charles was no pushover for the school bullies. Jackson declares that Charles had a reputation for being "arch and unlucky," a polite way of saying he was mischievous enough to get into scrapes, but not clever enough to avoid detection. His chivalry led him on one occasion to champion James Murray, a small Scottish scholar, who was being pushed around by the bullies. It was a service that James Murray never forgot, and when he became a notable Lord Mansfield, he gratefully renewed his friendship with Charles.

Charles Wesley became the second Wesley son to be made a king's scholar of Westminster, thus following in Samuel's steps. That was in 1721. Henceforth his expenses would be paid, and some of the financial pressure lightened. In 1725, he became captain of the school, a sort of president of the student body, and in 1727 he left Westminster for Christ Church, a college of Oxford University, which big brother John had left shortly before.

The Irish Connection

One of the Wesley connections was Mr. Garrett Wesley of Dangan and his wife, Katherine. Garrett Wesley was also a member of parliament for County Meath.

The Garrett Wesleys were childless and very eager to adopt an heir from some legitimate branch of the Wesley clan, a poorer branch if possible. Accordingly, their eyes fell on young Charles, still at Westminster when the episode opened. A letter was sent to the rector. Had the rector a son named Charles, and if so, was the rector agreeable that Charles should become the adopted son of Garrett and Katherine?

The rector was willing only that young Charles should make such a decision freely and personally, and despite Charles's appeal for counsel, the rector left it to him. Garrett Wesley himself called on Charles at Westminster and endeavored to persuade Charles to go back to Ireland with him. But young Charles, like Moses of old, "refused to be called the son of" Garrett and Katherine Wesley and to adopt the life of an Irish country gentleman, "choosing rather" the way of the Epworth Wesleys (Heb. 11:24, 25).

Charles as yet knew nothing of "the recompence of the reward" (v. 26), but as it turned out, he who might have been listed with the mere princes and dukes and such people is now listed in the peerage of the kingdom of heaven.

The benevolent Garrett Wesley died on September 23, 1728. Katherine survived him for 17 years. She left Dangan for Dublin, where she died in 1745. In Dublin she lived in a large house on Jervis Street, almost opposite St. Mary's Church, in which John Wesley preached. What thoughts did John have when he was at the house that might well have been the home of brother Charles?

2

The Academic Pursuit of Holiness

An Instant Saint?

The spring of 1726 was brighter than most at Epworth. In April, John Wesley was elected fellow of Lincoln College, and the rector's jubilation was almost unlimited.

"Wherever I am, my Jack is fellow of Lincoln!" Charles, too, rejoiced in his brother's success, but it was to mean for him a changed situation. He was going up to Christ Church, the college, but now his brother was to leave it because of his duties at Lincoln College. John would now have an income from Lincoln, whereas the rector was most unpromising, to say the least, about financial help for Charles.

The summer could not have been a happier one, however. It appears that the brothers walked to Epworth from London and spent the summer with their parents and sisters. John assisted his father in the duties of the rector and on the interminable "family incubus," the versified commentary on Job. John also talked very often and long with Susanna, went swimming, shot plover, and read a great deal. Miss Kitty Hargreaves, a local lady, received much of his attention and might have received more had not the rector "frustrated our meeting." The rector actually ordered the young woman off the premises! This so disturbed John that he promised never to touch Kitty's hand again.

But the sad tale of Hetty marred that summer. Having fallen in love with a young lawyer, she stayed out all night with him and fell foul of her father's legalism. John, up in arms in defense of Hetty, preached against his father's interpretation of the old law to which the rector made appeal, whereupon the rector threatened to invoke another ecclesiastical law. Charles carried this news to John, who almost immediately apologized to the rector, not for defending Hetty, but for breaking a law of the church. Thus passed the hot summer in the flushed fenlands of Epworth and Wroote, and in the fall Charles Wesley headed for Oxford.

All four of the Epworth Wesley males were Oxford men. Samuel, Jr., came to Oxford in 1711 at 20 years of age. There was nothing distinctive about him except his strong Anglican opinions and a fruity birthmark on his neck. He had, however, a reasonable appetite for learning. Susanna had considered him a little slower in the uptake than most of the Wesley brood.

Samuel, Jr., also graduated with his Oxford degree after what Adam Clarke laconically describes as "exemplary diligence."

John went up to Christ Church at Oxford from Charterhouse School in 1720, at 17 years of age. He carved out a distinguished academic career before he, too, graduated with his degree and later was elected fellow of Lincoln College.

Charles followed in the Wesley way. But he alone went up a Wesley by birth and a Wesley by choice.

Oxford town was in some ways a different place to young Charles from what it had been to his father, and very much different from our contemporary Oxford.

Charles's Oxford was just one mile in length and less in breadth. The north and east gates were still standing. There were no sprawling suburbs, but over cobbled streets hand-drawn and horse-drawn carriages rattled. Sedan chairs were common, as crinolined ladies or male fops were transported crazily around puddles of mud. The castle was almost totally in ruins, and what remained served as the county jail, beggaring all description for filth and misery. This jail later figured prominently in the Wesley story.

The main street ran east to west, and onto it fronted University College, Queen's College, and All Saints College, built in 1706-8. Historic Magdalen College also graced the main street. On the main street also stood, and stands, the University Church of St. Mary's, made famous by great preaching and momentous events of Christian history, especially in Reformation times. St. Mary's figures importantly in the Wesley saga.

Frank Baker summarizes:

> Our picture must be of a fair-sized city in which ugliness jostled beauty, and learning struggled with industry and dirt, just as there was traditional and sometimes bitter rivalry between town and gown. There were one or two broad streets, but for the most part they were narrow and paved with coarse cobbles, and down the center ran a "Kennel" or gutter overflowing with all kinds of rubbish.[1]

Charles Wesley's Oxford was crammed with clubs—the Amorous, the Pedicle, the Three Tuns, the Punning, the Witty, the Handsome, the Nonsense, etc. To these the young Charles would soon add the Holy Club. In the manner of the day the Wesleys met their friends at nearby inns and coffee houses and played billiards, backgammon, tennis, and cards, which—although forbidden in the Assembly Hall—was a game permitted in the private rooms.

Charles's moderate skill on the flute opened doors of friendship in the musical and social life of the university. The sudden release from the Westminster supervision of Samuel and his wife unsteadied Charles for a little time. He had, however, been equally suddenly thrown into his first real and continuing association with brother John. Indeed, it was at his going up to Oxford in 1726 that Charles Wesley began to form with brother John that partnership that eventually became the greatest evangelistic brotherhood in the history of the Christian Church.

But Charles found Oxford University a threat to personal spirituality. He later wrote:

> My standing here is so very slippery, no wonder I long to shift my ground. Christ Church is certainly the worst place in the world to begin a Reformation in. A man stands a fair chance of being laughed out of his religion at his first setting out, in a place where 'tis scandalous to have any at all.[2]

In that same year, John Wesley moved from Christ Church to Lincoln College to assume his new tutorial and fellowship duties there, but for the first time the brothers were resident at the same university in the same city and able to be in constant touch. The behavior of Charles in these months gave John concern, and John later said so.

> He pursued his studies diligently, and he led a regular, harmless life; but if I spoke to him about religion he would warmly answer; "What! Would you have me be a saint all at once?" and would hear no more.[3]

Charles had other reasons to be grateful to John. John's circle of friends cushioned Charles's arrival on the Oxford scene. He found a lively and interesting bunch of young people associated with John and set about really enjoying them. The group included Robert Kirkham, son of the rector of Stanton Harcourt; Kirkham's three sisters; and Mary and Anne Granville. Anne was a young widow who was later to make her mark on high society as Mrs. Delaney.

This fascinating group foregathered at the Kirkham home in the rectory of Stanton Harcourt, a sleepy but lovely village in the green Cotswolds. To make things more interesting, the young people adopted names from romantic literature. Mary Granville was Aspasia, Anne Granville became Selima, Betty Kirkham was Varanese, John Wesley was Cyrus, and Charles—whom John lost little time in introducing to the circle—became Araspes.

The undoubted grace, charm, and wit of the Kirkham girls fell over the Wesley brothers. The girls were pretty, charming, well read, and well able to hold up their end in discussion with the men from Oxford. It was all most enjoyable and openly innocent.

Varanese, especially, charmed the brothers. That John was in love with her was evident to the other members of the group. And she did him good, introducing him to the writings of Thomas à Kempis, Jeremy Taylor, and William Law.

Varanese had likewise a wholesome although less amorous effect on Charles. Indeed, in a letter written in 1735 while en route to Georgia, Charles refers to her and to Selima:

> Besides you two, I have no relations, no friends in England, whom I either write to, or find any ease in thinking of.[4]

Stanton Harcourt was near Oxford, so the group met often. They walked, rode, danced, read, and discussed the secrets of the life of Christian devotion. But in 1727, John left Oxford to act as his father's curate at Wroote, near Epworth, and his going left "a vacant place against the sky"—everyone's sky, but especially that of Charles.

Charles Wesley's awakening to spiritual values came suddenly and without obvious cause other than John's removal, unless he was influenced in the rebound from mild infatuation with a young actress quite ready to exploit the affair with the help of her mother.

He declared, however, that he had learned from the experience of loving an actress:

> I can without any regret resolve never to exchange another word with the pretty creature. . . . I shall be far less addicted to gallantry, and doing what sister Nutty (Samuel's wife) with less justice said you did—liking woman merely for being woman. . . . But enough of Molly—I'll blot my brain and paper no longer with her.[5]

This he wrote to John in January 1729, and we know from another letter to him, written in May of that year, that a sober but sincere mental change had come over Charles. We hear of no sudden enlightenment, no swift and overpowering illumination, but of single-minded and undramatic application to his immediate duty. He got down to real business in his studies, seeking counsel and help from John on how he might better apply himself, use his time to greater advantage, and keep a journal like his brother's; but somehow a persistent inability to concentrate on his studies hampered him, and only by strong effort did he at length succeed in properly handling the problem. He felt that he was less well equipped than John to be a scholar.

> I'm sure I'm less indebted to nature than you. I'm very desirous of knowledge, but can't bear the drudgery of coming at it so well as you could. In reading anything difficult, I'm bewildered in a much shorter time than I believe you used to be at your setting out. My head will by no means keep pace with my heart, and I'm afraid I shan't reconcile it in haste to the extraordinary business of thinking.[6]

But Charles was in earnest. A change was coming over him as 1728 merged into 1729. He was a diligent student but probably too eager to copy the methods of John. This is seen in his adoption of his older brother's way of writing résumés and extracts from his reading, his anxiety to become more than proficient in Latin and Greek, and his hankering after a method of "cipher"—a shorthand like John's—in order to keep a diary like his:

> I would willingly write a diary of my actions, but I don't know how to go about it. What particulars am I to take notice of? Am I to give my thoughts and my words, as well as what I do; and what besides? Must not I take account of my progress in learning as well as religion? What cipher can I make use of? If you would direct me to the same, or a like method with your own, I would gladly follow it, for I'm fully convinced of the usefulness of such an undertaking. I shall be at a stand till I hear from you.[7]

Charles Wesley had sobered, but for a little while he was in danger of becoming a hypochondriac. He stuck out his religious tongue at the mirror; he lived to make up for his deficiencies in some areas by overdeveloping his strength in others.

> I resolve that my falling short of my duty in one particular shan't discourage me from rigorously prosecuting it in the rest. . . . I won't give myself leisure to relapse, for I'm assured, if I have no business of my own the Devil will soon find me some.[8]

Charles was in earnest. He who had but recently resented the imposition of instant sainthood now applied himself almost grimly to the disciplines of sanctity as he saw them. More and more prayer, stricter preparation for Communion and more frequent "communicating," a more intense approach to reading and obeying the Scripture— by these means he sought peace of soul. The Methodist was breaking out; the Holy Club was in the offing.

> My first year at College I lost in diversions. The next I set myself to study. Diligence led me into serious thinking. I went to the weekly Sacrament, and persuaded two or three young scholars to accompany me, and to observe the method of study prescribed by

the Statutes of the University. This gained me the harmless nick-
name of Methodist.[9]

Charles's letter, dated May 5, 1729, permits us to underline the
origin of the Holy Club, the Oxford Methodists. There were to be other May days in the Wesley saga, but May 1729 marks the birth of the
Holy Club under the very first of the Methodists, Charles Wesley. It
was largely religion by rote and by method, but it was sincere and
earnest, and it was helpful to the group. The Holy Club was helpful
also to the poor people of Oxford, to Oxford's children, and to the piti-
ful prisoners lying in the hole at the end of High Street. Let not anyone less in earnest about loving God and his neighbor cast any stones
at the first Methodist.

With all his heart Charles wished that John were back at Oxford.
He kept John informed about the little group of young men gathering
around him. William Morgan from Ireland he described as "a modest,
humble, well-disposed youth [who] lives next to me." But William
had gotten into bad company, from which Charles "assisted in setting
him free." Charles then did his utmost to prevent William's relapse,
and worked and wept over him until he could write to John, "He . . . is
resolved to spare no pains in working out his own salvation." Another
member of the group was that mutual friend Robert Kirkham, brother
of the lovely ladies at Stanton Harcourt. Robert was a much more serious problem for Charles to handle, for he wanted an easier route to
heaven than Charles's newly found flinty path of self-denial. In a
word, Robert wanted to rough it a little more smoothly. Of him
Charles wrote to John:

> I'm afraid so he can but get to heaven any way, the less pains,
> he thinks, the better . . . you can't imagine how wretchedly lazy he
> is [perhaps a reference to Robert's difficulty with early rising] and
> how small a share of either learning or piety will content him. Four
> hours a day will spare for study out of his diversions, not so many
> hours for diversions out of studies! What an excellent invertor! Nay
> and to my knowledge he is not so scrupulous but half this will serve
> his turn at most times.[10]

These three men—Charles, William Morgan, and Robert Kirkham
—constituted the beginnings of the Oxford Methodists, but Charles
hankered after the return of John to Oxford from Wroote and Epworth. Later in life he wrote, "In half a year my brother left his curacy
at Epworth and came to our assistance." Even Stanton Harcourt and
Westminster became for him means of self-denial and of desires for
John's return. Of the former he wrote to John:

I'm so far from expecting but small satisfaction at Stanton, that all I fear is meeting too much. Indeed I durst on no account trust myself there without you.[11]

Of his visit to Samuel and Nutty at Westminster in the summer of 1729, he wrote to John:

What my entertainment here has been I shan't say at present, though very welcome I was without doubt to my sister, for I have lost my stomach. . . . If anything can prevent my ever disagreeing with you, 'twill be somebody's indignation that we agree so well. . . . They wonder here why I'm so strangely dull (as indeed mirth and I have shook hands and parted), and at the same time pay the compliment of saying I grow extremely like you.[12]

Poverty pursued Charles all through his Oxford course as an undergraduate. He was the least mercenary or money-minded of men; indeed, "money was to the end of his life the least and vaguest of Charles's preoccupations."

Charles poked fun at his own poverty. In the summer of 1729, he walked from Epworth to London—about 170 miles—to save the expense of coach travel. The trek took almost a week, but he was able to be jocular about it:

I was almost seven days upon the road, and consequently had I not met with the luckiest company 'twas possible, should not now have had ought of the nine shillings I brought into town with me.[13]

In explaining that poverty kept him from attending the theater to see a play, he wrote:

My Lord Charles' presence was wanting there for many reasons a person of your sagacity may easily guess at—supposing for want of a coat or a shirt. Such accidents aren't the first of this kind his Lordship has met with at Westminster, though he may have the wit to say they shall be the last.[14]

And just one short year before he left for what he expected to be yet another means of soul culture, but which almost became soul wrecking, Charles wrote to Samuel at Tiverton, saying that lack of time and money prevented his "coming over to help" with the gardening, adding:

This is no hint, take notice; for when need be, you can bear witness to my proficiency in begging explicitly.[15]

Thus the Wesley specter of poverty continued to haunt him to the extent that he considered selling the pictures on his study walls in order to buy clothing, remarking at that time, "If my shirts can hold out till spring, my good friend Horn . . . has promised then to help me out a little."

Meanwhile his deepest desire was granted. The authorities at Lincoln College, with the added help of D. Morley, rector of Lincoln, persuaded John that his gifts and calling would be of greater use to the church if he were to return to Oxford's Lincoln College. So to Lincoln College, Oxford, John Wesley returned in November 1729, and Charles with relief and gratitude pressed upon John the leadership of the Oxford Methodists as though simply acknowledging John's inborn authority.

The Return of the Fellow of Lincoln

That John Wesley became the leader of the Holy Club—of the Oxford Methodists—will surprise no one even slightly acquainted with the brothers. John was never shy of leadership, and Charles had no illusions about himself as a leader nor about his brother's leadership qualities. "My brother ever had the ascendancy over me," he wrote, as one guilelessly indicating a simple fact, and thus the transference of the leadership of the Holy Club was but typical of Charles's admiration of John.

Charles's outgoing nature and affability allowed him to bare his soul and his situation continually. Whatever else bound Charles Wesley, silence, solitude, and taciturnity did not. He did not find it "lonely at the top," for he was seldom there.

Thus when John returned from Epworth to Oxford in the last days of 1729, he became by almost involuntary but entirely unanimous approval the leader of the Holy Club. There were some factors that could have prevented it but did not. John refused to be bound to the Epworth living just when his acceptance of it would have kept the family home together for the sick and aging father and Susanna and three spinster sisters, and with that instinct he seemed to possess for the right direction, he headed for Lincoln College, Oxford. The curate of Epworth had become the active fellow of Lincoln and leader of the Oxford Methodists, and brother Charles was delighted and relieved to have it so.

The Life of the Oxford Methodists

With the return of John, the little society at Oxford increased to a magnificent four. One of the four has given a delightful vignette revealing both the impression made on him by the return of John and the relationships between the Wesley brothers at that time. The letter was written about five years later, so the impressions are fresh in the writer's mind. John Gambold was a constant companion to Charles Wesley. He wrote:

> Hardly a day passed, while I was at the College, but we were together once, if not oftener. After some time he introduced me to his brother John, of Lincoln College. "For," said he, "he is somewhat older than I, and can resolve your doubts better. . . ." I never observed any person have a more real deference for another, than he constantly had for his brother. . . . He followed his brother entirely . . . Mr. John Wesley was always the chief manager, for which he was very fit. For he not only had more learning and experience than the rest, but he was blest with such activity as to be always gaining ground, and such steadiness that he lost none.[16]

John's spiritual calm and poise impressed Gambold:

> I have seen him come out of his closet with a serenity of countenance, which was next to shining . . . always cheerful, but never triumphing, he so husbanded the secret consolations which God gave him, that they seldom left him. He used many arts to be religious, but none to seem so. . . . The first thing he struck at in young men was that indolence which would not submit to close thinking.[17]

Thus John quickly stamped his image on the group of young men. It was always a small group, for only an earnest young man "durst . . . join himself to them" (Acts 5:13). But among those who were soon to do so was George Whitefield, the third man in that incomparable evangelistic trio that was to contest the English-speaking world for Christ.

It was Charles Wesley who was instrumental in the spiritual awakening of George Whitefield, and of this George has left us in no doubt.[18]

George Whitefield

The early life and background of George Whitefield could hardly have been more of a contrast to Charles Wesley's. He was the son of the widowed hostess of the Bell Inn at Gloucester, which appears to have been, in Henry Fielding's term, "an excellent house indeed." The inn's landlord was later described as "the great preacher's brother, a very honest, plain man, absolutely untainted with the pernicious principles of Methodism."[19] But that was in 1749, while the Wesleys and the brother of "mine host of the Bell Inn" were overturning in God's name the mortified religion of Gloucester and all England.

Although so radically different from that of Charles Wesley, George's background was not devoid of religious influence. He was bereft of his father at two years of age and "was regarded by his

mother with a particular tenderness, and educated with more than ordinary care. He was early under religious impressions, but the bent of
his nature, and the general course of his younger years, as himself ac-
knowledges with expressions of shame and self-condemnation, was of
a very different kind."[20] But the depth of Whitefield's depravity appears to have been a love of card playing and what he described as "a
sensual passion for fruit and cakes."

George, like his later friend Charles, had a hankering after the
stage and acting. He often occupied a cheap seat at the Gloucester theater, where no doubt his natural aptitude for dramatics, coupled with
an unusually powerful and melodious voice and slight squint in his
left eye, laid some kind of base for his astonishing power as pulpiteer
and field preacher in Revival days.

Whitefield came up to Oxford University at 18 years of age. He
had a solid foundation in the Latin classics, an unquenchable thirst for
learning, and little or no money. Thus he came to Oxford as a servitor,
working his passage, and subsisting on such tips as he received from
the more well-to-do students he served.

In his 18th-century style, Gillies writes:

> Happy was it for Mr. Whitefield, that there was a Society of
> Methodists, at that time, in Oxford; but especially that he became
> acquainted with the Rev. Mr. Charles Wesley, by whom he was
> treated with particular kindness. Such benefit did he receive under
> his ministry, that he always accounted him his spiritual father. And
> Mr. Wesley's reciprocal affection for him, stands recorded in the
> verses at the beginning of Mr. Whitefield's second and third jour-
> nals.[21]

The circumstances surrounding the first meeting of Charles Wesley and George Whitefield, his "inalienable friend," make for revealing and somewhat romantic reading.

> The young men (the despised Methodists) were then much
> talked of in Oxford. I had heard of, and loved them before I came to
> the University; and so strenuously defended them when I heard
> them reviled by the students, that they began to think that I also
> should be one of them. For above a twelvemonth my soul longed to
> be acquainted with some of them, and I was strongly pressed to fol-
> low their good example, when I saw them go through a ridiculing
> crowd to receive the Holy Eucharist at St. Mary's. At length God
> was pleased to open a door. It happened that a poor woman in one
> of the workhouses had attempted to cut her throat, but was happily
> prevented. Upon hearing of this, and knowing that both the Mr.
> Wesleys were ready to every good work, I sent a poor apple-woman
> of our College to inform Mr. Charles Wesley of it, charging her not

to discover who sent her. She went, but, contrary to my orders, told my name.[22]

Charles Wesley had not missed seeing the friendly face in the hostile crowd and had often noted a rather lonely figure on the campus. He immediately invited George for breakfast on the following morning. And so began a most remarkable friendship, which weathered both distance and doctrinal controversy to emerge a stronger thing. Whitefield believed so: "Blessed be God! It was one of the most profitable visits I ever made in my life." Charles surrounded George with loving-kindnesses. He introduced him to John—of course!—and to the other members of the little band of brothers. Charles also loaned him books, including William Law's *Serious Call to a Devout and Holy Life*, of which George said:

> I never knew what true religion was till God sent me that excellent book by the hands of my never-to-be-forgotten friend.[23]

The result was that Whitefield now began to live by rule and to endeavor to account for every minute of his time by using it to the best advantage. In some ways it looked as if he would outstrip his "never-to-be-forgotten friend" in the rigor of his "Methodism." He went to Communion at every opportunity; he visited the sick, the prisoners, and the poor; he read the Bible and William Law to all whom he could find; and, at one time, he almost lapsed into mysticism. His health was undermined and his nervous system strained.

But his "never-to-be-forgotten friend" again providentially stopped him on this disastrous course and with wise counsel and medical help got George fully restored and back home to Gloucester for rest and recuperation. But George could not be corralled. Even while at Gloucester regaining his strength, he made it all his business to rouse the dead to newness of life.

> Thus were the days of my mourning ended. After a long night of desertion and temptation, the Star, which I had seen at a distance before, began to appear again, and the Day Star arose in my heart. Now did the Spirit of God take possession of my soul, and, as I humbly hope, seal, me unto the day of redemption.[24]

A Serious Call to a Devout and Holy Life

It is necessary that we turn for a moment to see the importance to Charles Wesley, and indeed to John, of a book. The book is that which so powerfully impacted George Whitefield, but let us remember that he had received it from Charles Wesley. Perhaps it was John who first introduced the book to the Oxford Methodists, for it was published just a few months before he returned. Whoever introduced the book upset the applecart.

The book is titled *A Serious Call to a Devout and Holy Life*. Its author was William Law, M.A., fellow of Emmanuel College, Cambridge University. William Law was, however, an ousted nonjuror. He had refused on grounds of reason and conscience to take the oath of allegiance to George I, a Hanoverian king on the throne of England.

Law was a very great man. He was great in spirituality, great in devotion, great in learning. He was fundamentally a preacher with no pulpit but his writer's desk, and his frustrations escaped through his quill. His standing as a writer remains very high, and he is regarded as one of the finest of all masters of English prose. His works, especially *A Spiritual Call*, *The Spirit of Love*, and *Christian Perfection*, have all retained top ranking among the classics of devotional writing.

Law's friendship with and influence upon the Wesley brothers, both Charles and John, is a full, long, and quite involved business that has become the subject of a number of helpful and insightful books. Enough here to note that while both brothers acknowledge their debt to Law, Charles was the more sympathetic to him and was recommending his writings to friends long after the outward breach that occurred with him. John, who regarded Law almost as an oracle, became much more critical of him sooner.

The Law-Wesleys affair is a story of cooling relationships. In 1725 John had what Evelyn Underhill described as "an awakening"—John called it entering "upon a new life"—when his friend Betty Kirkham introduced him to the writings of Thomas à Kempis, and a little later to those of Jeremy Taylor and William Law.

John returned to Oxford and began to apply Law's teaching to the life of the Oxford Methodists. All were profoundly affected: John, Charles, Whitefield, and Gambold—each witness to the impact of the book.

In 1732, when the Holy Club was under heavy fire of ridicule, John and Charles frequently walked the many miles from Oxford to Putney, south of London, to consult with Law. Thereafter, until the final break with Law in 1738, John frequently visited Law, seeking counsel.

"In November 1734, John spent three whole hours with William Law and records at length the benefit he received."[25] Very frequently indeed, especially between 1731 and 1736, Charles Wesley not only visited Law but also warmly recommended that people read *A Serious Call*, and he himself read the book aloud to individuals and families both in England and America. After Charles's evangelical conversion, he witnessed personally to William Law:

> I told him my experience. "Then am I" said he "far below you, (if you are right,) not worthy to bear your shoes." He agreed to our notion of faith, but would have it all men held it. . . . I told him, he was my schoolmaster to bring me to Christ; but the reason I did not come sooner to Him was my seeking to be sanctified before I was justified.[26]

That is about the sum total of the effect of Law's teaching on the Wesley brothers. But for it and their reverence for him, they might have entered soul peace years before they did. On July 27, 1739, 13 months after his conversion, John made much the same criticism of Law's teaching as Charles had done.

The Methodists of Oxford University nevertheless learned much from Law, chiefly with regard to the culture of the life of holy devotion once the soul is washed in the sanctifying blood of Jesus Christ. Therefore, at 70 years of age, Charles is still commending the reading of the book that so shook the Oxford Methodists, but this time it is to his own daughter Sally.

For his part, Law was rather mystified, writing about John Wesley:

> I was once a kind of oracle with Mr. Wesley. I never suspected anything bad of him, or ever discovered any Kind or Degree of Falseness, or Hypocrisy in him. But during all the Time of his Intimacy with me, I judged him to be monk under the power of his own Spirit.[27]

Law's book is one of the seminal books of history, influencing men as diverse as William Penn, Samuel Johnson, Edward Gibbon, and the members of the little society of Oxford Methodists. These latter it shook out of their self-obsessed religion, causing them to reach beyond themselves into the agony of need around them and to reshape their use of time to the greater advantage of others as well as of themselves. As Charles puts it, the book called for a more balanced life more equally proportioned

> 'Twixt the mount and multitude,
> Giving and receiving good.[28]

There is a very powerful connection between Law's presentation of the culture of holiness and that of Charles Wesley:

> Holy Lamb, who Thee confess—
> Followers of Thy holiness,
> Thee we ever keep in view,
> Ever ask "What shall we do?"[29]

But for all their sincerity, for all their devotion to methods of prayer, fasting, works of mercy and benevolence, peace of soul eluded them. Nor could William Law, apparently, point them to "the Lamb of God, which taketh away the sin of the world" (John 1:29). In Charles's words, as just noted, "[I was] seeking to be sanctified before I was justified." Thus, so far as personal salvation was concerned, all his rigorous striving profited him nothing!

Nevertheless, there was some benefit occurring from the Oxford Methodist days. Thirty-seven years later, in December 1772, John speaks for both brothers:

> I often cry out "Give me back my former life." Let me be again an Oxford Methodist! I am often in doubt whether it would not be best for me to resume all my Oxford rules, great and small. I did then walk closely with God and redeem the time. But what have I been doing these thirty years?[30]

Charles took his bachelor's degree in 1730 and his master's in March 1733, whereupon he had the privilege, or authority, of having pupils of his own. Whatever success he may have had with students in academics, he does not appear to have had much with them in the area of "Methodistical religion." He tried to thrust upon them the lifestyle of the Holy Club, together with the benefits of his outstanding mastery of the classics.

The pupils were few in number to begin with, but soon they became even fewer under the impact of his emphases on fasting, prayer, and frequent Communion. Charles actually pressed on the young men the duty of fasting on the grounds of his interpretation of a forgotten statute of the university! The number of pupils dwindled to one, nor did Charles seek for others despite the poverty that pressed him, and he had to confess by March of 1735:

> As to my title of "tutor," I shall lose it with Dick Smith, unless Sam Bentham succeeds, whom I shall be glad to take, and not sorry should he prove my last.[31]

The years of austere religion were beginning to take their toll of Charles. Fasting as severely as he did resulted in frequent sickness after eating. Deliberate denial of sleep left him tired and weary, and he began to look with envy on the dead! On one occasion he startled the mourners at a funeral by declaring, "What would I give to be on that deathbed!"

The Rector of Epworth Goes to Heaven

Old Samuel Wesley resigned the Epworth living in 1733. He was in rapidly declining health and, in the fall of 1734, was seized with an illness that dragged him to death in eight months. In March 1735 he became so ill that Charles canceled a holiday with big brother Samuel. He wrote:

> This spring we hoped to have followed our inclinations to Tiverton, but are more loudly called another way. My father declines so fast, that before next year he will in all probability be at his journey's end; so that I must see him now, or never more with my bodily eyes. My mother seems more cast down at the apprehension of his death than I thought she could have been; and what is still worse, he seems so to . . . I wish I durst send him Hilarion's words . . . , "Go forth, my soul; what art thou now afraid of? Thou hast served thy God these threescore and ten years, and dost thou tremble now to appear before him?"[32]

But, according to Charles, the rector "enjoyed a clear sense of acceptance with God" during his last protracted illness. "I heard him express it more than once although at that time I understood it not. 'The inward witness, Son, the inward witness' said he to me, 'this is the proof, the strongest proof, of Christianity.'"[33]

Both John and Charles were with the rector and his family at his release. Because Samuel was not present, Charles wrote him a most beautiful and moving letter:

> You have reason to envy us, who could attend him in the last stage of his illness. The few words he could utter I saved, and hope never to forget. The morning he was to communicate he could not without the utmost difficulty receive the elements: but immediately after receiving these followed the most visible alteration. He appeared full of faith and peace which extended even to his body; for he was so much better that we almost hoped he would have recovered. The fear of death he had entirely conquered, and at last gave up his latest human desires of finishing Job, paying his debts, and seeing you. He often laid his hand on my head, and said, "Be steady. The Christian faith will surely revive in this kingdom; you shall see it, though I shall not."[34]

Thomas Jackson is undoubtedly correct when he writes:

> The fact is, that, at the close of his life the father was far in advance of his sons, both in evangelical knowledge and spiritual attainments. He enjoyed the Christian salvation, the nature and method of which neither John nor Charles at that time understood. When their views of divine truth were corrected and matured, they simply taught what their venerable parent experienced and testified upon the bed of death.[35]

John wrote some years later to one of his critics:

My father did not die unacquainted with the faith of the Gospel, of the Primitive Christians, or of our first Reformers; the same which, by the grace of God, I preach, and which is just as new as Christianity. What he experienced before I know not; but I know that, during his last illness, which continued eight months, he enjoyed a clear sense of his acceptance with God.[36]

3

Georgia

Sailing into Georgia

The death of the rector was the death of a Wesley era. The old home was broken up. The rector's debts amounted to over a hundred pounds, a weighty debt for the times; so on the very day of his funeral, his livestock was seized to pay off one creditor. His private letters and papers were locked away until his chief "heir" Samuel could come. John took "the family incubus," *Job*, to pilot it through the press in London after he had himself completed the manuscript. Wise, proud Susanna left Epworth forever. She went first to her daughter at Gainsborough, then to Samuel's home at Tiverton before going for a while to live with her daughter and son-in-law, the Wesley Halls. Finally she lived in John's house at the earliest London Methodist Society chapel, the Foundry.

From the scenes of their childhood, Charles and John returned to Oxford, but changes were in the offing there as well. Within six months both brothers were on their way to America, ostensibly to offer to Indians and colonists that form of religion that had not saved their own souls.

John had dreams of a virgin land inhabited by simple but uncorrupted and noble natives whose salvation it would be a joy to behold, and whom to help would enable him to work out his own salvation.

But why did Charles go along? Most likely, Charles went because John pressed and persuaded his brother to accompany him, and it turned out much worse than he could ever have imagined.

Charles's whole life was in turmoil—"fightings without and fears within." The poor but well-loved Epworth home had gone, the bevy of sisters of his childhood were scattered, his mother was unsettled and for the time was not the strong tower of confidence as in the past. But most agonizing of all, Charles's soul was in upheaval, the quest for peace with God was unrewarding, and he was cast down like the sweet singer of Israel.

As Charles Wesley entered on his Georgian venture, he was in deep melancholia. On February 5, 1736, he wrote to Varanese and Selima.

> In vain have I fled from myself to America; I still groan under the intolerable weight of inherent misery! . . . go where I will, I carry my hell about me. Nor have I the least ease in anything, unless in thinking of S[elima] and you. O that you both might profit from my loss, and never know the misery of divided affections.[1]

That was Wesley's state of mind as he was launched on his Georgian fiasco. Shortly thereafter, he wrote a hymn, which, although not published until 1749, summed up his feelings of entrapment:

> Lo! On a narrow neck of land,
> Betwixt two unbounded seas I stand.[2]

The music man was the misery man. Why then had he gone to Georgia? The answer is a proper name—John!

> I took my degree, and only thought of spending all my days in Oxford. But my brother, who always had the ascendant over me, persuaded me to accompany him and Mr. Oglethorpe to Georgia. I exceedingly dreaded entering into Holy Orders but he overruled me here also, and I was ordained deacon by the Bishop of Oxford, and the next Sunday, priest by the Bishop of London.[3]

Charles was ordained deacon by Potter on October 5, 1735, and priest by Gibson on October 12, 1735. It is very clear that he was being pressured. For six years, John had virtually regulated Charles's life in a program of study, prayers, and fastings that undermined his health and by their very futility cast him into melancholia. Charles had an almost childlike dependence on John, and now he was committed to a task for which he was not merely unqualified but physically and temperamentally unsuited.

But the die was cast. John Wesley was appointed pastor and head missionary to the colonizers in Savannah. Charles was appointed personal secretary to Oglethorpe, the governor. Ingham was appointed lay reader, and Delamotte also went along. When the party embarked aboard the *Simmonds* at Gravesend on October 14, 1735—the Wesleys in one forecastle cabin and their friends in another—the heart of the Holy Club was afloat.

Governor Oglethorpe

It is helpful to have some knowledge of the man under whom the Wesleys were to work in Georgia. James Oglethorpe was the founder and governor of that state. Of him the historian wrote:

> While living, he was greatly venerated for his generous and philanthropic spirit, and since his death his fame has been growing as fast as men have learned to honor those who serve them above the men who inquire and destroy . . . he was open as day to every claim to charity, and ready to cheer others onward in every attempt to improve the condition and character of their fellowmen. He kept himself free from that strain of selfish ambition by which philanthropy is sometimes dishonored; which deprives it of all the beauty of holiness, and destroys more than half its power.[4]

Samuel Wesley, Jr., also wrote, stirred by Oglethorpe's championship of the prisoners and the disadvantaged, in a report that Oglethorpe turned in to Parliament in 1730:

> Yet Britain cease my Captives' Woes to mourn,
> To break their Chains, see Oglethorpe was born?[5]

Even if we allow for the poets' language of hero worship, Georgia has reason to be proud of her origins and founder. The modern Methodist, Leslie Church, says:

> Contemporary estimates of General Oglethorpe's life can no longer be accepted as satisfactory. Two hundred years have given us a new perspective, and his personality appears in a colder but clearer light.[6]

But men can be judged fairly only in the context of the age in which they lived, and thus judged, Oglethorpe emerges as one of the most remarkable benefactors of humanity.

This was the man chiefly responsible for discovering, publicizing, and actually operating the means and methods by which prisoners who had served their sentences, and whom the jails had vomited onto the streets of London without hope or resource other than to return to crime, were to be given new opportunity in the new bright lands of the West. To these were to be added the suffering Protestants of Salzburg—of whom 13,000 had entered England hopeful of a passage to America—and many displaced Irish and Scots, all eager to begin anew in Georgia. Unless we realize the heterogeneous nature of the early colony of Georgia, the things that happened there to both Charles and John Wesley will remain dark mysteries. And when we add to that the presence of the original native Indians in and surrounding the colony, and the constant threat of Spanish attack, we begin to see the complexity of Oglethorpe's task. But he was a noble leader who weathered the storms of intrigue, slander, and threat right bravely and well. Readers of the life of Charles Wesley and his work in Georgia simply must remember this:

> It is easy to see how the General was beset with perplexity and trouble. He too looked for something like simplicity of heart and kindness of feeling among the emigrants; but he found only bitterness and dissention, and was constantly stunned with complaints within, while he was threatened with dangers from abroad, which he saw no way to meet. His delusion with respect to [Charles] Wesley evidently grew out of the depression which this state of things occasioned; and it should be remembered, that he was ready to acknowledge his error, and receive his former friend to his full confidence again, which is by no means common with men in high station and almost unlimited in power.[7]

How the Wesleys Made Up Their Minds

Oglethorpe had long been a familiar name to John and Charles Wesley. Their father had once dreamed and planned to become a missionary with the Society for Promoting Christian Knowledge, which took deep interest in Oglethorpe's plans for Georgia. Susanna, too, had read all the missionary material she could get her hands on. John is described by Schmidt as one "possessed by the missionary idea in a manner rare in the whole history of the church."[8]

Their own concern for the prisoners in the castle prison at Oxford providing a strong impetus toward the work of Oglethorpe, John and Charles felt a kinship on that score alone. But the general had also been a contributor to the rector's *Job* project and was in London when John came to see it off the press.

The general's business included the choice and appointment of a chaplain for Georgia to succeed one Rev. Samuel Quincy, who had been fired by the London trustees of the colony.

The suggestion that John Wesley be appointed had come from Dr. Burton of Christ Church. John sought his mother's counsel:

"I am the staff of her age," said he, and to Susanna he went. Out of her poverty and sorrow came her proud, monumental reply, "Had I 20 sons I should rejoice if they were all so employed."[9]

Burton built up the pressure on John. What was needed, he said, was not popular preachers but men who had learned to be contemptuous of the world and its appeal, who cared nothing for "the ornaments and conveniences of life," who were "inured to bodily austerities and to serious thoughts." At that juncture in John's life, no other form of appeal would have had half the power of this one, and 10 days later John signed up and began to pressure Charles.

> "Jack knew his strength and used it," wrote big brother Samuel later, as he saw his power over Charles diminish. "His will was strong enough to bend you to go, though not me to consent. I freely own 'twas the will of Jack but I am not yet convinced 'twas the will of God."[10]

Oglethorpe, too, needed a little persuasion, but eventually the Georgia trustees appointed Charles as his secretary. When the *Simmonds* was held up at Cowes for more than a month, Charles preached in the parish church a few times to large congregations, for the departure of the four young men aroused considerable interest. But on December 10, the ship got under way at last.

On the evening before departure, the four men got together and drew up what they called *The Solemn Agreement*, which expressed their objectives and intentions. Once again the leadership of John can be seen in the document, although it was actually Benjamin Ingham who wrote it out:

> In the name of God, Amen. We, whose names are underwritten, being fully conscious that it is impossible, either to promote the work of God among the heathen, without an entire union among ourselves, or that such a union should subsist, unless each one will give up his single judgment to that of the majority, do agree, by the help of God;—first, that none will undertake anything of importance without first proposing it to the other three;—secondly, that whenever our judgments differ, any one shall give up his single judgment to the others;—thirdly, that in case of an equality, after begging God's direction, the matter shall be decided by lot.

> John Wesley
Charles Wesley
Benjamin Ingham
Charles Delamotte[11]

The journey took two full months, but we know little of it from the pen of Charles. Most of what we know comes rather from John's journal, although Ingham, too, spent considerable time putting down the daily life of passengers, crew, weather, and points of interest.

So far as the quartet of missionaries was concerned, they drew up and stuck to the kind of program they had used at Oxford. Not a moment of any day was to be wasted.

4 A.M.   —Rising, spending until 5 A.M. in private prayer

5 A.M.-7 A.M.. —Bible study

7 A.M.   —Breakfast

8 A.M.-9 A.M.	—Public prayer with all the passengers
9 A.M.-12 Noon	—Private exercises and study
12 Noon-1 P.M.	—Meeting to discuss what all had done since last meeting, and to tell what they planned to do before the next
1 P.M.	—Dinner
	Until 4 P.M. spent in public and private counseling
4 P.M.	—Evening prayers with exposition and catechizing
5 P.M.-6 P.M.	—Private prayer
6 P.M.-7 P.M.	—Reading; worshiped with the German passengers; Benjamin read to all who would listen; Charles [Wesley] wrote letters and prepared sermons.
7 P.M.-8 P.M.	—John met with German passengers for their evening prayers. The others likely remained in their cabins for reading and other pastimes.
8 P.M.	—The four met for fellowship and mutual instruction.
9 P.M.	—Bed

Benedict of Nursia or Anthony of Padua could hardly have demanded more of their monks, and some of the passengers felt that they were aboard a floating monastery. Mr. Johnson objected to the noisy public prayer meeting as being too close to his cabin for comfort. Mr. Horton, who loved his liquor, was not very fond of John Wesley, who didn't. To prove his point, Mr. Horton climbed to the roof of the Wesley cabin and performed a lengthy and noisy tap dance at midnight! Such incidents were the roots of some of the troubles met with by the Wesleys in Georgia. It appears that some passengers got the distinct impression that the famous four were saving their own souls at the expense of the rights and comfort of other passengers. That was probably true!

From 9 A.M. until 12 noon, John took up and mastered German with the help of the Moravians, while Charles wrote letters and prepared sermons. If we had only Charles's record of the passage, we would never guess just how terrible were some of the storms the ship encountered on its two months voyage.

It is true that the devil tempts the godly, but it is true also that the godly tempt the devil. Among the motley crowd of passengers aboard the *Simmonds* were two mischievous and scheming women. There was Beata, the wife of surgeon Dr. Thomas Hawkins; Anne Welch, the wife of a carpenter; and Mrs. Richard Lawley. Both Mrs. Welch and Mrs. Lawley were pregnant, and the likelihood is that others were also in a similar condition, for a midwife willing to sail with the ship had to be hired on the eve of its departure.

Beata and Anne were the subtle ones, playing up to John's obvious desire for their spiritual betterment by feigning a deep interest in religion. The story is an involved one and concerns John mostly, so we do not examine it here.[12]

John's naïveté is astounding. Charles looked on incredulously as John gave his attentions to the spiritual welfare of ladies Welch and Hawkins. Both Charles and Ingham tried to open John's eyes to the hypocrisy of his penitents, but John was not to be put off, for he was confident of their sincere intentions. After all, how few women were prepared to join him voluntarily in the reading of William Law—by the hour—and in making protracted preparation for Communion?

But Charles was more shrewd than John, in this instance at least, and the impatience extended also to Ingham. Indeed, Charles was so insistent on John's "overcharitableness" to Mrs. Hawkins and Mrs. Welch that John called him "perverse." Thus, with Charles describing John's behavior as "inimitable blindness," the two ladies who would also be a large part of the troubles of the Wesleys in Georgia injected discord into the cabins of the Oxford four.

Probably at this point, Charles Wesley began to feel—subconsciously at least—that his brother was neither infallible nor impregnable, and Charles's future disapproval of John's choice of Grace Murray for a wife may have been planted aboard the *Simmonds*.

When the women realized the failure of their schemes on John despite all the deliberate opportunities for flirtations that they gave him, their attentions turned to resentment and the hope of revenge and sowed the seeds of many a trouble for Charles.

Arrival

Through storm, sunshine, and sickness, the 124 souls aboard the *Simmonds* made the voyage. What troubles, fears, and problems they encountered, we must learn from John's *Journal*. Charles pursued his letter-writing duties for Oglethorpe and the preparation of sermons for himself, and on February 5, 1736, they landed at Savannah, where John was to be the pastor. In that evening, Charles's fears and apprehensiveness surfaced and found vent in a letter to Varanese and Selima. It makes for discouraging reading—the Atlantic storms were nothing compared with the emotional and mental storms in his soul. The writing of the letter was, however, a means of raising his spirit a little.

> On board the *Simmonds* off the Island of
> Tibey in Georgia. Feb. 5, 1736.

> God has brought an unhappy, unthankful wretch hither, through a thousand dangers, to renew his complaints, and loathe the life which has been preserved by a series of miracles. . . . If I

have never yet repented of my undertaking, it is because I could hope for nothing better in England—or Paradise.[13]

Fear, or homesickness, or some kind of depression had plunged him into darkness. But while he wrote, what he called "the strange expansion of heart" came over him, and he offers spiritual counsel to the addressees—only to drop again into the melancholy mood. Apparently the letter lay on the table for about a week before it was reread and completed with an almost apologetic tone:

> I am come to a crisis. The work I see immediately before me is the care of 50 poor families (also for them that they should be so cared for!), some few of whom are not far from the Kingdom of God. Among these I shall either be converted or lost. I need not ask your prayers; you both make mention of me in them continually. Obstinate pride, invincible sensuality, stand betwixt me and God. The whole bent of my soul is to be altered. My office calls for an ardent love of souls, a desire to spend and to be spent for them, an eagerness to lay down my life for the brethren.[14]

It was a long, depressing letter from a man of moods, written in a spirit and strain hardly hopeful for his future work. But on March 9, Charles landed in Frederica, and he began his *Journal*. His spirit has been revived.

> Tuesday, March 9th, 1736, about three in the afternoon, I first set foot on St. Simon's Island, and immediately my spirit revived. No sooner did I enter my ministry, than God gave me, like Saul, another heart.[15]

Ingham was the first to salute him, as he and Oglethorpe had preceded Charles by a month, together with the colonists. He greeted Charles heartily as usual, but his information was not good—already Ingham had run into difficulties "for vindicating the Lord's day." Shades of things to come!

Oglethorpe, too, received him very kindly, but within a few days trouble blew up from that angle as well! The people seemed overjoyed to see him, and he spent the entire afternoon in conference with them, a flush of loving anticipation on his soul. And so brother Charles was launched on his Georgian ministry, a ministry for which he was utterly unsuited.

The Georgian Ministry

Quite obviously, Charles Wesley had not wanted to come to Georgia, and now events were proving that he should not have allowed John to steamroll him into the venture. His knowledge and experience of life were extremely limited—a few years at Epworth in his childhood, and with only his sisters for company; a few more in a boys' school; and the insulated existence of the Oxford Methodists!

Charles was simply not equipped to deal with slanderous and scheming females, who were not for their part equipped for the rigorous, routine religion of Charles's Oxford Club transplant, which had them stand in the rain for prayers and run to the storeroom—which was used as a meeting place—at the bash of a drum!

Nor was Charles enamored of his work as Oglethorpe's secretary, for the seemingly unending letter writing got on his nerves. One week after arrival he was already writing:

> Tues. March 16th, I was wholly spent in writing letters for Mr. Oglethorpe. I would not spend six days more in the same manner for all Georgia.[16]

Although Charles loved the thick forest of oak, bay, cedar, gum, and other trees surrounding the settlement, he was not overfond of Frederica, either. Peabody says the settlement was "situated on the middle of a field of the Indians, where they had cleared and cultivated about forty acres." It was but a spot on the map as yet, poorly organized and surrounded by thieving Indians who did not at all conform to John Wesley's image of the "noble savage."

Frederica had no facilities for worship, education, or pastoral work, and so Charles pined for the quiet groves and churches and common rooms of Oxford. But his chief burden and torture was the declining relationship between his employer and himself.

The Oglethorpe Affair

Charles Wesley's inefficiency as a secretary and his rigidity as a parson soon began to show. Four times a day, by the beating of a drum, the colonists were summoned to the place of prayer, to sit or stand in sun or shower, while their new parson read to them the official prayers and lessons of the Prayer Book! One family lost a baby because the doctor was put in jail for firing a gun on the Sabbath day; another family was split into two parties because the new parson insisted upon baptizing their baby in the name of the Trinity. The people grew resentful of Charles:

> In the afternoon, while I was walking in the street with poor Catherine, her mistress came up to us, and fell upon me with the utmost bitterness and scurrility, said she would blow me up . . . she would be revenged, and expose my . . . hypocrisy, my prayers four times a day by beat of drum, and abundance more, which I cannot write, and though no woman, though taken from Drurylane, could

have spoken . . . In the evening hour of retirement I resigned myself
to God, in my brother's prayer for conformity to a suffering Savior.[17]

And Oglethorpe was perplexed: "How can it be," he asked
Charles, "that there should be no love, no meekness, no true religion
among the people, but instead of that, mere formal prayers?" It was a
searching question.

> Mr. Oglethorpe, meeting me in the evening, asked when I had
> prayers. I said, I waited his pleasure. While the people came slowly,
> "You see, Sir," said I, "they do not lay too great a stress on forms."
> "The reason of that is because others idolize them." "I believe few
> stay away for that reason." "I don't know that."[18]

In such an atmosphere, the mischief-maker thrives, and within a
month of his arrival Charles Wesley entered in his journal:

> Wed. March 24th. I was enabled to pray earnestly for my ene-
> mies, particularly Mr. Oglethorpe, whom I now looked upon as the
> chief of them.[19]

Very few parsons in Wesley's day applied themselves to their duties as conscientiously and scrupulously as Charles in Georgia. He led
four worship sessions a day, at which he habitually delivered an ex-
temporary exposition of the prescribed Scripture lesson. Because there
were no clocks to regulate their life, the worshipers were summoned
by the beating of a drum. They gathered in the open space near
Oglethorpe's tent when weather permitted, but when the weather was
poor, the colony's store tent became the sanctuary.

But for all his zeal, Charles's ministry was a miserable failure.
Jackson, endeavoring to trace the course of the failure, came to the
conclusion that three failures conspired together to create disaster.

1. Defective theology, which resulted in defective personal piety.
He tried to make unconverted sinners live like entirely sanctified
saints. He required men and women to behave like Christians while
they struggled under the load of unforgiven sin. Charles had no
gospel; he confused justification before God with sanctification of
heart and life. As the negro preacher put it, he could not give what he
did not have any more than he could come back from where he had
not been! This led inevitably to

2. The preaching of a purely negative religion of legalistic import.
The shadow of William Law fell over Frederica. Renunciation of the
world—by colonists who wondered what world he was talking about!
Mortification of the desires of the flesh, through self-denial such as
prayers and fastings, which had not produced the desired results of
Oxford, and stood less a chance in Frederica.

3. The enforcement of rigid ecclesiastical discipline; insistence upon priestly baptism, especially if the colonist had been previously baptized by a layman; insistence upon total immersion, three times, even of infants; scrupulous adherence to the Prayer Book services, special days, and total polity.[20]

Charles Wesley did not present "the truth as it is in Jesus," which the Holy Spirit certainly seals with His blessing; but he did present the truth as it is in William Law, which, as Peter once said in another connection, does "put a yoke upon the neck of the disciples, which neither our fathers nor we were able to bear" (Acts 15:10).

When we remember the agitated nature of those colonial days in Georgia, we can only marvel that Charles Wesley was so unbending. Frederica was a 40-acre parcel of promise, but it was as yet no paradise. Life was tough and irritatingly uncomfortable for all of the colonists. Men who had never wielded a spade nor handled a musket had to become farmers and soldiers simultaneously. Having never built more than a hen coop or a rabbit hutch, they now had to fell trees and build houses. Many who had been beggars and wastrels in London, and others who had been guilty criminals, were now expected to become the firm base of a new city. They were now to become pioneer colonists! They were the raw material of the gospel, but here was a prim priest taking them all as Prayer Book saints!

He had neither news nor comfort for people existing in tension with one eye on the coastline and the other on the forests, sandwiched between the threatening Spaniards and the thieving Indians.

But for Charles, the final crunch was the Oglethorpe affair. Oglethorpe had never been enthusiastic over Charles's appointment as personal secretary, although he respected his discipline and sincerity. John was Oglethorpe's ideal clergyman; and being a man of action used to handling life situations, Oglethorpe needed little prompting for his perverse attitudes to Charles and his work. But neither Charles nor his employer reckoned upon the evil machinations of the women Hawkins and Welch.

These had been the troublemakers of the *Simmonds*, and the men should have been ready for more trouble. They were, however, forewarned but unarmed—even John walked into their web. Mrs. Hawkins and Mrs. Welch determined to be the queen bees of the colony and saw in the unsuspecting Charles a temptation to mischief.

Feigning a penitent and humble spirit, these two made to Charles Wesley a bogus confession of adultery with Oglethorpe. Wesley, remembering preferential treatment given the women aboard ship by the cavalier general, swallowed the story whole but kept his mouth shut. The women, however, did not: they spread the tale around that Wesley had concocted and was spreading the adultery gossip. And further, said they, whispering into ears already off the Wesley wavelength, the parson was doing this and much more to undermine the authority of the general!

And now, since the general had not found Charles to be any kind of supersecretary, he became hostile, critical, and unkind to him. Neither man stopped long enough or early enough to seek the true facts. Charles Wesley's troubles now began in earnest. His first instinctive reaction was to shrink from his employer; but Oglethorpe, sensing this, took it as a sign of Wesley's guilt and began to make circumstances really hard on him. Charles's bed was taken away. He was subjected to indignities from the colonists, who simply took their cue from the estrangement obvious between the governor and his secretary. Common wastrels treated him as they would have done a criminal, and the colonists generally, with very few exceptions, made his life as miserable as possible. Having brought little with him from England, in expectation of living in the governor's quarters, he was flattened by an order issued by Oglethorpe to the servants that Charles was to be denied use of anything and everything belonging to the governor, including even the teakettle.

Oglethorpe, strong in knowledge of his own innocence of any wrongdoing with the women, assumed the guilt of Charles. Only friendship with the Wesley family back in England, especially Uncle Matthew Wesley, the apothecary, prevented him from putting Charles on trial immediately for immoral association with the women Hawkins and Welch, and for sedition. Charles, on the other hand, saw the governor's attitude in almost the same way: he became seriously ill and weaker by the hour, but no one cared; he was denied even boards to lie on and continued to lie sick and sore on the inhospitable ground.

> Wed. March 31st. I began now to be abused and slighted into an opinion of my own considerableness. I could not be more trampled upon, was I a fallen Minister of state. The people have found out that I am in disgrace . . . My few well-wishers are afraid to speak to me. Some have turned out of the way to avoid me. Others desired I would not take it ill, if they seemed not to know me when we should meet. The servant that used to wash my linen sent it back unwashed. . . . I . . . found the benefit of having undergone a much lower degree of obloquy "at Oxford."[21]

Charles nevertheless struggled to fulfill his pastoral duties, comforting the needy and counseling the perplexed. Meanwhile, he planned to starve himself to death rather than ask Oglethorpe for assistance.

John to the Rescue

Benjamin Ingham, concerned and faithful as ever, dashed off to Savannah to fetch John. With John's arrival in Frederica, things began to improve a little for Charles, for John stood very high indeed in Oglethorpe's respect. Before long John had talked Charles out of his "suicide by starvation" behavior. It is interesting that about the first thing the brothers did was to walk in the woods, with Charles leaning heavily on John for strength, to discuss in Latin—for fear of being overheard—the entire situation in Frederica.

Various conferences followed between John and Oglethorpe, John and the malicious women, and John and Charles. The elder brother was himself on the verge of troubles of the heart, but he did succeed in injecting some adult sense into the situation. Oglethorpe, who was responsible for the defense of the colony, frequently found trouble with the threatening presence of the Spaniards. This required occasional expeditions of a reconnoitering and deterrent nature. It occurred to him that it would not be a good thing to risk meeting his Maker with the Wesley affair on his mind. Unfortunately, Charles entered some of the paragraphs, important to this phase, in a personal cipher in his journal. We do know, however, that the governor sent for him and gave him a diamond ring to be retained by Charles in the event of Oglethorpe's death. The governor returned safely, and Charles returned the ring. The *Journal* reads,

> He condemned himself for his anger, which he imputed to his want of time for consideration. . . . He ordered me whatever he could think I wanted; promised to have me an house built immediately; and was just the same to me he had formerly been.[22]

The governor also allowed John and Charles to switch parishes for a while, and it was from John that Charles learned that he would be entrusted with correspondence from Oglethorpe to the London trustees of the colony.

Charles had, however, made up his mind to quit both job and Georgia.

> Wed. July 21st. I heard from my brother that I was to set sail in a few days for England. . . . Sun. July 25th. I resigned my Secretary's place, in a letter to Mr. Oglethorpe. . . .[23]

There was a quiet morning conversation, each assuring the other of the clear air between them, and Oglethorpe requesting Charles not to overpublicize his resignation, in case the trustees should appoint an office-seeking Presbyterian, or the like, who might obstruct the reception of the gospel among the heathen. Charles's resignation should be, in effect, tabled until Oglethorpe could have a say in the appointment of a successor. The governor took the chance to give Charles a little fatherly counsel:

> On many accounts I should recommend to you marriage, rather than celibacy. You are of a social temper, and would find in a married state the difficulties of working out your salvation exceedingly lessened, and your helps as much increased.[24]

Sailing out of Georgia

So on Monday, July 26, Charles Wesley "concluded the lesson, and my stay in Georgia." The final words in the lesson for that day were, "Arise, let us go hence," and he did just that, boarding the boat in Savannah at noon. "When the boat put off I was surprised that I felt no more joy in leaving such a scene of sorrows."[25]

John traveled as far as Charles Town (S.C.) with Charles, entrusted with letters from Oglethorpe to the lieutenant general. They tarried a day or two there, and Charles saw enough of the horror and inhumanity of the black slave trade to make him its enemy for life.

It was August 16 before the ship left Charles Town for Boston—a voyage so rough and storm-filled that Charles, who feared for his life more than once, never forgot it.

He waited in Boston for a more seaworthy boat with a less alcohol-loving captain, staying at the home of a friendly lawyer called Mr. Price. Charles's letters from Boston are cocktails of unhappy moanings, insecurities, uncertainties, and suspicions. Baker points out also that they are written in a strange mixture of Latin, Greek, and shorthand, as though the writer feared they might be intercepted.

Charles was very ill again in Boston, and when the time for embarkation came, he had to be almost carried aboard ship. The old spirit of despair returned. To John he wrote:

> I leave my journal and other papers with Mr. Price, which he will send you if I fall short in England.[26]

The people of Boston were kind to Charles. Ministers and people alike gave him a hospitable reception, but in his state of mind and body it was solitude and silence he craved:

> I am wearied with this hospitable people, they so vex and tense me with their civilities. They do not suffer me to be alone. The clergy, who came from the country on a visit of this New England, are more pleasant even than the old. I cannot help exclaiming, O! Happy country that cherisheth neither flies, nor crocodiles, nor inform-

ers. About the end of the week we shall certainly go on board the ship, having to pay a second time for our passage: even here nothing is to be had without money. . . . My disorder, once removed by this most salubrious air, has again returned. All my friends advise me to consult a physician, but I cannot afford so expensive a funeral.[27]

That was written on October 5, but it was still three more weeks before he went aboard the *Hannah* to sail for England, three weeks of serious illness during which many well-wishing friends pressed him not to embark until he recovered. When the time came, he had to be almost carried aboard by his friends, but he wrote to John:

At present I am something better: on board the Hannah, Captain Corney: in the stateroom, which they have forced upon me. I have not strength for more. Adieu.[28]

The voyage was a rough one, with seas so high and so heavy that the livestock aboard—sheep, hogs, and fowl—were washed overboard. Four men were kept continually at the pumps; the mizzenmast had to be cut down; and the passengers despaired of seeing land alive. But Charles, who recovered sufficiently to read prayers with all who would listen, wrote:

In this dreadful moment I bless God I found the comfort of hope, and such joy in finding I could hope, as the world can neither give nor take away. I had the conviction of the power of God present with me, overbalancing my strongest passion, fear, and raising me above what I am by nature, as suppressed all rational evidence, and gave me a taste of the divine goodness.[29]

Passing safely through this storm and a slightly lesser one, the good ship *Hannah* finally arrived off Deal on December 3, 1736, and the missionary from Georgia gratefully set his feet on terra firma again! Charles's first action was to give thanks.

I knelt down, and blessed the Hand that had conducted me through such inextricable mazes; and desired I might give up my country again to God, when He should require it.[30]

=4

Twin Converts

The Making of the Minstrel Begins

It was easier for Charles Wesley to shake Georgia's grit from his shoes than her grip from his soul. He had left America, but America would not leave him.

The early weeks of 1737 meant for him visits with his family and old friends, privileged contacts and interviews, dinner with royalty, and many another pleasure most welcome after the isolation and deprivations of the colony. But Georgia still called, and in his heart Charles felt drawn to the land of his humiliation and failure. Sickness and popularity alike seemed allies of Georgia. The former was like an accusing master summoning him to return and continue the job he had abandoned, the latter like a charming hostess not quite fulfilling her promises. All year long, the thoughts of return nibbled at his mind.

Oglethorpe had returned to London, as promised, just a few weeks after Charles, and Charles seems to have been thinking that if he could return to Georgia—not in his hated former capacity as secretary but as a properly appointed and accredited missionary—he would really find the niche of God's appointment.

January 1737 was a full month for him. He found that he was a bit of a public personality, especially in the religious and governmental worlds. It seemed that because of John's Georgian journals, which were now becoming known among the elite of literary-minded circles, and because of growing interest in Oglethorpe's Georgia experiment, all of the religious leaders of London wanted to hear a firsthand report of the work being done in the colony. Charles lodged first at the friendly home of the Rivingtons, publishers of the rector's commentary on Job, and associates of the Wesley family. As their house was in St. Paul's Yard, Charles was in a hospitable home among familiar friends, in a well-loved place, and able conveniently to worship again at St. Paul's Cathedral. He later moved to the home of his friend James Hutton in Westminster and was able to attend the meetings of the small religious society that met there every Sunday evening.

Big brother Samuel had left a letter with Hutton for Charles, a letter revealing the affection of Samuel and his wife, Nutty, and assuring Charles of their happiness at his return to England. The letter was a means of grace to Charles, who cherished it to the end of his life. No accusations, no "I told you so," no upbraiding—just a warm, loving letter from affectionate people. Charles wrote on it the words *"Notue in fratris amina paterni,"* or "Let my widow preserve this precious relic."

Charles had conferences with the dignitaries of the church, at which he discussed not only Anglicanism in Georgia and the work of the S.P.G. but also the desirability of closer Anglican-Moravian relationships. For, as with John, the Church of the Moravian Brethren, the *Unitas Fratrum,* had left a deep imprint on his spirit because of the joyful faith and trust of the Moravians in the face of death at sea. In February, he met Oglethorpe and pressed him to secure his appointment as a missionary to Georgia. He attended the meeting of the trustees of the colony and then set out on a round of calling on family and friends. Susanna Wesley was then at the Tiverton home of brother Samuel. That astonishing lady was indisposed and confined to her room, but the meeting was unusually demonstrative; for if John was Susanna's special charge, Charles was her baby son, even if she had turned him into a later edition of her husband. "I went to comfort my mother," he wrote in his *Journal.*

And then it was over to Stanton Harcourt, where he was again given a right royal welcome, "especially by my first of friends, Varanese."

But Georgia tugged more strongly as the weeks went past. Charles was now more than willing to accept the hazards of colonial life in return for a renewed opportunity to work out his own salvation. Oglethorpe, who was willing to let Charles try again, had made the requested nomination.

What was bugging Charles? Was it just a strong attack of "Wesleyitis" that was unwilling to accept failure? Was it a subconscious impulse to redeem himself in his own eyes, a sense of vocation, or just plain egotism? Whatever it was, the trustees appointed him missionary, giving him a special assignment to draw up plans for an orphanage in Georgia. Their decision was some kind of vindication of Charles.

By the early winter of 1737 the Moravian influence, too, was getting stronger over Charles. The Moravian settlement at Herrnhut in

Germany was running a close second to the English settlement in Georgia. He had established contact with the Moravian leader and guide, Count von Zinzendorf—no doubt during discussions between Zinzendorf and the Anglican authorities in London—and now Charles wrote the count, seeking his prayers and letters:

> At last, with difficulty and hesitation, I seem to be rising again. I would once more play the warrior, and force my way into freedom. May thy prayers and the prayers of the community at Herrnhuth, and I beg, may thy letters follow me as I return to Georgia. Pray God on my behalf that I may be willing to be free, that I may thirst for Him alone, that I may fulfill my ministry . . . I take with me a young man named George Whitefield, a minister of fervent spirit . . . God has wondrously aroused by his means the twice-dead populace.[1]

Charles's spirit was abundantly willing, but the second mission was not to be. He wrote to Whitefield, "To go I am resolved on if anyone will set me on horseback and I can keep my seat," for the flesh was once again very weak and sick, and dysentery was immobilizing him. Further, Susanna, with strong maternal instinct, and even stronger feminine force, "vehemently protested" this time, unwilling that even one of her hypothetical "20 sons" should throw his life away. His doctors, too, absolutely forbade him to go. Nevertheless, Charles did make the attempt, reaching Gravesend on December 31, 1737, just in time to bid Godspeed to George Whitefield, already aboard the *Whittaker* and ready to set sail for Georgia.

Two months later Charles, suffering a new and more violent attack of sickness, finally dismissed the idea of returning to Georgia. On April 3, 1738, he submitted the resignation he had withheld at Oglethorpe's request.

Meanwhile, on Wednesday, February 1, 1738, another disillusioned missionary from Georgia arrived in England. Big brother John, having made a rather undignified evacuation from Georgia, was home again, and once more the duo was together.

"The Change Which God Works"

"The change which God works" is but a phrase from one of the most moving and familiar testimonies to the transforming grace of God to be found in religious biography. Although the words are John Wesley's, they express equally well the experience of Charles. The words might indeed stand as the text Charles was expounding from May 21, 1738, until the end of his life. They certainly summarize the whole message of the gospel he preached.

The entire account reads:

> About a quarter before nine, while he was describing the change which God works in the heart through faith in Christ, I felt my heart strangely warmed. I felt I did trust in Christ, Christ alone for salvation; and an assurance was given me that He had taken away my sins, even mine, and saved me from the law of sin and death.[2]

Compare John's witness with that of Charles in a hymn written on the first anniversary of his "great change," that is, on May 21, 1739. The entire hymn is one of glorious Christian freedom and the rapture of praise it spawns!

> *Then with my heart I first believed,*
> *Believed with faith Divine;*
> *Power with the Holy Ghost received,*
> *To call the Savior MINE.*[3]

If any man had the right to sing loud, long, and lovingly of "the change which God works," it was Charles Wesley; for if any man knew the utter misery into which a religion of hard labor and heartbreaking legalism can plunge one, it was he. We have tried to show a little of it; but for the black despair that enveloped him, even as he did his best to work his passage to heaven, there is no language unless it be his own:

> *Sudden expired the legal strife;*
> *'Twas then I ceased to grieve;*
> *My second, real, living life*
> *I then began to live.*[4]

Three factors were involved in the great change that God worked in Charles Wesley on May 21, 1738, just three days before John, too, experienced it. These were a man, a book, and a Voice.

The Man Called Peter

His name was Peter Böhler, just as John Wesley spelled it, though sometimes the umlaut is dropped to make it Bohler. His gravestone in the old Moravian burial ground spells it in Latin, Petrus Boehler. Born in Frankfurt am Main in 1712, he was John's junior by about nine years and Charles's by about five. In some ways he would resemble Whitefield to the Wesleys, Böhler being born of an innkeeper father and relying on the local gymnasium for his elementary education, but pressing on to graduate from the University of Jena.

Böhler arrived in England on Tuesday, February 7, 1738. On that very day John Wesley, who had arrived home but one week previously, met him in the home of a Dutch merchant in London. John writes,

Finding they [Böhler and the two others] had no acquaintance in England, I offered to procure them a lodging, and did so near Mr. Hutton's, where I then was. And from this time I did not willingly lose any opportunity of conversing with them, while I stayed in London.[5]

The timing of Böhler's brief stay in England was divinely perfect. He arrived on February 7, en route to Georgia, and he left on May 4 for Carolina; but those three months proved to be the hinge of history and of destiny to the Wesley brothers and the entire English-speaking world. John Wesley enshrined both dates in his *Journal*. At Böhler's departure, he wrote:

> Oh what a work hath God begun, since his coming into England! Such an one as shall never come to an end till heaven and earth pass away.[6]

The Lord has His moments, and He also knows His men. Böhler was the right man at the right moment for Charles and John Wesley. He was well informed and a solid student of the Bible: he knew *what* he believed as well as *why* he believed it. Böhler was spiritually-minded, warmly evangelistic, yet unoffensive in witness, and he was a devotedly disciplined Christian. Further, he enjoyed his religion, whereas the Wesleys were enduring theirs as a leaden load on their lives.

It is interesting to read the opinion of Böhler on the brothers Wesley at this time. Writing to Zinzendorf, he said,

> The elder, John, is a goodnatured man; he knew that he did not properly believe in our Savior, and was willing to be taught. His brother is at present very much distressed in mind, but does not know how he shall begin to be acquainted with the Savior.[7]

Böhler, who was very much at home with Latin, was clumsy and hesitant with what little English he knew. Consequently, his usefulness was extremely limited. He therefore put himself under the tuition of Charles Wesley to improve his English. The pair conversed mostly in Latin, but Böhler lost little time in pressing salvation by faith on tutor Charles. During February, while John was visiting friends and winding up his Georgian matters, Böhler was with Charles, who was then ill at Oxford. On February 24, Charles, being in very great pain, asked Peter to pray for him. Reluctantly, Peter agreed, and "prayed for my recovery with a strange confidence."

> Then he took me by the hand and calmly said, "You will not die now . . ." He asked me, "Do you hope to be saved?" "Yes." "For what reason do you hope it?" "Because I have used my best endeavours to serve God." He shook his head, and said no more. I thought him very uncharitable, saying in my heart, "What, are not my en-

deavours a sufficient ground of hope? Would he rob me of my endeavours? I have nothing else to trust to."[8]

Charles was gravely ill at that time, and the doctors worked hard with him. Sister Kezzy was brought in and lovingly nursed him. As he noted earlier, his proposed return to Georgia was forbidden by doctors and friends. But Böhler held on.

Partial recovery enabled Charles to get around somewhat feebly. On May 4, Böhler, who had divided his time between the two brothers, had to leave for Carolina. He had kept up his witness to the last, and although successful in persuading John that salvation is by faith and can be instantaneously received, he failed with Charles, who regarded John's acceptance as a betrayal of the faith of the church.

But the seed was sown, and the harvest would come. A week after Böhler's departure Charles decided to move lodgings. He was on the point of doing so when, to quote him,

> God sent Mr. Bray to me, a poor ignorant mechanic, who knows nothing but Christ; yet by knowing Him, knows and discerns all things . . . Mr. Bray is now to supply Bohler's place.[9]

The move from the home of Hutton, Sr., was necessitated by Mr. Hutton's antipathy to the interest being taken by the Wesleys in the Moravian doctrine of faith and instantaneous salvation. The elder Wesley had acknowledged his agreement with this before Böhler left London and had for some little time been engaged in condensing the biography of the Scottish Presbyterian Haliburton. This was, as Charles Wesley said at the time, "one instance, and but one, of instantaneous conversion," of which he was not as yet personally convinced.

Mr. Hutton, Jr., was a publisher and willing to handle John's *Life of Haliburton,* but his father forbade him. Charles Wesley was undiplomatic enough to read the book aloud to the family; thus tension crept into the situation. This was the immediate reason for Charles's decision to move from the comfortable Hutton home to that of "the poor mechanic" Mr. Bray, although Charles was still looking for proof that instantaneous conversion is not God's way with man's soul!

Being unable to walk, Charles was carried by sedan chair from the Huttons' to Mr. Bray's in Little Britain, off Aldersgate Street and near to St. Paul's. Thus Charles went from unusual comfort to a brazier's home, where that happy Christian lived prayerfully, holily, and in loving joy.

The Book

Martin Luther's writings form another link between the conversion of Charles and that of John. In John's case, the Luther writing seems to have been his *Preface to the Roman Epistle*. In Charles's case, it was Luther's *Commentary on Galatians*.

On May 12, Charles awoke with a great yearning for God and righteousness. For a few days past, his opposition had been dwindling, and he had been coming to the conclusion that faith must be the porch of peace with God, but it must be faith in the atoning Christ. The reading of the prophet Isaiah convinced him that the promises of the gospel were not simply general, but personal. They were for the "whole wide world, *and me!*"

At every opportunity Peter Bray read the Scriptures to his household and joined Charles in urgent prayer for health and holiness. Ten days went past in this earnest manner. Charles was visited by some other remarkable men who had peace with God.

A certain Mr. Ainsworth's openness to truth moved Wesley deeply, and this may indicate that his last defense against simple faith alone was crumbling, for Ainsworth was a classical scholar of some distinction, as was Charles.

Mr. Holland, one of Charles's Anglican friends in fellowship with the Moravians, and who was probably the reader of Luther's *Preface to the Romans*, which had so affected John Wesley, on May 17 introduced Charles to Luther on the Galatians. The book shook Charles profoundly.

> I marvelled that we were so soon and entirely removed from him that called us into the grace of Christ, unto another Gospel. Who would believe that our Church had been founded on this important article of justification by faith alone? I am astonished I should ever think this a new doctrine . . . Salvation by faith alone— not an idle, dead faith, but a faith which works by love, and is incessantly productive of all good works and all holiness.[10]

Whatever his big brother had to say later about Luther,[11] it was Luther who set both brothers before the door of faith and put their hands on its handle. "I spent some hours this evening in private with Martin Luther," wrote Charles, "especially his conclusion of the 2nd chapter."

> *I laboured, waited, and prayed, to feel*
> *"Who loved ME, and gave himself for ME,"*

which was precisely Luther's counsel in the book.

> When nature, near exhausted, forced me to bed, I opened the book upon, "For He will finish the work, and cut it short in righteousness, because a short work will the Lord make on the earth." After this comfortable assurance that He would come, and would not tarry, I slept in peace.[12]

Two days later, on May 19, Charles was visited by another Moravian—a lady this time. He quizzed her closely on her personal experience of Christ, and her answers completely satisfied him that here was yet another undeniable witness to salvation by faith alone, in the atoning Christ alone, resulting in peace with God.

> Her answers were so full to these and the most searching questions I could ask, that I had no doubt of her having received the atonement; and waited for it myself with a more assured hope.[13]

The following day was spent in reading the Scriptures with Mr. Bray, who was troubled at Charles's deferred faith. The portion that brought most comfort was Matthew 9, which relates the healing of the palsied man. Charles writes:

> It was a long while before he could read this through, for tears of joy: and I saw herein, and firmly believed, that his faith would be available for the healing of me.[14]

Thus Charles Wesley went to bed on Saturday evening, May 20, 1738.

That night, John Wesley and a few of his friends, fearing that Charles was about to die, spent the entire night in prayer for him.[15] The answer surpassed all their asking.

The Voice

It was Sunday, May 21, 1738. The Christian calendar declared it to be Pentecost Day; the Anglican calendar called it Whitsunday—the white day of the Church. To most Christians, it was the day of the Upper Room gift of the Holy Ghost, from the Father, through the Son, to the Church—but to Charles Wesley it was the day of deliverance, the day of his life: the day for which he will borrow the experience of Peter in the jail of Herod, or Paul in the prison at Philippi, and the language of David, Isaiah, and Jesus Christ:

> *Long my imprisoned spirit lay,*
> *   Fast bound in sin and nature's night.*
> *Thine eye diffused a quick'ning ray.*
> *   I woke; the dungeon flamed with light!*
> *My chains fell off, my heart was free;*
> *I rose, went forth, and followed Thee.*[16]

Many volumes, written over many years, crammed with multiple metaphors, backed by countless examples, will not suffice for Charles Wesley to say what he feels and knows about the events of this day of all days. It was May Day in his soul.

In a rapture of joy,
    My life I employ
        The God of my life to proclaim!
    'Tis worth living for this,
    To administer bliss
        And salvation in Jesus's Name![17]

At this point in his *Journal*, however, Charles recounts plainly and directly just what occurred, and the best description is his own.

Charles heads the section in bold capitals that stress the day's importance to him.

The Day of Pentecost

The words have no doctrinal significance, nor ought we to force any into them. They are rather a simple recognition of a special day in the Christian year that became an extraspecial day to him. He then writes:

THE DAY OF PENTECOST

Sun., May 21st, 1738. I waked in hope and expectation of his coming. At nine my brother and some friends came, and sang an hymn to the Holy Ghost. My comfort and hope were hereby increased. In about half-an-hour they went: I betook myself to prayer; the substance as follows:—"O Jesus, thou hast said, 'I will come unto you'; thou hast said, 'I will send the Comforter unto you'; thou hast said, 'My Father and I will come unto you, and make our abode with you.' Thou art God who canst not lie; I wholly rely upon thy most true promise: accomplish it in thy time and manner." Having said this, I was composing myself to sleep, in quietness and peace, when I heard one come in (Mrs. Musgrave, I thought, by the voice) and say, "In the name of Jesus of Nazareth, arise, and believe, and thou shalt be healed of all thy infirmities." I wondered how it should enter into her head to speak in that manner. The words struck me to the heart. I sighed, and said within myself, "O that Christ would but speak thus to me!" I lay musing and trembling: then thought, "But what if it should be him? I will send at least to see." I rang, and, Mrs. Turner coming, I desired her to send up Mrs. Musgrave. She went down, and returning, said, "Mrs. Musgrave had not been here." My heart sunk within me at the word, and I hoped it might be Christ indeed. However, I sent her down again to inquire, and felt in the meantime a strange palpitation came of heart. I said, yet feared to say, "I believe, I believe!" She came up again and said, "It was I, a weak, sinful creature, spoke; but the words were Christ's: he commanded me to say them, and so constrained me that I could not forbear."

I sent for Mr. Bray, and asked him whether I believed. He answered, I ought not to doubt of it: it was Christ spoke to me. He knew it; and willed us to pray together: "but first," said he, "I will read what I have casually opened upon: 'Blessed is the man whose unrighteousness is forgiven, and whose sin is covered: blessed is the man to whom the Lord imputeth no sin, and in whose spirit is no guile.'" Still I felt a violent opposition and reluctance to believe; yet still the Spirit of God strove with my own and the evil spirit, till by degrees he chased away the darkness of my unbelief. I found myself convinced, I knew not how, nor where; and immediately fell to intercession.

Mr. Bray then told me, his sister had been ordered by Christ to come and say those words to me. This she afterwards confirmed, and related to me more at large the manner of her believing. At night, and nearly the moment I was taken ill, she dreamt she heard one knock at the door: she went down and opened it; saw a person in white; caught hold of and asked him who he was, and answered, "I am Jesus Christ," and cried out, with great vehemence, "Come in, come in!"

She waked in a fright. It was immediately suggested to her. "You must not mind this: it is all a dream, an illusion." She continued wavering and uneasy all Friday till evening prayers. No sooner were they begun than she found herself full of the power of faith, so that she could scarce contain herself, and almost doubted whether she was sober. At the same time she was enlarged in love and prayer for all mankind, and commanded to go and assure me from Christ of my recovery, soul and body. She returned home repeating with all joy and triumph, "I believe, I believe:" yet her heart failed her, and she durst not say the words to me that night.

On Sunday morning she took Mr. Bray aside, burst into tears, and informed him of the matter; objecting she was a poor weak sinful creature, and should she go to a Minister? She could not do it; nor rest till she did. He asked whether she had ever found herself so before. "No never." "Why, then," said he, "go. Remember Jonah. You declare promises, not threatenings. Go in the name of the Lord. Fear not your own weakness. Speak you the words: Christ will do the work. Out of the mouth of babes and sucklings hath he ordained strength."

They prayed together, and she then went up, but durst not come in till she had prayed again by herself. About six minutes after she had left him, he found and felt, while she was speaking the words, that Christ was with us. I never heard words uttered with like solemnity. The sound of her voice was entirely changed into that of Mrs. Musgrave. (If I can be sure of anything sensible.) I rose and looked into the Scripture. The words that first presented were, "And now, Lord, what is my hope? truly my hope is even in thee." I then cast down my eye, and met, "He hath put a new song in my mouth, even a thanksgiving unto our God. Many shall see it, and fear, and shall put their trust in the Lord." Afterwards I opened upon Isaiah xl.1: "Comfort ye, comfort ye my people, saith your God: speak ye comfortably to Jerusalem, and cry unto her, that her warfare is accomplished, that her iniquity is pardoned; for she hath received of the Lord's hand double for all her sin."

I now found myself at peace with God, and rejoiced in hope of loving Christ. My temper for the rest of the day was, mistrust of my own great, but before unknown, weakness. I saw that by faith I stood; by the continual support of faith, which kept me from falling, though of myself I am ever sinking into sin. I went to bed still sensible of my own weakness, (I humbly hope to be more and more so,) yet confident of Christ's protection.

Mon., May 23rd. Under his protection I waked next morning, and rejoiced in reading the 107th Psalm, so nobly describing what God had done for my soul. I fell asleep again, and waked out of a dream that I was fighting with two devils; had one under my feet; the other faced me some time, but faded, and sunk, and vanished away, upon my telling him I belonged to Christ.

To-day I saw him chiefly as my King, and found him in his power: but saw little of the love of Christ crucified, or of my sins past: though more, I humbly hope, of my own weakness and his strength. I had many evil thoughts darted into my mind, but I rejected them immediately (yet not I). At noon I rose, continually fainting, nevertheless upheld. I was greatly strengthened by Isaiah xliii., which God directed me to.

My brother coming, we joined in intercession for him. In the midst of prayer, I almost believed the Holy Ghost was coming upon him. In the evening we sang and prayed again. I found myself very weak in body, but thought I ought to pray for my friends, being the only Priest among them. I kneeled down, and was immediately strengthened, both mind and body. The enemy did not lose such an opportunity of tempting me to pride: but, God be praised, my strength did I ascribe unto him. I was often since assisted to pray readily and earnestly, without a form. Not unto me, O Lord, not unto me, but to thy name be the glory![18]

Surprise! Surprise!

Why Charles's conversion should have been a surprise to brother John surprises us as well, unless John assumed that, as the first of the fraternal pair to acknowledge the truth of Böhler's teaching on saving faith, he would likewise be first to find faith. Having spent the night of Saturday, May 20, in prayer, on Sunday he went to church at St. Mary-le-Strand to hear his friend Dr. Heylyn preach. It was

a truly Christian sermon (on "They were all filled with the Holy
Ghost"; "and so," said he, "may ALL YOU be, if it is not your own
fault") . . . I received the surprising news that my brother had found
rest to his soul. His bodily strength returned also from that hour.
"Who is so great a God as our God?"[19]

On Wednesday, May 24, the voice of William Holland reading the
words of Martin Luther brought faith, peace, and assurance to the
troubled heart of John Wesley.

> I felt I did trust in Christ, Christ alone for salvation; and an as-
> surance was given me that He had taken away MY sins, even
> MINE, and saved ME from the law of sin and death.[20]

John discovered, as Charles had done three days previously, that
Luther was right: "experimental religion lies in the personal pronouns!"

The Special Number—a Duet

John's friends in the meeting room rejoiced with great joy at his
testimony. It was but a short walk across the street and along to Little
Britain. A turn in to the right, and there on the corner stood the building in which Charles lodged with Bray. Never did "a troop," as
Charles described John and his companions, cover the distance quite
so speedily, and within minutes John was standing in Charles's bedroom, crying, "I believe! I believe!" Twin converts! It was the birth—or
was it the sealing?—of a partnership.

Twin Converts

Seen in retrospect, the progress of the Wesley brothers toward
May 1738 is like viewing from a hilltop two interweaving footpaths—
meeting, crossing, and merging, only to diverge again, but ultimately
joining the main road at the same gate.

Although Charles arrived and passed through the wicket gate only about three days before John, they were really fellow travelers and
Methodist good companions. To change the metaphor, they were really spiritual twins. They had the same father in Christ, namely Peter
Böhler, who placed the seed of the Word in their hearts. In Edwards'
phrase, Peter Böhler was "the main precipatory influence in their conversion."[21]

Böhler found John to be much more open and willing to face the
facts, hear the witnesses, weigh the evidence, and reach a verdict than
Charles. Böhler found Charles to be difficult: he seemed unpredictable
and impetuous, subject to depression, ready to jump to unwarranted
conclusions about himself. At times his *Journal* reads like a clinical

chart on the end of a bed. Under God only could the admirable Böhler and the patient Bray have been able to cope with him in the distress of his soul travail.

Martin Luther, that colossus of Christian history, wrote tenderly enough to point Charles to the personal pronouns of the Pauline gospel, but powerfully enough to penetrate John's impeding philosophy until he, too, felt the force of Paul's pronouns. With Charles, it was Luther's *Galatians*—the message of Christian freedom through personal faith. With John, it was probably Luther's *Preface to the Romans*. Paul's gospel includes the words of God's grace—"free to all," "free in all," and "free for all." These were the Lutheran fires that warmed the Wesley hearts.

How fitting it was that in the final phase of their own salvation, two of the greatest communicators of the Word of God to the 18th century should receive the Word through human voices. In Charles's case, it was Mrs. Musgrave's voice; in John's case, it was the voice of William Holland. But in each case the word was the Word of the Lord from Paul through Martin Luther.

The End of the Beginning

The conversion of the brothers was the end of their seeking and the beginning of their mission. From here on, they will continue to seek God's face in an ever-growing knowledge of His will. They will in the highest sense remain seekers all of their lives. Now they were not joyless servants seeking rest, but joyful sons seeking to do their Father's will. They were on the launching pad—not into space orbit, but into the highways and hedges, the smelly alleys and streets, fashionable mansions, and well-cushioned pulpits. The conversion experience was "not the end, nor even the beginning of the end; it was just the end of the beginning." Their conversion brought them to their mission, and their mission to them.

With all the Wesleys' ups and downs, the changes of tone, time, and key, the record of that mission indeed reads and sounds like a great oratorio under the baton of the mighty Maestro—the Holy Spirit!

The Opening Chorus

Before parting company on that tremendous evening of May 24, 1738, the brothers Wesley "sang the hymn with great joy."[22] What hymn? "It would be interesting," wrote Methodist hymn writer and musician Luke Wiseman, "to know the strains of this opening chorus of the great Methodist Oratorio." No doubt it would. The words are our first interest, however, as expressing the soul and the sentiments of the twice-born twins.

Some discussion has gone on around the identity of the hymn in question, but the present writer sees no good reason for rejecting the hymn beginning,

> Where shall my wondering soul begin?

They had just been brought from darkness into the marvelous light, lifted from the pit of noise and dirt to the rock of rejoicing, and there was a golden mist of marvel over their minds and hearts. Not many days ago, Charles had been singing

> Weary of struggling with my pain,
> Hopeless to trust my nature's chain,
> Hardly I give the contest o'er,
> I seek to free myself no more.
>
> With simple faith, to Thee I call,
> My Light, my Life, my Lord, my all:
> I wait the moving of the pool;
> I wait the word that speaks me whole.[23]

But now? The chains are off, the Spirit has breathed, the waters have moved, the Lord has spoken! It is now time for Te Deum, not dirge, for this is not a pleasing little experience—it is life from the dead! It is the bursting of prison walls! It is an explosion of grace! It is therefore time for the Methodist music man to open up, to pull out all the stops, to call on all the strings and woods and winds and cymbals of the redeemed soul, and to crash in on the scene like the opening chords of a Handel oratorio in a chatter-filled Georgian ballroom! The hymn is calling, "ATTENTION, PLEASE! Let us praise the Lord!"

The hymn sung by the brothers on the night of nights was one that Charles had written the day before. He refers to it in his *Journal* for May 23, 1738:

> At nine I began an hymn upon my conversion, but was persuaded to break off, for fear of pride. Mr. Bray coming, encouraged me to proceed in spite of Satan. I prayed Christ to stand by me, and finished the hymn. Upon my afterwards showing it to Mr. Bray, the devil threw in a fiery dart, suggesting, that it was wrong, and I had displeased God. My heart sunk within me; when, casting my eye upon a Prayer-book, I met with an answer for him. "Why boastest thou thyself, thou tyrant, that thou canst do mischief?" Upon this I clearly discerned it was a device of the enemy to keep back glory from God. And it is most unusual with him to reach humility, when speaking will endanger his kingdom, or do honour to Christ. Least of all would he have us tell what things God has done for our souls,

so tenderly does he guard us from pride. But God has showed me, he can defend me from it, while speaking for him. In his name therefore, and through his strength, I will perform my vows unto the Lord, of not hiding his righteousness within my heart, if it should ever please him to plant it there.[24]

A careful reading of the hymn will reveal all the notes of the glad gospel of pardon and freedom: verse 3 shows the temptation Wesley has spoken of; verse 4, normally omitted from hymnbooks, gives us his reply to the devil—a hearty resounding "NO!"—and his affirmation to preach the gospel.

The hymn has roused criticisms, valid and invalid, some of them very wily, by men who just don't like the idea of the best of news for the worst of people and object, moreover, to the company in which the hymn puts them! But all the grand old simplicities of the gospel are here. Further, the hymn is sometimes severely cut to accommodate both the critics and lazy modern congregations. I quote it from *Poetical Works* (1:91-92), where it is headed "Christ the Friend of Sinners," and begins part II of *Hymns and Sacred Poems*, published in 1739.

> *Where shall my wondering soul begin?*
> *How shall I all to heaven aspire?*
> *A slave redeem'd from death and sin,*
> *A brand pluck'd from eternal fire,*
> *How shall I equal triumphs raise,*
> *And sing my great Deliverer's praise!*

* * *

> *Outcasts of men, to you I call,*
> *Harlots, and publicans, and thieves!*
> *He spreads His arms to embrace you all;*
> *Sinners alone His grace receives:*
> *No need of Him the righteous have,*
> *He came the lost to seek and save.*

* * *

> *Come, O my guilty brethren, come,*
> *Groaning beneath your load of sin!*
> *His bleeding heart shall make you room,*
> *His open side shall take you in.*
> *He calls you now, invites you home:*
> *Come, O my guilty brethren, come!*

5

All My Business

*P*ROBABLY NO HYMN OF CHARLES WESLEY'S
sums up more aptly and fully his mission as he saw it than does that
magnificent evangelistic manifesto:

> *Jesus! the Name high over all*
> *In hell, or earth, or sky;*
> *Angels and men before it fall,*
> *And devils fear and fly.*

The hymn goes on through six glorious verses on the power of
the Lord Jesus and includes Charles's exposition of the Wesleyan mission. Here are two:

> *O that the world might taste and see*
> *The riches of His grace.*
> *The arms of love that compass me*
> *Would all mankind embrace.*

> *His only righteousness I show,*
> *His saving grace proclaim;*
> *'Tis all my business here below*
> *To cry, "Behold the Lamb!"*[1]

Slowly regaining his health, Charles was the means of the salvation of one of two people to whom he witnessed during June 1738. He
witnessed also to others, who listened eagerly. Among these was Dr.
Byrom, the scientist of Manchester and "an ingenious poet," as Whitehead puts it. He spoke in small meetings in London, and 30 persons
were converted.[2] Also about this time, Charles recovered sufficiently
to conduct public worship once again. In these services, too, a number
of people were converted.

But Charles's path had its ups and downs for a month or two. As
Frank Baker puts it,

> Depression was still to dog his footsteps, for it was one of the
> predominant traits of his volatile nature. . . . Henceforth, however,

72

Whitsuntide was always to be a time of peculiar blessing for him. Underlying the choppy surface of his Christian experience were the calm deeps of his new certainty of God's love for him, a more confident reliance upon that love filling every moment of his life. . . . There was a new enthusiasm, a new glow, a spiritual buoyancy which found its most lasting expression in the lilt of Gospel song, but which also revealed itself in his letters.[3]

Charles witnesses with surprising frankness to his feelings during those early days of new life. He was an emotional person who was extremely sensitive to "atmosphere" and who became depressed when he could not feel things in his soul.

> I was troubled to-day, that I could not pray, being utterly dead at the sacrament. . . . I was still unable to pray; still dead in communicating; full of a cowardly desire of death. . . . My deadness continued, and the next day increased.[4]

These quotes record Charles's feelings on three consecutive days: June 1, 2, and 3. It was a reaction involving the interaction of a spiritual high and a physical low; but before June 3 was over, his spirits were restored and his faith radiant. He had also learned that one way out of the depths is to praise God and to help others. He compared his reaction with his former experiences of depression:

> I could not help asking myself, "Where is the difference between what I am now, and what I was before believing?" I immediately answered, "That the darkness was not like the former darkness, because I was satisfied there was no guilt in it; because I was assured it would be dispersed; and because, though I could not find I loved God, or feel that he loved me, yet I did and would believe that he loved me notwithstanding."

And in a few hours he is rejoicing:

> We were all full of joy and thanksgiving. Before we parted, I prayed with Mr. Brown [whom he had just led into saving faith], and praised God, to the great confirmation of my faith. The weight was quite taken off. I found power to pray with great earnestness, and rejoiced in my trials having continued so long, to shew me that it is then the best time to labour for our neighbour, when we are most cast down, and most unable to help ourselves.[5]

It was good for Wesley that during those weeks he had Mr. Bray at his elbow, for that godly mechanic was both brother and counselor to him.

There were three general phases in Charles Wesley's ministry after his conversion.

1. There was an opening phase in which personal evangelism dominated. Charles was a zealous and efficient personal worker until

his death, but this is most marked in the first and the final phases of his ministry.

2. There was the period during which field preaching and itinerant evangelism predominated. Here again, he never ceased to be an evangelist, but he did cease to be an itinerant.

3. There was the period when his ministry, both in Bristol and in London, was more directly a pastoral one.

Personal Evangelism

Beginning in June 1738, Charles Wesley's *Journal* is crammed with instances of his witnessing and with cases of conversion. Already he is showing what "all his business" is, and unconsciously demonstrating his own proposition.

"What we have felt and seen, with confidence we tell!" He has good news, and he cannot and will not keep it dark. Person after person receives his witness, and many of them are converted. In the London churches his preaching bemuses his former friends. Charles Rivington is forthrightly hostile to "instant faith," as is Mrs. Delamotte, who

> fell abruptly upon my sermon, for the false doctrine contained therein. I answered, "I staked my all upon the truth of it." She went on, "It is hard people must have their children seduced in their absence. If every one must have your faith, what will become of all the world?" . . . Much dispute ensued. She accused my brother with preaching an instantaneous faith. "As to that," I replied, "we cannot but speak the things which we have seen and heard. I received it in that manner; as have above 30 others in my presence." She started up, said she could not bear it, and ran out of the house.[6]

But Mrs. Delamotte, too, came into living faith about two weeks later, grateful indeed for the gentle sincerity of Charles, who excused her unkindly behavior by remembering how intransigent he himself had been when first confronted with the demand for "instant faith."

From Tiverton, big brother Samuel, mystified by all that was transpiring, wrote Charles a letter "full of heavy charges."

But by far the most important events of that first year of Charles Wesley's new life were, first, his taking up an evangelistic ministry to the criminals; and second, his following the example of George Whitefield in the strategy of field preaching.

The Shadow of the Cross Falls over the Gallows

From the early days of the Oxford Methodists, Charles had been strongly drawn to work among the prisoners in the jails of Oxford and

London. William Morgan had persuaded the Oxford Methodists as early as 1730 to visit the prisoners in the castle jail there. The visits were soon extended to take in the debtors' prison known as the Bocardo. In Georgia as well, Charles had on occasion dealt with prisoners discharged on condition that they go to the colony. But his jail ministry in those days, although compassionate and comforting, totally lacked any vestige of evangelical concern. Now, however, it was different. On Monday, July 10, Charles definitely committed himself to obeying his Master by visiting the prisoners. It was a vital Methodist ministry, which, beginning with Charles, was to involve some of the most remarkable evangelists of the modern Church. Among these was Silas Told, one of John Wesley's converts who left the slave trade—and later his business—and gave 30 years to traveling in the death wagon to Tyburn with the condemned criminals.

Charles found a powerful ministry in this form of evangelism. The records surpass description and make strange reading in these days when the Church of Christ is making a belated rediscovery of this great field of human woe and misery.[7]

> Mon. July 10th [1738]. At Mr. Spark's request I went with him, Mr. Bray, and Mr. Burnham, to Newgate; and preached to the ten malefactors, under sentence of death; but with a heavy heart. My old prejudices against the possibility of death-bed repentance still hung upon me; and I could hardly hope there was mercy for those whose time was so short. But in the midst of my languid discourse, a sudden spirit of faith came upon me, and I promised them all pardon, in the name of Jesus Christ, if they would then, as at the last hour, repent, and believe the Gospel. Nay, I did believe they would accept of the proferred mercy, and could not help telling them, "I had no doubt but that God would give me every soul of them."[8]

He was back two days later, and on this occasion dealt personally with a prisoner for whom he felt specially deep compassion, namely,

> a poor black that had robbed his master. I told him of one who came down from heaven to save lost sinners, and him in particular; described the sufferings of the Son of God, his sorrows, agony, and death. He listened with all the signs of eager astonishment; the tears trickled down his cheeks while he cried, "What! was it for me? Did God suffer all this for so poor a creature as me?" I left him waiting for the salvation of God.[9]

That same evening he dealt equally directly with Mr. Washington from Queen's College, and on the next morning he was back again at Newgate jail:

> I read prayers and preached at Newgate, and administered the sacrament to our friends, with five of the felons.[10]

Next day he is at Newgate again, where he

> spake strongly to the poor malefactors; and to the sick Negro in the condemned hole, moved by his sorrow and earnest desire for Jesus Christ.[11]

And again the following day, Saturday, July 15:

> I preached again with an enlarged heart; and rejoiced with my poor happy Black; who now *believes* the Son of God loved him, and gave himself for him.[12]

The hangings were scheduled for Wednesday, July 19. Charles was at Newgate on July 16 and 17, persuading criminals in Christ's stead to be reconciled to God. The black man had great soul peace. Another felt his heart "all on fire," believing Christ died for him, and yet another was "strongly moved." On the 18th, Charles counseled the black and eight others condemned to die, then administered Communion to them. That night, Charles and Bray had themselves locked in the death cell with the condemned men.

> We wrestled in mighty prayer. All the criminals were present; and all delightfully cheerful. The soldier, in particular, found his comfort and joy increase every moment. Another, from the time he communicated, has been in perfect peace. Joy was visible in all their faces. We sang,
>
> > Behold the Savior of mankind,
> > Nail'd to the shameful tree!
> > How vast the love that him inclined
> > To bleed and die for thee, etc.
>
> It was one of the most triumphant hours I have ever known.[13]

As the dreadful hour approached, Charles spent the remaining time with his 10 new brethren. He describes without ornamentation how the "irons were knocked off." He tells of the ride to the Tyburn gallows in the cart with the condemned, and—dreadful as it was—he speaks of "the children appointed to die."

He prayed with, and kissed, the men. All were in good spirits:

> They were all cheerful; full of comfort, peace, and triumph; assuredly persuaded Christ had died for them, and waited to receive them into paradise. Greenaway was impatient to be with Christ.[14]

The whole scene, which by all natural reason should have been pathetic and sorrowful, was by supernatural grace one of incredible confidence and praise! "I never saw such calm triumph," wrote Charles. The hymn was sung again, and the spirits of the 10 were commended "to him that judgeth righteously" (1 Pet. 2:23). The cart drew off, but the men remained calm. Not one of them struggled, but all "meekly gave up their spirits." At exactly 12 midday at Tyburn they were with Christ in paradise. It was triumph all the way!

> I spoke a few suitable words to the crowd; and returned, full of peace and confidence in our friends' happiness. That hour under the gallows was the most blessed hour of my life.[15]

From that hour spent on the gallows under the shadow of the Cross, Charles Wesley's life for the next 15 years takes on the color and tone of "that Glorious Monotony" ascribed to the labors of his brother John, and is a running commentary on his own words:

> *'Tis all my business here below*
> *To cry "Behold the Lamb!"*

Not to Be Muzzled: Proclamations of Grace

Throughout the summer of 1738, John Wesley was on the Continent. He had gone to visit Zinzendorf at the Moravian settlement in Herrnhut, Germany, and to see "where the Christians lived." Had he been in London, perhaps he would have counseled his brother not to accept an Islington appointment, for it appears that although Charles had taken it on the express invitation of the minister, Mr. Stonehouse, ecclesiastical procedure required that he also have approval from the bishop. This Charles did not have, and the church wardens of the congregation knew so. For two reasons, then, he could not last at Islington: he lacked the proper legal authority, and his new message of salvation by faith was offensive to the church wardens, although the minister was not strongly against it. Therefore, there was trouble ahead at Islington.

In September he preached in Westminster Abbey on "Salvation by Faith" and conducted the Communion service. On the same day he had a full house at St. Botolph's on Aldersgate to hear him expound Romans 2. On September 19 he preached three times and complained of a sore throat, but rejoiced that the evening congregation of 300 was "attentive" and that "another lost sheep was now brought home." In a day or two he persuaded a certain Mrs. Metcalf of her need of repentance and faith and left her rejoicing in the Lord. On September 16 he was back at Newgate jail preaching "Christ to four condemned prisoners," and that evening John returned from Herrnhut.

> At night my brother returned from Herrnhuth. We took sweet counsel together, comparing our experiences.[16]

The following day Charles again preached three times, and in each service announced and emphasized the need of repentance and faith. In brief, Charles Wesley would not be muzzled. Grace is an

amazing thing, and a Christian is a person to whom an amazing thing
has happened that cannot be kept dark. As Charles had written earlier
that year, a single tongue would not do the theme justice. He longed
for a thousand:

> *O for a thousand tongues to sing*
> *My great Redeemer's praise!*

but at present he would make the one he had do the work of a thousand!

One seemingly unimportant event occurred in October. Charles
gave it only five lines in his *Journal*, but it was probably of immeasur-
able importance to the coming Revival.

> Seeing so few present at St. Antholin's, I thought of preaching
> extempore: afraid; yet ventured on the promise, "Lo I am with you
> always;" and spake on justification from Romans iii, for three quar-
> ters of an hour, without hesitation. Glory be to God, who keepeth
> His promise for ever.[17]

The importance of this development should be neither ignored nor
diminished. Whatever opinion we may hold on the debate about sermon delivery, it does appear that Charles Wesley would have been ill-
fitted and unprepared for preaching in the streets and on the hillsides
and fields of England and Ireland if he had not first "ventured on the
promise" and preached extempore at St. Antholin's. The method had
danger for him, magnificent preacher though he was—indeed, there
were those who declared him more powerful than Whitefield. His one
great shortcoming in this respect was his tendency toward insufficient
sermon preparation, always the snare of the extemporaneous preacher.

Field Preacher and Itinerant Evangelist:
With Whitefield onto the White Fields

Not since the Quaker George Fox, "the man in the leather breech-
es," and before him not since Wycliffe's Lollards, had the common
people of England seen the like of George Whitefield. Returning from
America in December 1738, George found that he was increasingly
unwelcome in the churches of London. But he also found that the
multitudes for whom Christ died were not in the churches. Therefore,
he went where the people were—to the streets and squares of the city,
and to the wide-open spaces of Moorfields and Kennington Common.

George was the John the Baptist of the Revival, and the Wesleys
were like Andrew and John Zebedee who followed him to those "re-
gions beyond" the churches.

Soon after John Wesley returned from Herrnhut, the brothers
were called upon to answer complaints about their preaching of faith

and assurance. They appeared together before the bishop of London on October 12, 1738, to reply to charges of antinomianism. The charge was absurd, of course, and the brothers emphatically said so:

> "If by assurance," said Bishop Gibson, "you mean that inward persuasion whereby a man is conscious in himself . . . that he is in a state of salvation, I do not see how any good Christian can be without such assurance."[18]

The brothers declared that such was their preaching, and the interview ended with an amicable agreement that the Fetter Lane Society, with which the brothers were at that time associated, was not in violation of the law concerning conventicles. The good bishop assured them that his door was open to them at all times, and John and Charles left.

Meanwhile, the Islington affair was cooking, and this time Charles alone was called on the bishop's carpet. Ostensibly, the interview concerned Charles's intention to press the point that baptism by Dissenters or schismatics is invalid, but the bishop soon got around to the Islington church affair and asked if Charles was a licensed curate. Charles replied that he had proper invitation and agreement with the minister.

> "But do you know," asked Gibson, "that no man can exercise parochial duty in London, without my leave?" "Does your Lordship exert that power? Do you now inhibit me?" Charles asked. But the bishop was by now exasperated and said loudly, "O why will you push matters to an extreme? I do not inhibit you . . . you knew my judgment before, and you know it now; good morrow to you!"[19]

But if the bishop of London did not "inhibit" Charles, the church wardens at St. Mary's Islington did. As preached by Charles, the gospel of faith alone, in Christ alone—a message so welcomed by the condemned criminals of Newgate—was most unwelcome in many London churches. What the criminals accepted as the best of news for the worst of people, the sinners of St. Mary's Islington rejected as the worst of news for the best of people.

It was preposterous, after all, for decent people to be told that their religious hearts were as sinful as Wesley's "poor black" in Newgate death row, and that all their good religious works were dirty and tattered rags, quite useless as the means of salvation, since that is by faith alone in Christ alone! Hence in the *Journal* we soon come to this:

> After prayers Mr. Stonehouse made way for me to the pulpit: I offered to go up, when one Cotteril, and a Beadle, forcibly kept me back. I thought, "The servant of the Lord must not strive;" and

yielded . . . Mr. Streat advised to ask Mr. Stonehouse to discharge me from ever preaching again.[20]

Though Mr. Stonehouse held on to his curate for a few more months, the writing was on the wall. Thus Charles records on June 15, 1739, that the minister had reluctantly acceded to the request of his board and "consented that I should preach no more."[21]

What was to be done? With a fire burning in his bones and the London pulpits closing against him one after another, he began to see the inner meaning of Whitefield's ministry. Charles's objective was the salvation of souls. The method was principally preaching: he must preach where the souls were, and Whitefield had revealed that. The common people were thronging to hear him, 5,000 here, 10,000 there. His congregation on Kennington Common was reported to be around 15,000, rising on occasion to 20,000.

George needed help. Would his dearest friend Charles "come over . . . and help" him (Acts 16:9)? On December 11, 1738, the friends stood together in the field as George preached to "a vast throng at St. Helen's." In April Charles stood with him as he preached in Islington Churchyard. On May 29 Charles preached in farmer Franklyn's field to about 500 people on "Repent: for the kingdom of heaven is at hand" (Matt. 4:17). It is apparent that, unlike John at that time, Charles was not troubled at becoming "more vile." But he did have a strong deposit of ecclesiastical propriety in his soul, and he balked at the starting line.

On June 24, however, all hesitancy was taken away. Significantly enough, it was St. John the Baptist's Day on the church calendar—a pretty significant precedent of field preaching.

> Sun. June 24th. St. John Baptist's day. The first Scripture I cast my eye upon, was, "Then came the servant unto him, and said, Master, what shall we do?" I prayed with West, and went forth in the name of Jesus Christ. I found near ten thousand helpless sinners waiting for the word, in Moorfields. I invited them in my Master's words, as well as name: "Come unto me, all ye that travail, and are heavy-laden, and I will give you rest." The Lord was with me, even me, his meanest messenger, according to his promise. At St. Paul's, the Psalms, Lessons, &c., for the day, put fresh life into me. So did the sacrament. My load was gone, and all my doubts and scruples. God shone upon my path; and I knew this was his will concerning me.[22]

And later that same day:

> I walked on to the Common, and cried to multitudes upon multitudes, "Repent ye, and believe the Gospel."[23]

So emerged the singing crusader of Christ. Before long he became in many places the most popular of the trio of field preachers during the opening years of the 18th-century revival of religion in England. By April 2, 1739, big brother John, as his famous phrase puts it, had "submitted to be more vile" and, at the coaxing of Whitefield, had preached to 3,000-4,000 people from a little eminence in the brickyard at the farther end of St. Philip's plain in Bristol.

Charles had been most reluctant to see John go off to Bristol from London. He was even convinced that John would not return alive.

> We dissuaded my brother from going to Bristol, from an unaccountable fear that it would prove fatal to him. . . . He left a blessing behind. I desired to die with him.[24]

John, on the other hand, described his going to Bristol as entering upon "this new period of my life."[25] It must be admitted that, when the idea was discussed in the Fetter Lane Society in London, some of the scriptures—apparently jabbed at random by the brethren—were not actually encouraging. The four verses quoted by John appear to have been the source of Charles's apprehensiveness, for each verse speaks of death and burial![26] Thus the promise Charles received from the Bible seemed even more confirmatory that he was about to lose John. It said:

> Son of man, behold, I take from thee the desire of thine eyes with a stroke: yet shalt thou not mourn or weep, neither shall thy tears run down.[27]

The group, in all sincerity, had yet another try. This time they landed catches from 2 Samuel and 2 Chronicles; but these were not helpful either, so the verse-plucking idea was abandoned, and the group decided by lot that John should go to Bristol after all.

George Whitefield had gone into the fields because the churches were closed to him, and he had to obey his Master's command. Charles had gone because of George's example and because the sacred flame burned in his soul. John had gone because Scripture and George Whitefield laid necessity upon him. He did not die, but lived, and toward the end of August 1739, he requested that Charles, too, go to Bristol. Not only did Charles go, but also on the way there he preached at Evesham and at Gloucester to thousands who hung upon his every word.

It is interesting that at Gloucester, Charles preached in a field made available to him by Whitefield's brother, proprietor of the Bell Inn! At Charles's first preaching there, 2,000 listened attentively to him. This must have left the local parson rather astounded, for he had refused Charles the use of the church, saying civilly that he would "gladly drink a glass of wine" with him "but durst not lend him his pulpit for 50 guineas"!

In a letter to John, Charles describes his encounter with "an old intimate acquaintance" of the brothers. For at Gloucester the adversary made an attempt to turn Charles off field preaching.

> I went to the field at five. An old intimate acquaintance (Mrs. Kirkham) stood in my way, and challenged me, "What, Mr. Wesley, is it you I see? Is it possible that you who can preach at Christ-Church, St. Mary's, &c., should come hither after a mob?" I cut her short with, "The work which my Master giveth me, must I not do it?" and went to my mob. . . . Thousands heard me gladly, while I told them their privilege of the Holy Ghost, the Comforter, and exhorted them to come for him, to Christ as poor lost sinners. I continued my discourse till night.[28]

The "discourse" was about a three-hour sermon!

Charles Wesley was in time to make Bristol his town, a fact memorialized by Methodists in the outstanding life-size bronze statue of him that now stands in the courtyard of the famous New Room in the Horsefair, Bristol, close to the preachers' horse stables and facing the main street. The statue represents Wesley with his right hand outstretched and his field Bible in the left, as though still pleading as of yore,

> All ye that pass by,
> To Jesus draw nigh.
> To you, is it nothing that Jesus should die?
> Your Ransom and Peace,
> Your Surety He is!
> Come! See if there ever was sorrow like His.

A great beginning in a tough place!

The brothers spent Charles's first Bristol evening both together and with the group meeting in the Horsefair, a meeting marked by the continual bawling of a drunken Quaker at his wife. Charles was impressed, however, by the large attendance at the 6 A.M. prayer meeting of

> our brethren and sisters, who have learned of Christ to come to the temple, early in the morning [cf. John 8:2]. None of them as yet think it part of their Christian liberty, to forsake the means of grace.[29]

The following day was spent visiting society members and being introduced to them by John; but on Friday, August 31, 1739, Charles Wesley was left in charge and immediately began his ministry of Bible exposition.

I entered upon my ministry at Weaver's-hall, and began expounding Isaiah, with much freedom and power. They were melted into tears all around. So again at one, when the bands met to keep the church-fast. We were all of one heart and of one mind . . . fell all at once into the strictest intimacy with these delightful souls; and could not forbear saying, "It is good for me to be here."[30]

Focus on Background Features

The great work God wrought in Britain in the 18th century was very strongly influenced by three or four brands of traditional Protestantism. For the analysis of the Revival, we leave aside discussion of Scotland. Scotland had its own revival, in which Whitefield played a small part, but Wesley none at all, for Wesley's Methodists had a hard time trying to set the heather on fire because of the entrenched Genevan Presbyterian Calvinism of the steely John Knox brand.

The influences permeating the Revival in England were the Puritan or Presbyterian type of Anglicanism. This was in many places strongly Calvinistic and was influential also in Wales and Ireland. There was also the so-called Arminian influence, but this was of two general types: the philosophical, which was spiritually arid, and the evangelical, which was the spring of the theology of the Wesley brothers. Evangelical Arminianism held strongly to possible salvation for all—for each person who exercised personal God-given faith in Jesus Christ. There was also the Lutheran influence, which in England took the shape of Moravianism. The Moravians were the fruit of the Pietist movement, which had arisen earlier within Lutheranism as a kind of "reformation of the Reformation." The Moravians were becoming the most remarkable evangelistic movement in Christian history prior to the rise of Methodism. In some things, such as predestination, election, and their concept of sanctification, the Moravians differed little from the Calvinists.

In Wales and in the west of England, the Revival took on a clear Calvinistic color and centered around the remarkable men Howel Harris, John Cennick, and George Whitefield. Whitefield's Calvinism was strong but tender, and the man himself most reluctant to lead any party. In England, from the Scottish border to the English and Bristol channels, the Revival was dominantly evangelical Arminian under the preaching and teaching of the Wesley brothers and their cohort of circuit-riding preachers.

The Moravianism found in England about the time the Revival began was really somewhat of a distortion of the real thing. It had taken on an unhealthy pallor. Its cheeks were sickly with mysticism, that is, the idea that such means of grace as worship, the sacraments, preaching, etc., were not needful. Moreover, a strange practice (?) called "stillness" had been introduced by Philip Molther into the society at Fetter Lane. This was the immediate reason why the Wesleys and their disciples pulled out from this society on July 20, 1740. Mainstream Moravianism recovered somewhat from these distortions and was to make its own peculiar contribution to the Revival, especially in Ireland and in the northern Midlands of England.

What About Anglican Attitudes to the Revival and Its Leaders?

Because Whitefield moved in and out of the country so much, the more constant leaders of the Revival were John and Charles Wesley. George Whitefield continued to make a powerful impact on the populace, but it was necessarily spasmodic because of his American interests—he made six round trips across the Atlantic and one one-way trip, a considerable feat of endurance.

As we have seen, all three men were ordained clergymen of the Church of England and therefore expected to minister under Anglican direction, jurisdiction, and permission. But the Wesleys saw clearly—John more clearly than Charles—that the spread and consolidation of the Revival was compelling them into circumstances that would lead to the adoption of means and methods likely to be troublesome to their Anglican fellow ministers and bishops. These were matters more of practice than of doctrine, and they lay mainly along three lines:

1. The matter of preaching in dioceses in which they had no license.
2. The matter of field preaching, which was related closely to number 1, and which became the chief reason for offense.
3. The matter of lay preaching, which was highly irregular in Anglican terms and repugnant to the clergy and to the bishop. But without the lay preachers, it seems clear that the work of the Wesleys would have been stymied.

We must constantly remember the importance of the parish system to the Church of England. The entire country, including Wales, was cut up into parishes under parish ministers. The parishes in turn were organized into dioceses under bishops, while the whole was governed by two archbishops—York and Canterbury—the latter being the primate of all England. The system badly needed modernizing. It could not have adequately served the populace even had the common people attended church or desired so to do.

The cumbrous machinery of the Church of England was no
more able to adopt itself to the changes of the Industrial Revolution
than the antiquated, unreformed parliamentary system, and the creation of the new parishes lagged as far behind the times as the for-
mation of new parliamentary constituencies.[31]

By 1818, when Parliament finally set about providing more and
more churches to minister in the rapidly growing industrial areas, the
opportunity for change was lost. As Stuart Andrews writes, "But by then
it was too late: Methodism had already contrived to fill the vacuum."[32]

But, as many writers have indicated, it was not just that the
Methodist preachers preached in the new expanding industrial areas
and in the neglected parishes; they also preached in a new way, with a
new fervor, and a new message—or, at any rate, a new emphasis.
Whereas men who knew their times and their national church were
critical of it and bored with it, the lively and powerful meetings of the
Methodists soon began to grab attention; and after the first years of
Pentecostal onslaught and the consequent persecution, Wesley's soci-
eties popped up in every city, town, and hamlet in England. John
Wesley himself provides an interesting comparison.[33]

Such a state of affairs inevitably meant that the Wesleys often fell
afoul of the accepted rule of not preaching on another parson's pitch,
a fact that was aggravated because many parsons did not preach there
themselves and simply resented others who did so. Thus a wedge was
driven that resulted in persecution for the evangelists; both Charles
and John could fulfill their mission only by apparently ignoring the license rule. It must be remembered, however, that wherever they
went, they preached before or after church hours, and generally only
after contacting the vicar or curate of the parish. Their field preaching
annoyed the authorities because the parish system was basic to the established national church, of which the brothers were ministers.

Lay preaching had been a bugbear to the Church of England for a
couple of centuries. The only concession it had ever made, if concession it was, was the demand that the church say who should have the
authority to be a lay preacher or reader. But men who had been lifted
from the pit of iniquity and suddenly let loose in the world were not
disposed to wait for, or bend to, the lifeless whims of ecclesiastical
lawmakers deader than the extinct dodo.

The meager education of the lay preachers of Methodism gave
concern to both brothers, especially to Charles, who was such a loyal
son of the English church, and together they did much to improve the
condition. For example, John prepared his magnificent Christian Li-
brary, which consisted of twoscore digests of Christian classics, and

also the *Explanatory Notes upon the Old Testament* and *Explanatory Notes upon the New Testament*. But it was late in the century before Methodism produced her own scholars who were, many of them, among the very finest in the land. Again we must remember that the two men who led them, plus those who later came to the standard of the Cross—John Fletcher, Adam Clarke, Thomas Coke, and others—were scholars fit to hold their own in any learned company. Meanwhile, the laymen, learned or not, must blast Satan's kingdom, and never a more noble army did so. Remember also that not all Anglican vicars shared the view of their peers in this respect. There were men such as Berridge, Venn, Grimshaw, Fletcher, and a score of others who were delighted to help spread the gospel among the forgotten legions of England.

As for doctrinal divergences, the Wesley brothers ever maintained their adherence to the 39 Anglican Articles of Religion.

There is one important doctrine that cannot be traced in the Prayer Book, however: the doctrine of Christian perfection, that John declared to be that "grand depositum" that God lodged with the Methodists. There is also the fact that John did not feel bound to defend everything in the Prayer Book: "Nay, there are some things in the Common Prayer Book itself which we do not undertake to defend."[34] In brief, the doctrine preached by the Wesley brothers as they crisscrossed and zigzagged up and down England ought not ever to have offended any informed and sincere Anglican, whatever his rank or office.

There remains the most important matter of all: how to reach the multitudes of England with the gospel of pardon and holiness? And how to do this in the teeth of fierce opposition, across a landscape ill prepared for communication, to a people lying in darkness in desolate villages and degrading towns? And yet not to forget the sinful middle and so-called upper classes and the not-so-noble nobility?

But, as that is the point at which we left Charles in Bristol, let us now rejoin him in his mission.

=6

To Spend and to Be Spent

SPANNING THE PERIOD 1739-41, Charles Wesley's early Bristol ministry prepared him for a wide-ranging evangelistic ministry as impressive in many ways as that of brother John. The two had drawn ever more closely together: they were now "brothers in battle."[1] Both were convinced as to the experience of saving faith; both had passed through the narrow gate of new birth onto the way of life; both were convinced that they had gospel truth in trust for transmission; both were convinced that field preaching was God's method for reaching the masses; both saw that they must conserve the fruits of evangelism by means of fellowship and Christian culture; both of them believed that they had a divine mandate to tell every man everywhere of the everlasting love of God; finally, both brothers had preached before the University of Oxford. The similarity between them was striking to the dean and to the heads of the colleges. In fact, Charles's sermon found an abiding place as sermon no. 3 of the *Standard Sermons of John Wesley*.[2]

But it is in the intensity and sweep of their evangelism over the years, from 1738 until Charles's marriage in 1749, that the Wesleys are most alike and for which they are probably mostly remembered. The tender power of their united ministry is summed up in Charles's prayer, so abundantly granted by the Lord of the Church:

> *I want an even, strong desire,*
> *   I want a calmly present zeal,*
> *To save poor souls out of the fire,*
> *   To snatch them from the verge of hell,*
> *And turn them to a pardoning God,*
> *And quench the brands in Jesus's blood.*
>
> *I would the precious time redeem*
> *   And longer live for this alone,*
> *To spend and to be spent for them*

Who have not yet my Saviour known:
Fully on these my mission prove,
And only breathe to breathe thy love. . . .

My every sacred moment spend
In publishing the Sinner's friend. . . .

And lead them to thy open side,
The sheep for whom their Shepherd died.[3]

Charles and John regarded themselves as a team and should be so regarded by all who would really know them. It was John who wrote early in the Revival that "no two men in Europe were doing a similar work," and later:

> Are we not old acquaintances? Have we not known each other for half a century? Are we not jointly engaged in such a work as probably no other two men on earth are? . . . We, at least, should think aloud and use to the uttermost the light and grace on each bestowed. We should help each other,
>
> *Of little life the best to make*
> *And manage wisely the last stake.*[4]

The letters that passed between them are frank and affectionate, revealing personal feelings, and often conditions of soul, with a sincerity that gives us the accusing sense of opening someone else's mail. The concern that each has for the other in the bloody battles with the adversary and his mobs is a profoundly moving element in the Wesley saga.

For upwards of 15 years, Charles was an itinerant evangelist as intrepid as, and in some ways more effective than, John. In many parts of England, Wales, and Ireland Charles faced wild and murderous mobs with a courage that was almost whimsically nonchalant: he was Christ's cavalier. At Walsal, for example, the riffraff crowded him to the ground. But he got to his feet, dusted himself off, gave thanks to God on the spot, and dismissed the mob with the benediction before walking homeward through the heart of it. At Sheffield, a barrage of bricks and rocks smashed through windows of the meetinghouse where Charles was preaching, injuring a number of listeners. Charles calmly announced that the service would continue—outside! "Outside," said he, "I can preach and look my enemy in the face!"

He did so. Stones struck him full in the face, and an officer of the army rushed at him with drawn sword. However, as Charles would put it, "the soldier of Christ" arose, bared his breast, and dared the man to have a thrust, saying, "I fear God and honor the king!" Faced with that infectious smile, the officer sheathed his sword and stormed off in disgust!

At Devizes, the mad mob commandeered the fire engine and fire-fighting equipment and stormed the preaching house, the preacher, and the congregation. At first they brought only the small engine, but in their craziness they soon "rushed out to fetch the large engine" as well:

> They now began playing the larger engine, which broke the windows, flooded the rooms, and spoiled the goods. We were withdrawn to a small upper-room, in the back part of the house, seeing no way to escape their violence. They seemed under the full power of the old murderer. Our brother who keeps the Society they laid hold on first, dragged him away, and threw him in the horse-pond, and broke his back, as was reported . . . We gave ourselves to prayer, believing the Lord would deliver us, how or when we saw not, nor any possible way of escaping. Therefore we stood still to see the salvation of God.[5]

The siege and assault went on for hours, the mob replenishing the engine's water supply from time to time and resuming a battering-ram tactic on the doors. It is a dramatic episode occupying eight pages of Charles's *Journal*, "a day never to be forgotten!"[6] Eventually help came in the person of the "persecuting Constable," who offered Charles a compromise:

> He said, "Sir if you will promise never to preach here again, the gentleman and I will engage to bring you safe out of town." My answer was, "I shall promise no such thing . . . I make no promise of not preaching here when the door is opened; and don't you say that I do."[7]

The escape that night was like a thriller novel—the constable collecting "his posse," as Charles describes it, the ride out through the mob-ruled street, fierce bulldogs unleashed against horses and riders, and the arrival at the town of Droxal. It is all unbelievable! Charles later wrote a hymn-prayer for the brethren at Devizes, and a most moving one it is.

The concern of the brothers for each other in those threatening times is well illustrated by the Stafford incidents, as viewed from the side of Charles:

> Fri. June 24th, [1743] . . . I found my brother in the marketplace, calling lost sinners to Him that justifieth the ungodly. He gave notice of my preaching in the evening. From him I had the first account of our brethren's persecution at Wednesbury. Their unhappy Minister was the contriver of all.[8]

A society of nine members was organized on that occasion, and within a few months Charles, when revisiting the society, records that it had been "sifted like wheat by their two potent enemies, stillness and predestination."[9] He spent several hours rescuing one of their victims, then on the following day John arrived from Wednesbury:

> My brother came, delivered out of the mouth of the lion. He looked like a soldier of Christ. His clothes were torn to tatters. The mob of Wednesbury, Darlaston, and Walsal, were permitted to take him by night out of the Society-house, and carry him about several hours, with a full purpose to murder him. But his work is not finished; or he had now been with the souls under the altar.[10]

Though John's *Journal* gives his own account of what happened,[11] Charles learned the details from the Wednesbury Methodists:

> My brother, they told me, had been dragged about for three hours by the mob of three towns . . . Some cried "Drown him!" . . . Some, "Hang him upon the next tree!" Others, "Away with him! away with him!" and some did him the infinite honour to cry, in express terms, "Crucify him!" . . . but they were not agreed what death to put him to. In Walsal several said, "Carry him out of the town: don't kill him here: don't bring his blood upon us!"[12]

It is a long, horrific tale of human depravity and blindness, sponsored and prompted by ministers, ignored by justices of the peace, and executed by degenerate mobsters. Nothing but a divine miracle could have saved John, and the Lord worked that miracle!

> The instrument of his deliverance at last was the ringleader of the mob, the greatest profligate in the country. He carried him through the river upon his shoulders. A sister they threw into it. Another's arm they broke. No farther hurt was done our own people; but many of our enemies were sadly wounded.[13]

Nevertheless, in a matter of 36 hours, Charles—by agreement with John, who had other commitments—was riding back into the riot zone!

> I found the brethren assembled, standing fast in one mind and spirit, in nothing terrified by their adversaries. The word given me for them was "Watch ye, stand fast in the faith, quit yourselves like men, be strong." Jesus was in the midst, and covered us with a covering of his Spirit. Never was I before in so primitive an assembly [in reference to the primitive church in Acts]. We sang praises lustily, and with a good courage; and could all set to our seal to the truth of our Lord's saying, "Blessed are they that are persecuted for righteousness' sake."[14]

Before leaving town, Charles received into society membership the young man whose arm had been broken in the riot, and Mr. Munchin, "the late captain of the mob," who had rescued John. Charles asked him what he thought of John.

"Think of him!" said he: "That he is a mon of God; and God was on his side, when so mony of us could not kill one mon!"[15]

It would be as easy to fatten a greyhound as to do literary justice to the evangelistic adventures of the Wesley brothers and to the Methodists they raised up and had to leave in the battle zones to fight and suffer for Jesus Christ. As for Charles, the Methodist music man, probably he had a reckless joy in it all!

Such a spirit enabled this singing cavalier of Jesus to put the verve and the nerve of the gospel into the Methodist societies all over England, Wales, and Ireland, and to give them the soul-stirring words to sing as they came up from campaign to Conference bearing on their bodies the marks of Christ:

> And are we yet alive,
> And see each other's face?
> Glory and praise to Jesus give
> For His redeeming grace!
> What troubles have we seen,
> What conflicts here we past;
> Fightings without and fears within,
> Since we assembled last?
> But out of all the Lord
> Hath brought us by His love,
> And still He doth His help afford,
> And hides our life above![16]

The Lord's Horsemen

We must remember, when reading the Wesley saga of "travels oft," that John and Charles were also "in perils oft," not only perils in the city and perils among the false brethren but also perils from rivers, robbers, and roads—especially the roads (cf. 2 Cor. 11:25-29).

Much of the country was accessible only over roads that were at best but footpaths in the summertime and rivers of mud in winter. When the Wesleys' crusade commenced in 1739, there were not more than four "good roads" in the land. Their evangelism was well advanced before any attempt was made to improve the roads in the 1760s. But by then the brothers had long been riding their noble steeds up, down, and across the land, seeking sinners where they were and how they were.

It is reported by Daniel Defoe, Arthur Young, and Boswell, all of whom went on periodic travels, that negotiable roads probably numbered no more than a half dozen, that they were all very short, and all in the south of England. Even the old Roman road system had been allowed to fall into decay. The so-called Great North Road out of London was only 10 miles long. The remainder of the route to Newcastle and the Scottish border—about 220 miles—was a narrow, landlocked thing with horse tracks on either side. There was another short stretch of "new road" to London's southwest, a little bit more to the south, and Wales had a short stretch out of Cardiff. The rest of the country had only messy, muddy pack tracks that were traceable by their quagmires, pits, and boggy holes. Big brother John humorously recounts how his horse stumbled over the top of a gatepost submerged in mud.

At intervals, travelers found ditches or "grips" about four feet deep, supposedly for straining off the water, but which were more effective for laming horses and upturning carts and coaches. What were called "ridings," especially in the north, were supposedly shortcuts through open country or woods. In fact, they were "deep cuts" described by the elder brother as "sufficient to lame any horses and shake any carriage to pieces." In many of these, the mud was "belly-deep," with the rider's legs immersed! As Samuel Johnson writes, "I took the stage 16 days to travel about 300 miles between Edinburgh and London with many an adventure between." Such conveyance never appealed to the Wesleys, who were seeking souls, few of whom ever saw the inside of a coach, much less traveled in one.

Add to it all the droves of cattle, herds of sheep and swine, and flocks of fowl being walked between towns and markets.

Nor was travel itself the only danger. Highwaymen lurked in the lanes and ridings. The stage holdup was about as frequent there as it later became in the American West! Dick Trupin on his Black Bess, Black Jack the loner, and many another haunted the "highways." Both John and Charles Wesley were at different times held up by highwaymen.

The dangers were not over when the riders reached the cities:

> As I was riding to Rose Green (Bristol) in a smooth, plain part of the road, my horse suddenly pitched upon his head and rolled over and over. I received no other hurt than a little bruise on one side; which for the present I felt not, but preached without pain to six or seven thousand people.[17]

And remember the weather! The visitor to England is probably in no danger of forgetting it. But often we read in the brothers' journals: "belly-deep in snow," or "hail and rain frozen on face," or "gave the horse its head in the storm."

We have normally associated it all with John, and with good reason he has been described as "the Lord's horseman"; but in reality that whole first generation of holiness preachers were the Lord's horsemen. John was the general of that calvary, and Charles his chief lieutenant.

Charles Wesley was for above 15 years as mobile as John. For example, ignoring his rides between London and Bristol, and his trips into Wales and Cornwall, after the drama at Devizes Charles zigzagged half of England in a mere seven months, and before a year was out, he had covered much of the other half. He had been all around Bristol and the west country, down into Devon and Cornwall, across to Cardiff and Wales, up in Staffordshire, and across to Durham. He had preached in Newcastle, Epworth, and Wiltshire, and had circuited the famous Methodist triangle of Bristol, London, and Newcastle!

Charles kept it up until his marriage in 1749 and for 5 years thereafter, when by arrangement with John he took on heavy pastoral responsibilities in the societies in London and Bristol. But let us remember the horseback travels of the Methodist music man, not only preaching everywhere at the slightest opportunity but also "witnessing both to small and great" (Acts 26:22-23) and teaching all England to sing "the songs of salvation" (cf. Deut. 31:19; Isa. 42:12).

The Singer's Sermon *(Text: Lam. 1:12; Mark 15:29)*

It is a thrilling thought and an impressive picture we have of Charles Wesley dismounting his little horse at the crossroads or on the village green, unsheathing his field Bible, holding both hands forward—palms uplifted in entreaty—and crying,

> *All ye that pass by,*
> *To Jesus draw nigh.*
> *To you, is it nothing that Jesus should die?*
> *Your Ransom and Peace, Your Surety He is!*
> *Come! See if there ever was sorrow like His.*
> *For what you have done,*
> *His blood must atone,*
> *The Father hath punished for you His dear Son;*
> *The Lord, in the day*
> *Of His anger, did lay*
> *Your sins on the Lamb, and He bore them away!*

I LOVE THIS.

He dies to atone
For sins not His own,
Your debt He hath paid and your work He hath done!
Ye all may receive
The peace He did leave
Who made intercession, "My Father, forgive!"

His death is my plea;
My Advocate see,
And hear the blood speak that both answered for me:
My ransom He was
When He died on the Cross
And by losing His life he has carried my cause.[18]

= 7

Family Affairs
(and a Brace of Brides!)

Two Deaths

Samuel Wesley, Jr., that quiet, good man, died suddenly in November 1739. He had been an upright and conscientious churchman, a kindly husband, and a brother indeed to the younger members of the Wesley clan. Moreover, there have been few sons who have so sincerely and constantly cared for their parents. But Samuel had found it extremely hard even to begin to understand the attitude and activities of his younger brothers over the 18 months between May 1738 and November 1739. Perhaps in time he would have learned to live with the reputation of being a big brother of a pair of firebrands, but Providence denied him the opportunity.

His death was a serious loss to the aging Susanna. It is doubtful that she ever recovered from the shock. She was then 70, and Samuel had been but 47 and a solace and strength to her. Within 3 years Susanna died also, in the upstairs bedroom of John's home in City Road, London. She died in Christian triumph on July 30, 1742. Perhaps this is not the place to eulogize one of the most amazing women and mothers of church history. Few people would care to deny her eminence or her right to the honor and respect of posterity. It is impressive that John should insert in his *Journal* two of his mother's striking letters, one to her husband the rector, the other to John the scholar. John inserts them at the point where he describes his mother as "a preacher of righteousness" and as one "entrusted with the care of a numerous family."[1] Clearly, John regarded his mother with great affection and respect as a woman of impressive gifts used in a striking way. Adam Clarke was powerfully impressed by her as well and said so in no less a place than his famous commentary. In his remarks on Prov. 31:10, he wrote that Susanna was "more than the equal," as wife and mother, of the "Hebrew woman there described."[2]

Strangely, Charles was not at Susanna's deathbed. There is a large gap in his *Journal* for that year, so we do not know precisely where he was when his mother died. However, he did receive a full account of her passing from John, and another from sister Anne.

With the exception of Kezzy, who had died the previous year at age 31, all the Wesley women were present at Susanna's exodus. It was a joyous affair despite their loss. Susanna had but lately received the assurance of God's forgiveness, not having even imagined—as John puts it—"that this was the common privilege of all believers." But that assurance was hers in the end.

> We stood round the bed, and fulfilled her last request, uttered a little before she lost her speech: "Children, as soon as I am released, sing a psalm of praise to God."[3]

Sing they did, but the Methodist music man was not present! Had he been present at the hours of victory, perhaps he would have written a better poem than the stilted, formal, and half-dead thing he wrote for her epitaph—the poorest of all his hymns on Christian death.

A Bride for the Music Man

During the first 10 years of the Revival, the Wesley brothers published a number of hymnbooks in which virtually all the original compositions were by Charles and the translations by John. In 1749, however, Charles had need of a dowry. He had been attracted to, and had fallen deeply in love with, a fine and sweet little lady whose mother was rather reluctant, to say the least, to see her lovely daughter married off to a penniless traveling preacher. So Charles set about raising some worldly wealth, although material affluence was ever his least and last concern. He published in 1749, therefore, two volumes of hymns under his own name, and by subscription. These were the two volumes of *Hymns and Sacred Poems,* published to help him pay his marriage expenses.

His prospective bride was Miss Sarah Gwynne, the daughter of a Welsh country squire, Gwynne of Garth. "My Sally," as he was fondly to call her, was half his age, but—by every known account—ideally fitted to the wife of the revivalist poet.

As with most men in love, Charles was utterly enamored of his lady. He first met her in August 1747, when, with her father and another family member, she visited him as he left for Ireland:

> Mr. Gwynne came to see me at Mr. Philips's, with two of his family . . . My soul seemed pleased to take acquaintance with them.[4]

So reads Charles's first written reference to Sally; but absence made his heart grow fonder, so upon his return to Wales from that trip to Ireland, he made straight for Garth. He was ill and in much pain from the moment he landed at Holyhead, off the Isle of Anglesey, but he pushed on in the teeth of a high wind, crossed the narrow strip of sea in an overcrowded small boat, and pressed on to Caernarvon before taking "a little rest." He was away again by seven in the morning and, but for his companion, would have gone earlier.

With the rain pelting down and "sharp wind full in my teeth," Charles rode all day in pain and physical misery, pressed forward by his heart, drawn onward by the vision of "my Sally." Another restless night at Tan-y-bwlch, and on again early the following morning, at five this time, and in hard rain! All day long he pushed on toward Garth and his heart's desire. He spent the next night in a small village, trying to warm himself and to dry his clothes at a small fire supplied by a kindly neighbor, who also nailed up the window to keep out the wind. "I had no more rest," writes Charles, "than the night before."[5] But it was up and on again at five the next morning:

> The weather grew more severe. The violent wind drove the hard rain full in our faces. I rode till I could ride no more; walked the last hour; and by five dropped down at Garth. All ran to nurse me. I got a little refreshment, and at seven made a feeble attempt to preach. They quickly put me to bed. I had a terrible night, worse than ever. Sat., March 26th, and the five following days, I was exercised with strong pain . . . My short intervals were filled up with conference, prayer, and singing.[6]

Thus did Charles Wesley go a-courting! The Gwynne family nursed him back to health, and on his way he went again.

In June, he took Sally and her dad to Kingswood to meet his Christian friends—"my principal ones especially at Kingswood," writes Charles. He testifies that "the Lord made our souls as a watered Garden," and that he "was much revived in singing with Miss Burdock and Sally." It was Sally's first visit to Kingswood, but not her last. After conducting her and her father to London "to visit the Church," he made the return trip to Bristol. While he was passing through Windsor, his horse threw him—was Charles really looking where he was going? At Cirencester he preached in a yard from the text, "The redeemed of the Lord shall return, and come with singing . . ." (Isa. 51:11).

So the story goes on and on throughout the latter part of 1748 and the earlier part of 1749. Charles preached and sang at Bristol, London, and most points between. Though he made another of his fruitful Irish trips, Sally was never out of his thoughts, and he had made up his mind to ask her to marry him.

Now this brought up the arrangement of the brothers and their helpers—that no one of them would seek matrimony without the consent of the others. Therefore, Charles sought John's approval. John was not a very reliable judge of women, but already—perhaps knowing and remembering Oglethorpe's counsel to Charles a decade earlier—John had drawn up a list of "desireable" young ladies. It pleased Charles to discover that Sally was on the list! There was, however, the nagging question of income. Charles was a poor man with only his fellowship and a small legacy recently received from a Mrs. Sparrow. The brothers subsisted on what little their new societies could afford to give them, and John was eyeballs deep in debt as a sole trustee of the Methodist meetinghouses. So Charles returned to Garth, armed with but 50 pounds to ask the daughter of a reasonably affluent home to marry him!

Sally's mother was sincere in her admiration of Charles. "I would rather give my daughter to you than to any man in England," said she, "were it not for your want of fortune."

Charles then asked whether an assured income of 100 pounds a year would please Mama. It would, so back to London went Charles to seek collateral. There were his hymns, which, as the vicar of Shoreham assured Mrs. Gwynne by letter,

> are even at this time a very valuable estate . . . and . . . will be much more valuable . . . They are works which will last and sell while any sense of true religion and learning shall remain among us.[7]

John, too, had previously made that proposal, and since almost all the hymns were Charles's, the arrangement was equitable and just. When Mrs. Gwynne still appeared reluctant, she was assured and reminded that "real" estate on earth is a most unreal affair to those who "set [their] affection on things above" (Col. 3:2)!

So the marriage was set for April, and the waiting period was filled with poetry in letter form, or letters in poetic form, or whatever the poet's imagination created.

As Charles's wedding day approached, it was John who got cold feet. John was afraid that Charles's reception into such a family would impede his mission. Or was John subconsciously fearful that a wedge was about to be driven into their unique partnership? Charles's *Journal* seems to imply this.[8] In any event, by the day and time of the wedding in Garth, John was cheerful again:

We talked over matters with Mrs. Gwynne; and all my brother's fears were scattered. We read over the settlement. Mrs. Gwynne proposed a bond, till it could be signed. My brother signed the bond; Miss Becky [Sally's sister], and Miss Musgrave witnessed it.[9]

Bridal day dawned clear and beautiful on the Welsh hills. Charles rose at four and spent more than three hours in prayer and singing, some of that time with Sally, Becky, and John. "Sweet day!" he wrote, "so cool, so calm, so bright, the bridal of the earth and sky." At eight o'clock, "I led my Sally to Church"; and on April 8, in the quiet little chapel of Llanlleonfel, John Wesley united his brother to Sarah Gwynne, "giving Sally away" to Charles, as he says, "under God." As Charles later wrote,

It was a most solemn season of love! Never had I more of the divine presence at the sacrament. My brother gave out the following hymn:

Come, Thou everlasting Lord,
By our trembling hearts adored . . .

and 40 lines more! ending with

Own, midst the rich repast,
Thou hast given the best at last;
Wine that cheers the host above,
The best wine of perfect love![10]

Thus was Garth transformed into Cana of Galilee for Charles Wesley and his Sally! Yet, on that very day, the nervously happy bridegroom wrote to his friend Ebenezer Blackwell:

Garth, April 8, 1749

My dear friend,

Pray for me. I want your prayers rather than your congratulations. Yet I believe God has lent me a great blessing this day, and that I ought to be thankful, and employ every blessing and every moment to His glory. The following hymn we sang at the altar.

Come, Thou everlasting Lord,
By our trembling hearts adored . . .[11]

Honeymooning in the Bride's Home

Rev. and Mrs. Charles Wesley spent two weeks honeymooning at the Gwynne home. Charles preached every day and at the end of the second week rode to Bristol, leaving Sally at Garth for a little while. Being extremely eager to answer any doubt remaining in John's mind as to the harmful effect of matrimony on mission, Charles plunged into the work—and into sickness.

As he recovered, he wrote to John:

> I was too eager for the work, and therefore believe God checked me by that short sickness . . . More zeal, more life zeal, more life, more power, I have not felt for some years.[10]

By the end of May, Charles had rented a house in Bristol, although Mother Gwynne had hoped that Garth would be the couple's home for a year or two. Having sealed and signed the bond with John in Ludlow at the beginning of August, Charles and Sally went home to Bristol and to the house in Charles Street.

The Wesleys took up residence in Bristol in 1749—Friday, September 1, being specially marked in Charles's *Journal*.

> Fri., September 1st. By eleven we saluted our friend Vigor. I saw my house, and consecrated it by prayer and thanksgiving. I spent an hour at the preaching-room in intercession. I began the hour of retirement with joint prayer. Alone, I was in some measure sensible of the divine presence. I opened the book on those words, "While they spake, Jesus stood in the midst of them, and said, Peace be unto you." At six our first guests, Mrs. Vigor and her sisters, passed an useful hour with us. I preached on the first words I met, Rom. xii. 1: "I beseech you therefore, brethren, by the mercies of God, that ye present your bodies a living sacrifice," &c. The power of God was with us. Half-hour past nine I slept comfortably in my own house, yet not my own.

> Sat., September 2nd. We had family prayer at eight. I began the New Testament. I passed the hour of retirement in my garden, and was melted into tears by the divine goodness.

> Sun., September 3rd. Sally accompanied me to our feast in Kingswood. Poor Betsy was kept away by illness.

> Mon., September 4th. I rose with my partner at four. Both under the word and among the select band, we were constrained to cry after Jesus with mighty prayers and tears. We sang this hymn in my family:—

> *God of faithful Abraham, hear*
> *His feeble son and thine,*
> *In thy glorious power appear,*
> *And bless my just design:*

> * * *

> *Me and mine I fain would give*
> *A sacrifice to Thee,*
> *By the ancient model live,*
> *The true simplicity;*

> *Them, as much as lies in me,*
> *I will through grace persuade,*
> *Seize, and turn their souls to Thee*
> *For whom their souls were made;*

*   *   *

> *Bring them to the' atoning blood,*
> *(Blood that speaks a world forgiven,)*
> *Make them serious, wise, and good,*
> *And train them up for heaven.*

In the evening was that word fulfilled, "Him that cometh unto me, I will in no wise cast out," by the reception of a poor sinner to the favour of God in Christ Jesus.[13]

For the next 22 years, Bristol was home for the Wesleys, Charles supervising the Methodist Society and fanning out across the country in his evangelistic tours.

Brother John, a little fearful of what marriage would do to his brother's evangelistic activities, found that for the present at least those fears were groundless, for while it was physically possible, Sally rode for Christ with her husband. She had a very fine voice and was careful to use it in the work of evangelism. She also arrested much attention and admiration, not only by her singing but also by her loveliness and charming spirit. "All look on Sally with my eyes," wrote Charles tenderly. It was indeed a love match from beginning to end. A few months after traveling, since at that time they had no settled home, the couple finally took up residence in what later became Charles Street, Stokes Croft, Bristol.

Hymns for the Use of Families

The hymn the Wesleys sang on the dedication of their Bristol home was one of Charles's own.

Hymns for the Use of Families ran to 200 pages. Its 166 hymns cover almost every conceivable aspect of married life. Included are some most unusual but often necessary hymn-prayers (e.g., "For an unconverted husband," "For an unconverted wife," "For a persecuting husband," "For an undutiful son," "For a family in want," etc.). Of these beautiful hymns Henry Moore wrote:

> Numberless examples might be given of the genius and taste of the Rev. Charles Wesley. But, however unfashionable it may appear, I cannot but give the palm to this "Family Hymn Book." Such accumulated strength and beauty of expression, in presenting the daily wants, pains, trials, and embarrassments of a family, to the God of the families of the whole earth, surely never before was pre-

sented to the suffering children of men . . . We expect a man of real genius to be great where the subject is inspiring; but to be great in the privacies of common life, to be a true poet (while the man of God equally appears) in those littlenesses, so-called, of daily occurrences, shows an elevation and spirituality of mind that has been rarely, if ever, equalled.[14]

The Bristol Home

The 22 years' Bristol residence of the Wesleys was marked by what Edgar Guest called "a heap o' living." As in many another home, joys and sorrows chased each other across life like the shadows of clouds on a sunlit hillside, but their God-born nuptial love held and grew stronger as the years passed, and to the end of life they were still holding hands.

A Bride for Brother John

Grace Murray, the sea captain's widow; Mrs. Vazeille, the rich widow; and John Wesley, the traveling Methodist preacher—the story has the basic elements of a soap opera.

The friends and followers of John Wesley have very great difficulty trying to either justify or to excuse brother Charles for his finicky meddlesomeness in John's complicated romance with Grace Murray, the sea captain's widow. For whatever the consequences might have been had John properly wooed and married Grace, Charles was the intractable obstacle to the union. Himself happily married with John's agreement and assistance, Charles hopped around like a delirious grasshopper to prevent his brother's union with the one woman who might have proved a suitable partner in the work of the Lord. Thus he did by engineering the marriage between Grace and John Bennett, the Methodist preacher.

Everyone loved Grace Murray, or so it seemed, and everyone who could have married her would have done so. Grace appears to have been the pick of the pack at Newcastle Methodist fellowship. Men easily fall in love with their nurses, and Grace was a gracious nurse to a number of Methodist preachers when they pulled in at the orphan house out of the cold, hard, and hateful world.

Charles Wesley had received Grace Murray into Methodist membership in the London Society in 1740. Her conversion had been a real one, and her membership with the Methodists cost her a great deal of domestic unpleasantness from her husband, Captain Murray. The captain was lost at sea on one of his voyages, however, and Grace returned to Newcastle to be with her mother. Here John Wesley met her and was impressed. She had a natural charm and tact that endeared her to all the men and women alike. Perhaps she was, as Jones says, "as much a sower of discord in her way as Helen of Troy,"[15] but it seems more likely that she possessed much more than the normal degree of female charm found among women in 18th-century Methodism. That moved Charles to meddle in the promising romance of his brother. Again, Charles was clearly under the impression that Grace Murray was already betrothed to John Bennett. What he apparently did not realize was that his brother John had reason to believe that the Murray-Bennett affair was over and done with when he proposed marriage to Grace.

Whatever his chief motivation, as soon as Charles learned of the proposed union with Grace, he was spurred into an almost feverish activity and hopped from one city to another in an effort to prevent it by urging Bennett and Grace to marry! That would dissolve the crisis. But Charles it was who tragically misunderstood the whole affair. As Nehemiah Curnock noted,

> In reality the case was the other way around. Too late Charles Wesley discovered that he had persuaded John Bennett to marry his brother's betrothed fiance . . . It was indeed, not a "Comedy," but a tragedy of Errors.[16]

Only the impassioned tenderness of George Whitefield and John Nelson, the great Yorkshire lay preacher, averted a dreadful disaster for Methodism. Indeed, it looked at one point as though the brothers Wesley would be utterly sundered apart, and it is doubtful if their relationship with each other was ever the same again. Only John's sweet spirit of forgiveness ultimately averted the almost unthinkable rupture, but Charles Wesley must bear the blame for the tragic episode, whatever may be said on his behalf.

One poignant feature of the whole regrettable interlude is the fact that a very important letter sent by John Wesley to John Bennett via William Shent was "not delivered at all." The letter carries John Wesley's reasoned and reasonable address to Bennett and might well have been sufficient to prevent the unfortunate consequences of the situation; most certainly it would have moderated Charles Wesley's behavior had he known it—but he didn't.[17]

John Takes No Chances

Toward the beginning of 1751, when John Wesley decided to marry another widow, the wealthy London lady Mrs. Vazeille, he took no chances with Charles! Since he was in London when John returned from Oxford, Charles simply records how flabbergasted he was at the news John gave him:

> My brother, returned from Oxford, sent for and told me *he was resolved to marry!* I was thunderstruck, and could only answer, he had given me the first blow, and his marriage would come like the *coup de grace.* Trusty Ned Perronet followed, and told me, the person was Mrs. Vazeille! one of whom I had never had the least suspicion. I refused his company to the chapel, and retired to mourn with my faithful Sally. I groaned all the day, and several following ones, under my own and the people's burden. I could eat no pleasant food, nor preach, nor rest, either by night or by day.[18]

It was thus apparent that Charles would have opposed this romance also, had he known about it, but John was taking no chances.

But why did Charles find the idea of John's marriage so repugnant? As Jackson indicates,

> His distress could not proceed from any feeling of personal or family dislike of Mrs. Vazeille . . . A friendship also subsisted between her and the Gwynne family, whom she had recently visited; and Mr. and Mrs. Charles Wesley had lately spent several days in her house.[19]

It is probable that Charles's reaction is a reflection of his concern for the work of God. He feared that marriage with Mrs. Vazeille would curtail and limit John's leadership of the Revival, especially in itinerant preaching, with divisive results in the relationships of the societies. He need not have worried, for John "maintained his itinerant ministry with unimpaired efficiency to the end of his life."[20]

It was not long before Mrs. John Wesley discovered that her husband had but one passion, and that was for his Lord and Master, Jesus Christ. At first she carried her complaints to Charles, and for a while he was able to help comfort her; but soon she turned bitter toward him and Sally. Jackson maintains that Mrs. John Wesley's mental condition was unstable.[21] If so, perhaps Charles's reservations were more reliable in the case of the woman John had married than they had been in the case of the woman he might have married!

=8

Charles Wesley: Husband and Father

*F*EW MARRIAGES IN THE 18TH CENTURY were as close to being ideal and remaining idyllic as that of Sally Gwynne and Charles Wesley. In all Britain, Charles could not by searching have found a more gracious, fitting, and loving partner— and lovely withal!

The matrimonial happiness of Charles and Sally makes for touching reading, almost the antithesis of the misery attendant on the marriage of John Wesley and the widow Vazeille. As John Telford wrote, "The children of the Epworth Parsonage have almost become a proverb for their unhappy marriages. But no shadow ever fell on Charles Wesley's marriage."[1] Frederick Gill points out further that

> During his absence Charles kept Sally well posted with news, and his letters, though unfortunately mostly undated, express the warmest affection. His love for Sally increased with the years and always he wrote to her, no matter how busy, a lively account of his family and concern for their welfare . . . He could never be too grateful for the love she had brought into his life, or for the kindness of her parents.[2]

The letters from Charles to Sally can be read in volume 2 of his *Journal*, together with his accounts of his family. The following extracts reflect the spirit and content of the entire corpus of these letters.[3]

XIII.

Moorfields, April 10th, Easter-day.

My prayer for my dearest partner and myself is, that we may know Him, and the power of his resurrection.

The Lord (we found this morning) is risen indeed! At the table we received the Spirit of prayer for my dear desolate mother, the Church of England. O pray for the peace of Jerusalem! they shall prosper that love her . . .

Do not neglect your short-hand; do not neglect your music; but, above all, do not neglect your prayers.

My love to S. Gwynne, and our other friends . . .

My heart is with you. I want you every day and hour. I should be with you always, or not at all; for no one can supply your place. Adieu.

XVI.

March 29th.

MY BELOVED SALLY,—Go to Garth in the strength of the Lord, that you may return the sooner . . .

How many of Lampe's tunes can you play? I am afforded an exceeding fine harpsichord for sixteen guineas! What engagement do you give me to purchase it for you?

The alarm here continues and increases, through the daily accounts we receive of more earthquakes. I am printing more hymns and a sermon on the occasion. Next Sunday I expect strength to administer the sacrament at both chapels. I trust my ever-dearest Sally finds her strength and health confirmed. Wait upon the Lord, and you shall renew your spiritual strength also. I most earnestly commend your soul and body to his preserving care, who has loved you with an everlasting love, and prepared a kingdom for you from the foundation of the world.

Salute in my name all our Christian friends; above all, our dearest F. and M. Jesus be with you always!

XIX.

London, August 17th.

I often reflect on that hard saying, "Son of man, behold, I take away the desire of thine eyes with a stroke;" and ask myself, Could I bear Ezekiel's trial? Whether I shall ever be called to it, God knoweth; for known unto Him are all his works. But it is far more probable that my beloved Sally will see many good days in the vale, after my warfare is accomplished, and my weary soul at rest. Here indeed we have laid the foundation of an eternal friendship, and hasten to our consummation in bliss above. Till then we scarcely begin to know the end of our meeting upon earth. O that we may fully answer it, by helping each other on to heaven, and by bringing very many with us to glory!

God, I humbly hope, will hear my prayers, and give me to find you well on Wednesday. On this day se'nnight, at twelve, I have appointed to preach in Leominster . . . My heart is with you, and your dear worthy parents and relations. Blessed be God, that they are mine also. O that we all may be joined to the Lord, and one spirit with Him!

My brother is deeply engaged with his classes; but salutes you in great love. God owns and blesses him much. Last Sunday was a time of great refreshing. Many here inquire after you, out of true affection, and bewail you settling in Bristol.

Thursday afternoon.

Yours of August 13th has just now brought me mournful news of your increasing illness. Yet would I say, "It is the Lord; let him do as seemeth him good." Still my hope of you is steadfast, that hereby you shall be partaker of his holiness, who in tenderest love chastens you for your good. And you may be bold to say, "When He has tried me, I shall come forth as gold."

XXV.

Norwich, August 29th.

MY DEAREST OF FRIENDS,—Are you indeed so near me as London? or does Charles Perronet only flatter me? In your last you expected to reach Mrs. Boult's by Saturday. I shall lose no time, but take horse on Monday morning, and, with the blessing of God, seize you on Tuesday evening at your lodgings.

Every hour of every day you are laid upon my heart; so that I make mention of you in *all* my prayers. I cannot doubt but our next will be our happiest meeting. You *will* allow time for private prayer, while in London. My heart is with you and dear Betsy. The Lord Jesus keep and water you every moment!

XL.

London, March 17th.

MY DEAREST FRIEND,—Grace and peace be multiplied upon you and yours, who are mine also. One letter in a week does not half satisfy me, under your absence. I count the days since we parted, and those still between us and our next meeting. Yet I dare not promise myself the certain blessing, so many are the evils and accidents of life. *Accidents* I should not call them; for God *ordereth* all things in heaven and earth. Who knows his will concerning this wicked city? or how near we may be the fate of Lima or Port-Royal? Blessed be God, many *consider* in this day of danger and adversity. The Bishop of London has published a seasonable, solemn warning. Our churches are crowded as at the beginning. Last night I preached, for the first time, at the French chapel in Spitalfields, my scruples being at last removed. It was full as it could hold. "The poor have the Gospel preached unto them" was my text; and the Lord was with us of a truth . . .

The poor weavers, English and French, filled the place, and heard me gladly. Here is surely a door, great and effectual, and, as yet, *not* many adversaries. I must endeavour to keep up the awakening by preaching every morning of next week. . . .

Not a word of your music! That is a bad sign; a sign of idleness, I fear. When you would have me look out after a harpsichord for you, you will tell me so.

LXIII.

Westminster, Whitsunday, 1760.

MY DEAREST SALLY,—This I once called the anniversary of my conversion. Just twenty-two years ago I thought I received the first grain of faith. But what does that avail me, if I have not the Spirit now? "I account that the longsuffering of the Lord is salvation;" and would fain believe He has reserved me so long for good, and not for evil.

Eleven years ago He gave me another token of His love, in my beloved friend; and surely He never meant us to part on the other side of time. His design in uniting us here was, that we should continue one to all eternity.[4]

The Sorrows of Sally

As with her mother-in-law, Susanna Wesley, and many other women of 18th-century England, Sally had sorrow enough to shatter her tender disposition. Eight babies were born to her and Charles during their residence in Bristol, but only three grew to maturity. They named their first child after John Wesley, but the child died of smallpox when but 16 months old. Martha Maria died when 1 month old. Their Susanna died at 11 months, Selina at 5 weeks, and John James—the last baby—at the age of 7 months. Sally lovingly preserved a lock of hair from each of the little ones.

The three who survived childhood were Charles, Jr., born in 1757; Sarah, Jr., born in 1759; and Samuel, born in 1766.

The Word of a Wife

As for Sally herself, although family affairs terminated her traveling around with Charles, her whole heart and soul went with him everywhere. She sustained him with her prayers and assurances of love, and waited his return with all the eagerness and joy with which she had greeted him at Garth.

Sally wrote an informative preface to the volume of Charles's sermons published after his death. It is an intimate and interesting document. Concerning Charles and brother John, for example, Sally wrote:

The character of the brothers was distinctly different. John was born with a temper which scarcely any injuries could provoke, ingratitude ruffle, or contradiction weary. This disposition peculiarly qualified him to govern; but he was so far from arrogating authority, or demanding submission, and his gentleness and forbearance rendered him so the object of love amongst the people who placed themselves under his care that they considered "their sovereign pastor as a sovereign good."

It has been remarked that public men do not often shine in private life. Though he regarded all the world as his parish and every man as his brother, he was amiable in his domestic circle and kind to his relations, especially to those who were dependent upon him or whom he thought neglected and oppressed.

Charles was full of sensibility and fire, his patience and meekness were the effect of neither temperament nor reason, but of divine principle. John affectionately discharged the social duties, but Charles seemed formed by nature to repose in the bosom of his family. Tender, indulgent, kind as a brother, a husband, a father, a master; warmly and unalienably devoted to his friend; he was a striking instance that general benevolence did not waken particular attachments, discerning in the character of men, incapable of disguise, and eminently grateful. The peculiar virtue of John was forgiveness of enemies. He has been frequently known to receive into his confidence those who had betrayed it shared his affection; nor was it easy to convince him that anyone had willfully deceived him; or, if it were attested by facts, he would only allow it had been so in that single instance.

Equally generous and kind was his brother, respecting enemies, and capable of an entire reconciliation; but he could not replace his confidence where he had experienced treachery. This formed some variation in their conduct, as also the higher church principles of Charles, who manifested them to the last, by desiring to be buried in consecrated ground.[5]

His most striking excellence was humility; it extended to his talents as well as his virtues; he not only acknowledged and pointed out, but delighted in the superiority of another, and if there ever was a human being who disliked power, avoided pre-eminence and shrunk from praise, it was Charles Wesley.[6]

The daughter of the wealthy Welshman took patiently to the privations and risks, not to mention the dangers, of life as the wife of a Methodist preacher, and this in times when even the rumor of such involvement was frequently reason enough for violent persecution. Charles died in 1788 (on which more later), but Sally lived on for many years after her husband's death. She died in Marylebone in London in 1822 at 96 years, and the Methodists cared for her welfare right to the end of her life. William Wilberforce, the antislavery campaigner, loved her deeply and helped provide her with an annuity of £60.

Throughout her long widowhood Sally told story after story, in a delightful manner, of the blissful demands made on the wife of the Methodist music man.

Father and Children

Charles Wesley has left us not only letters from which we may glean knowledge about his children but also accounts of his boys.

Three children grew to adulthood: Charles, whom we shall distinguish from his father by calling him Charles, Jr.; Sarah, whom we shall name Sally; and Samuel, who is Sam. The two boys were musical prodigies, and the Methodist music man was intensely proud of them. With his daughter he could have been more patient, but he loved her deeply. As Frank Baker has written,

> Although he seems to have been a little heavy-handed with his only surviving daughter (we remember that he was fifty-one when she was born), so that she turned with something of relief to her uncle John, there is no doubt of his deep love for young Sally. And it was to her that he turned for comfort during his last autumn at Bristol in 1787. "Probably you will have the office of Milton's daughter in my last days," he wrote to her; and so it was to fall out.[7]

Charles, Jr., and Sam were the musical wonders of London. Of their talents, Robert Stevenson wrote:

> Charles Wesley the hymn-writer had two sons both of whom possessed truly extraordinary gifts in music. Dr. William Boyce, the Vestor of 18th-century musicians, compared the younger of them with Wolfgang Amadeus Mozart, and probably did not exaggerate unduly.[8]

Sam Wesley

Writing of the younger brother, Sam, Lightwood says:

> Sam's early attempts at composition were elementary but certainly very thorough. He would place some words before him and sing them through, and it would appear that he never forgot the melodies that came to him, storing them up in his mind for future use. As an example we have the well known story how at the age of six he composed airs for an oratorio on the story of Ruth. Two years later he wrote them down, and this product of his youthful genius is now preserved in the Manuscript Room at the British Museum.[9]

Presenting Sam and his son, that is, Charles Wesley's grandson—named after Bach—the *Oxford History of Music* says:

> In the musical history of the 19th century the works of the two Wesleys (Samuel and Samuel Sebastian) is of real importance. . . .

They tower above their English contemporaries, laymen or church-men.[10]

With brief reference to the music man's grandson, Samuel Sebastian Wesley: he is to be found in most English hymnals as the composer of several "classic" hymn tunes, notably "Aurelia," composed originally for "Jerusalem the golden," hence the title from *aureolus*, or golden.[11]

The Methodist music man was justifiably proud of all three children but took special delight in the talents and accomplishments of the two boys. Of the younger son, Sam, he wrote:

> The first thing which drew our attention was, the great delight he took in hearing his brother play. Whenever Mr. Kelway came to teach him, Sam constantly attended, and accompanied Charles *on the chair*. Undaunted by Mr. Kelway's frown, he went on; and when he did not *see* the harpsichord, he crossed his hands on the chair, as the other on the instrument, without ever missing a time.

> He was so excessively fond of Scarlatti, that if Charles ever began playing his lesson before Sam was called, he would cry and roar as if he had been beat. Mr. Madan, his godfather, finding him one day so belabouring the chair, told him he should have a better instrument by and by.

> I have since recollected Mr. Kelway's words, "It is of the utmost importance to a learner *to hear the best music;*" and, "If any man would learn to play well, let him hear Charles." Sam had this double advantage from his birth. As his brother employed the evenings in Handel's Oratorios, Sam was always at his elbow, listening and joining with his voice. Nay, he would sometimes presume to find fault with his playing, when he thought he could know nothing of the matter.

> He was between four and five years old when he got hold of the Oratorio of Samson, and by that alone taught himself to read words. Soon after he taught himself to write. From this time he sprung up like a mushroom; and, when turned of five, could read perfectly well, and had all the airs, recitatives, and choruses of Samson, and the Messiah, both words and notes, by heart . . .

> He was full eight years old, when Dr. Boyce came to see us, and accosted me with, "Sir, I hear you have got an English Mozart in your house: young Linley tells me wonderful things of him." I called Sam to answer for himself. He had by this time scrawled down his Oratorio of Ruth. The Doctor looked over it very carefully, and seemed highly pleased with the performance. Some of his words were, "These airs are some of the prettiest I have seen. This boy writes by nature as true a bass as I can do . . ."

> Mr. Madan brought Dr. N—— to my house, who could not believe that a boy could write an oratorio, play at sight, and pursue

any given subject. He brought two of the King's boys, who sang over several songs and choruses in Ruth. Then he produced two bars of a fugue. Sam worked this fugue very readily and well, adding a movement of his own, and then a voluntary, on the organ, which quite removed the Doctor's incredulity.[12]

Accompanying his elder brother, Charles, to St. Paul's for one of Charles's rehearsals, Sam again met Dr. William Boyce, famous London organist, whose words Charles, Sr., records in his *Journal:*

> At the rehearsal at St. Paul's, Dr. Boyce met [again] his *brother* Sam, and, showing him to Dr. H., told him, "This boy will soon surpass you all." Shortly after, he came to see us, took up a *Jubilate* which Sam had lately wrote, and commended it as one of Charles's. When we told him whose it was, he declared he could find no fault in it; adding, there was not another boy upon earth who could have composed this; and concluding with, "I never yet met with that person who owes so much to nature as Sam. He is come among us, dropped down from heaven."[13]

The following is a letter from Uncle John Wesley to nephew Charles, Jr. , when Samuel became Roman Catholic for a time.

May 2nd, 1786.

DEAR CHARLES,—I doubt not both Sarah and you are in trouble because Samuel has "changed his religion." Nay, he has changed his opinion and mode of worship; but that is not religion, it is quite another thing. "Has he then," you may ask, "sustained no loss by the change?" Yes, unspeakable loss; because his new opinion and mode of worship are so unfavorable to religion that they make it, if not impossible to one who once knew better, yet extremely difficult. What, then, is religion? It is happiness in God, or in the knowledge and love of God. It is faith working by love, producing righteousness, peace, and joy in the Holy Ghost. In other words, it is a heart and life devoted to God; or communion with God the Father and the Son; or the mind which was in Christ Jesus, enabling us to walk as He walked. Now, either he has this religion or he has not. If he has he will not finally perish, notwithstanding the absurd unscriptural opinions he has embraced, and the superstitious and idolatrous modes of worship. But these are so many shackles, which will greatly retard him in running the race that is set before him. If he has not this religion, if he has not given God his heart, the case is unspeakably worse—I doubt if he ever will, for his new friends will continually endeavor to hinder him, by putting something else in its place, by encouraging him to rest in the forms, notions, or externals, without being born again, without having Christ in him the hope of glory, without being renewed in the image of Him that created him. This is the deadly evil.

I have often lamented that he had not this holiness, without which no man can see the Lord. But though he had it not, yet, in his hours of cool reflection, he did not hope to go to heaven without it. But now he is, or will be taught, that, let him only have a right faith—that is, such and such notions—and add thereunto such and such externals, and he is quite safe. He may indeed roll a few years in purgatorial fire, but he will surely go to heaven at last. Therefore you and my dear Sarah have great need to weep over him.

But have you not need also to weep for yourselves? For, have you given God your hearts? Are you holy in Heart? Have you the kingdom of God within you—righteousness, and peace, and joy in the Holy Ghost, the only true religion under heaven? Oh, cry unto Him that is mighty to save for this one thing needful! Earnestly and diligently use all the means which God hath put plentifully into your hands, otherwise I should not at all wonder if God permit you also to be given up to a strong delusion. But whether you were or were not, whether you are Protestants or Baptists, neither he nor you can ever enter into glory unless you are now cleansed from all pollutions of flesh and spirit, and perfect holiness in the fear of God. —I am, dear Charles, your affectionate uncle,

JOHN WESLEY.[14]

Of the reaction of father Charles Wesley to this unfortunate development, his biographer Jackson wrote:

Mr. Charles Wesley passed through various sorrows in the course of his eventful life; but nothing grieved him so much as his Samuel's entrance into the idolatrous Church of Rome, against which he believed the severest threatenings of Holy Scripture to be levelled. He regarded that community as thoroughly corrupt, and therefore a declared object of the divine vengeance. In his closet, when he thought of his son, his feelings rose to agony, as his private papers most affectingly declare. He wept and made supplication for his child, whom he now regarded as lost to him and the rest of the family. The very sight of one who was so dear to him, now a captive in nuptic Babylon, caused his heart to bleed afresh.[15]

Sam's sister Sally, observing the pathetic sorrow of father Charles, made an entry in one of the father's notebooks against a prayer for the recovery of Sam from smallpox as a child. Her entry reads:

Alas! this prayer was raised for his son Samuel! How little do parents know what evils are prevented by early death![16]

Thus, as Jackson so pertinently indicates, while Charles mourned and wept and prayed, John Wesley sought to reclaim the delinquent by direct action. Perhaps the difference in the evangelists may here be noted. How else would Charles Wesley the poet express his agony than in poetry?[17]

Charles: The Elder Brother

For a few years in their childhood, the elder brother Charles overshadowed Sam the younger and was to Sam somewhat of an idol. Later events show, however, that Sam benefited more than anyone realized from the musical ability and performance of his elder brother. Standing by the harpsichord while Charles played, scraping his little fiddle, and beating time was probably a vital learning experience for Sam, whatever his father said about pen mending. For Charles was a child prodigy, recognized so by all who heard and knew him, and that group included some of the most accomplished and informed musicians and vocalists of the day. The friendships of Charles with tutors and professional musicians who seem to have vied with each other to get to teach him or to be permitted to listen to him were to be a boon to Sam in more mature years.

Of young Charles's talents and ability, father Charles Wesley has left us what amounts to a catena of opinions of musical experts woven onto a background of paternal pride. In his *Journal* he wrote:

> Charles was born December 11th, 1757. He was two years and three quarters old, when I first observed his strong inclination to music. He then surprised me by playing a tune readily, and in just time. Soon after, he played several, whatever his mother sung, or whatever he heard in the streets.
>
> From his birth she used to quiet and amuse him with the harpsichord; but he would never suffer her to play with one hand only, taking the other and putting it on the keys, before he could speak. When he played himself, she used to tie him up by his back-string to the chair, for fear of his falling. Whatever tune it was, he always put a true bass to it. From the beginning he played without study, or hesitation; and, as the learned declared, perfectly well.
>
> Mr. Broadrip [a composer] heard him in petticoats, and foretold he would one day make a great player. Whenever he was called to play to a stranger, he would ask, in a word of his own, "Is he a musicker?" and if answered, "Yes," he played with all readiness.
>
> He always played *con spirito*. There was something in his manner above a child, which struck the hearers, whether learned or unlearned.
>
> Mr. Madan [minister of the Lock Hospital] presented my son to Mr. Worgan [doctor of music], who was extremely kind to him, and, as I then thought, partial. He told us he would prove an eminent master, if he was not taken off by other studies. He frequently entertained him on the harpsichord. Charles was greatly taken with his

bold, full manner of playing, and seemed even then to catch a spark of his fire.[18]

Mr. Charles Wesley was concerned on account of the elder of his sons (Charles) because he was a stranger to the spirit of Christianity, though moral and harmless; but he had reason to be much more anxious for Samuel, who was less tractable, and in whom the absence of true piety was more apparent. Mr. Madan, who was an adept in music, was Samuel's godfather; and when the boy displayed his early powers as a musician, this clergyman carried him from place to place, among his friends, as a sort of prodigy. The child, though very young, was sensible and observant. He therefore felt that he was degraded, and conceived a prejudice against his father for suffering him to be thus exhibited as a boyish wonder.[19]

Father Charles Wesley devoted page after page to quoting the opinions and verdicts of many outstanding contemporary giants of the music world. All united in the praise of his elder son's prowess on the organ and harpsichord. A certain Dr. Shepherd went further by introducing young Charles to King George III, whose favorite musician he became, and also the recipient of many royal favors.

The association with royalty continued under George IV, who, as crown Prince of Wales, had made Charles his private friend, and who, as king, extended great respect and confidence to him.

Jackson's *Memoirs of the Rev. Charles Wesley* carries an interesting story of the royal connection. Charles was seeking appointment as organist in St. Paul's, but

At St. Paul's Charles was rudely repelled by the Reverend gentleman in charge of the appointment with the abrupt and unseemly answer, "We want no Wesleys here!" being apprehensive, it would seem, that, under his "volant touch," the tones of the organ would imbue the worshippers with the spirit of Methodism. The King heard of their incivility, and sent for the unfortunate organist to Windsor, where he expressed regret at what had occurred; and added, "Never mind. The name of Wesley is always welcome to me."

After the king had lost his sight, Mr. Charles Wesley was one day with His Majesty alone, when the venerable Monarch said, "Mr. Wesley, is there anybody in the room but you and me?" "No, your Majesty," was the reply. The King then said, "It is my judgment, Mr. Wesley, that your uncle, and your father, and George Whitefield, and Lady Huntingdon, have done more to promote true religion in the country than all the dignified Clergy put together."[20]

Ultimately, however, it would appear that John Wesley's misgivings were well founded. "He probably thought," wrote Jackson, "that the professional advantages which his nephews might reap from this display of their talents would be more than counter-balanced by their exposure to the temptations of the gay world which they were not prepared by deep personal piety to meet and resist. Their temporal interest was perhaps advanced; but their spiritual dangers were increased."[21]

And so it turned out. We have noted Sam's deflection from the ways of the Methodists to which father and uncle had given their lives in revival fervor; and the elder brother, whatever his musical achievements, proved no more of an evangelical Methodist than his brother. Father Charles's concern for the spiritual welfare of his boys was real and sincere, and he took comfort from young Charles's indications of sincere humility in youth. His letter to Sam when that boy was but seven years of age also gives us a feel of this concern:

> God made you for Himself, that is to be forever happy with Him. Ought you not therefore to serve and love Him?[22]

Nevertheless it must be said that in these terms the boys would have benefited in richer values than music can afford, had Charles, Sr., respected his brother John's sentiments concerning the early London concerts. One other facet of the musical activities of the Wesley family must be noted. That is the holding of concerts in their London home in Marylebone.

In 1770 Charles and Sally were offered and accepted the gift of the lease of the town residence of a certain Mrs. Gumley.

It was a large house situated in Chesterfield Street in the Marylebone section of London. Together with the extended lease, the good woman provided all the required furniture—handsome stuff indeed! —and everything that the family could need domestically. All the Wesleys had to pay was the ground rent.

Although Mrs. Wesley and the family moved from Bristol to London earlier than Charles Wesley (who had pastoral oversight of the Bristol societies and whose itinerant evangelism kept him more or less fixed on the Bristol center), by the end of 1778 he, too, had moved to London.

At that time, the idea of holding a series of concerts in the very large drawing room of their new home had been discussed among the family. The first two series of these concerts were quite sensationally successful, church and government leaders being especially prominent among the guests. General Oglethorpe was there, and the bishops of London and Durham, plus an earl or two and the lord mayor.

The concerts continued each year from 1770 until 1785, with more and more outstanding public leaders attending.

Young Samuel and Charles provided almost all the music, Samuel playing the violoncello and Charles the organ.

It would seem that John Wesley was not altogether happy with these concerts. He did attend one concert on January 25, 1781;[23] but after the concerts terminated, he wrote to his brother Charles on April 13, 1786, "I am not sorry your concerts are come to an end."[24]

Probably John Wesley was more sensitive to the widespread reaction likely to be roused among Methodist people by these concerts. For the people called Methodists were mostly the common people of England; there were "not many mighty, nor many noble" among them (1 Cor. 1:26). The common people were likely to view suspiciously this hobnobbing with aristocracy on the part of Charles Wesley and his sons.

For his part, father Charles himself was not altogether at ease over the drawing-room concerts. The music was classical, chiefly that of Handel, Corelli, Geminiani, and Scarlatti. The admission price was three guineas—a sizable sum in the 18th century—and the appeal was therefore to the upper class. There was understandable perplexity, therefore, among the common Methodist folks.

Charles Wesley, Sr., sought therefore to explain his action. To his brother John he wrote:

> My reasons for letting my sons have a concert at home are:
>
> 1. To keep them out of harm's way: the way (I mean) of bad music and bad musicians who by a free communication with them might corrupt their taste and their morals.
>
> 2. That my sons may have a safe and honourable opportunity of availing themselves of their musical abilities, which have cost me several hundred pounds.[25]
>
> 3. That they may enjoy their full right of private judgment, and likewise their independency: both of which must be given up if they swim with the stream and follow the multitude.
>
> 4. To improve their play and their skill in composing: as they must themselves furnish the principal music of every concert, although they do not call their musical entertainment a concert. It is too great a word. They do not presume to rival the present great masters who excel in the variety of their accomplishments. All they aim at in their concert music is *exactness*.
>
> If they excel in any degree it is in composition and play. Here then they chiefly exert themselves, as sensible that "many accompaniments may hide and cover bad play," that the fewer the accompaniments are, good play is the more conspicuous.
>
> I am clear, without a doubt, that my sons' concert is after the will and order of Providence. It has established them as musicians,

and in a safe and honourable way. The Bishop (of London) has since
sent us word that he has never heard any music he liked as well,
and promises Charles five scholars next winter.[26]

J. A. Maitland and Dannyreuther give high praise indeed to the
musical prowess of the sons of Charles Wesley. The former ranks
them with the Bachs in Germany, and the latter with Mendelssohn,
Liszt, and Franck!

Samuel, the younger son of the Methodist music man, has left us
quite a delightful cameo of his family in his *Autobiography:*

> My father was extremely fond of music, and in the early part of
> life, I believe, performed a little on the flute. He was partial to the
> old masters: Purcell, Corelli, Geminiani, Handel; and among the En-
> glish Church composers Croft, Blaw, Boyce, Green, etc. were
> favourites with him. He had a most accurate ear for time, and in
> every piece which had repetitions, knew exactly which part was to
> be played or sung twice, which, when any failed to do, he would
> immediately cry out, "You have cheated me of a repeat."
>
> He had not a vocal talent, but could join in a hymn or simple
> melody tolerably well in tune. I never heard that my grandfather
> had any particular partiality to music, nor the contrary.
>
> My mother had very considerable vocal talent, played prettily
> upon the harpsichord, and sang sweetly. In Handel's oratorio songs
> she much excelled, being blessed with a voice of delightful quality,
> though not of very strong power or extensive compass. Always ex-
> actly in tune and in good taste, but free from the least affectation or
> pretension to luxuriant embellishments or rapid cadences, which
> are too often employed to the detriment and disfigurement of the
> melody, and are foreign to the nature and genius of the composi-
> tion.
>
> My father used to say of my brother and me, "The boys have
> music by the mother's side," meaning that he had no claim to any of
> the talent which she certainly possessed.[27]

"Little Sally"

The birth of the sole surviving daughter of the Methodist music
man occurred in Bristol in 1759. To that city she returned in late life,
and there she died and is buried. She was two years younger than
Charles, Jr., and seven years older than brother Samuel, and had naturally much more in common with Charles who, as George Stevenson
says, "was destined to be her life-long companion."

We read much less about her from her father's writings than we
do about her musically brilliant brothers, but we learn enough one
way and another to gain a profile of her life and character. Neverthe-

less, the heavily disproportionate amount of information is a disappointment to all who know what little there is.

No single member of the Wesley family has done more in proportion to their means and opportunities to preserve the family honour than Sarah, the daughter of the Rev. Charles Wesley, yet of her own personal history scarcely a continuous page can be found anywhere.[28]

Her father was over 50 years old when she was born, and although he loved her dearly and did his best to bridge the generation gap, it was glaring. Writing to his wife, Sally, he said,

I feel thankful that Charles is better, and Sally also. She *should* take after me, as she is to be my child. One after another give me presents for Charley, but nobody takes notice of poor Sally—even her godmother seems to slight her.[29]

In his letters to his wife, Charles's references to little Sally are almost all of them oblique. "Little Sally" was the family's way of distinguishing the daughter from her mother.

Perhaps the relative obscurity of little Sally was due to the tone of the times. Perhaps, too, it was due to the astonishing talents of her brothers and the publicity and attention received by them. Add to these little Sally's inclination to withdraw from society even as a child. Another factor was the disfigurement caused by the dreadful smallpox, which also blighted her mother's beauty. But for whatever cause or reason, little Sally's life is not documented as fully as those of her gifted brothers. What we know must be gleaned from her father's letters, one or two references in the writings of her Uncle John Wesley, the testimony of her brother Charles and Dr. Adam Clarke, Sally's own letters and poems, and the references of Miss Tooth, Sally's executrix.

In point of fact, little Sally eventually proved to be the most "Methodistical" and "Wesleyan" of all the Charles Wesley family, in some ways more akin to her father and his values than were either of her brothers. When she died, she was a member of the Society of the People Called Methodists, with her Society Class ticket in her pocket.

What formal education little Sally received, she got first of all at Miss Temple's Bristol school for girls, her father pitching in to teach her Latin as with the boys. Her education was completed at Guildford near London. In London, too, as a child, she was introduced to Dr. Samuel Johnson, of which introduction her brother Charles wrote:

Dr. Johnson much distinguished my sister in her youth. She was not, like many others, afraid of him; indeed, the doctor was always gentle to children; and no doubt my aunt Hall (Charles Wesley's sister, Martha) had spoken kindly to him of her. She used to show him her verses, and he would pat her head and say to my aunt, "Madam, she will do."[30]

The letters to the youthful Sally from her father were perennially firm but always affectionate and loving, while his references to her are frequently rather wryly humorous:

> I am in daily expectation of a letter from Sally at Wimbledon: I suspend my pity or censure till I hear how she got her fall. If by the fashionable *heels* she may thank herself. Such a fall she had two years ago.[31]

Father Charles's concern for his daughter went much deeper than the matter of fashionable heels. He wrote also offering spiritual counsel and guidance which, even if somewhat stilted by modern standards, was nonetheless sincere. The following letter to Sally was written by Charles in 1778:

> To Miss Wesley, at the Rev. Bankes's, Wimbledon Common, Surrey.
>
> Both my dear Sally's letters I have received, and rejoice that you have so soon recovered your fall. If it was occasioned by the narrow fashionable heels, I think it will be a warning to you, and reduce you to reason. Providence saved you from a like accident at Guildford. Beware the third time!
>
> You gained by the despised Methodists, if nothing more, the knowledge of what true religion consists in; namely, in happiness and holiness; in peace and love; in the favour and image of God restored; in paradise regained; in a birth from above, a kingdom within you; a participation of the Divine nature. The principal means or instrument of this is faith, which faith is the gift of God given to every one that asks.
>
> The two grand hindrances of prayer, and consequently of faith, are self-love and pride, therefore our Lord so strongly enjoins on us self-denial and humility. "If any man will come after me, let him deny himself, and take up his cross daily, and follow me." And, "How can ye believe who receive honour one of another, and seek not the honour which cometh from God only?" Here, you see, pride is an insurmountable obstacle to believing. Yet the desire of praise is inseparable from our fallen nature. All we can do, till faith comes, is not to seek it, not to indulge in our own will, not to neglect the means of attaining faith and forgiveness, especially private prayer and the Scriptures.
>
> My brother thinks you were in some measure awakened while you met in band. Great good may be got by Christian fellowship, or (if you are unequally yoked) great evil. I left you entirely to yourself here, being always afraid you would meet with some stumbling-

block in the Society, which might give you an unjust prejudice against religion itself.[32]

Young Charles's letter has an interesting reminder of a famous incident in the life of John Wesley. The great man was particularly and remarkably fond of little Sally, whose temperament was so alike to his, that her father once declared she should have been John's daughter. Charley wrote to Adam Clarke, quoting Sally:

> I think it was the year 1775 (December 11th), my uncle promised to take me with him to Canterbury and Dover. At that time his wife, Mrs. Wesley, had obtained some of his letters which she used to the most injurious purposes, misinterpreting expressions, and interpolating words. These mutilated letters, she intended publishing in the Morning Post—which she did. My dear father, to whom the reputation of my uncle was far more dear than his own, saw the importance of refutation, and set off to the Foundry, to induce him to postpone his journey, while I, in my own mind, was lamenting such a disappointment, having anticipated it with all the impatience natural to your years. [She was then about 18.] Never shall I forget the manner in which my father accosted my mother on his return home. He said, "My brother is indeed an extraordinary man. I placed before him the importance of the character of a minister, the evil consequences which might result from his indifference to it, the cause of religion, stumbling-blocks to the weak, and urged him by every relative and public motive to answer for himself and stop the publication." His reply was, "Brother, when I devoted to God my ease, my time, my life, did I except my reputation? No. Tell Sally I will take her to Canterbury tomorrow."[33]

So to Canterbury with Uncle John Wesley went Sally!

Sally also accompanied Uncle John to Holland and appears to have always been good for him among the pressures of his society work and chaotic domestic affairs. Certainly he had few stauncher supporters than Sally! She shared his basic love of solitude. As Brother Charley wrote,

> My sister hated company, and avoided it whenever she could, entreating to be left at home when we dined out, excepting when we went to the good Methodists or Quakers—people who much loved the quiet little girl—and where she was permitted to take her book. She loved her school-fellows, and was much beloved by them, and she entertained them with stories which she had read.
>
> She sung remarkably well, and would have been a fine instrumental performer, I do not doubt, had she cultivated music, for she had an accurate ear and fine taste; but my dear father telling her she must devote two hours a day to practice, she immediately gave it up, preferring a book to anything.

With my worthy uncle John Wesley she was a great favourite, and with my admirable aunt Hall also, and with all the servants, especially those who were Methodists.[34]

She shared also his passion for books and reading:

When we resided at Bristol, one day the dinner-bell rang, and my father (who never waited above two minutes) having searched for my sister in vain, sat down to dinner, supposing she had been detained at the lady's [Miss Temple's] school. She was afterwards found in an upper room behind a box, finishing her book, which she preferred to dinner.[35]

Little Sally appears to have had a strong strain of the traditional independence of her grandmother Susanna and her uncle John, to say nothing of her more removed forebears:

You know, my good sir, our family were brought up with great reverence for kings, and consider Charles I a martyr. My dear sister could not think of him as he did. My father gave her Dr. Smith's Sermons to convince her. After perusing those sermons, especially that on January 30th, she persisted in her opinion, which made father say with a smile, "I protest, the rebel blood of some of her ancestors flows in her veins." To politics she always had an aversion, though she rejoiced in the demolition of the Bastille, and abhorred the treatment of poor unfortunate Louis and the French royal family [in the revolution of 1792]. Some prejudiced people called my sister a Jacobin.[36]

But in one respect at least, she was her father's daughter: she loved to versify, even though her father's encouragement on this score was not encouraging. "She early wrote verses," says Charley, "though she did not like to show them to her father because he took away a play she was writing, and because he laughed at a Greek name of a king in the play which my father had not heard before . . . He disheartened her without reproving her."[37]

Father Charles did, however, work with her on her verses. From time to time, they would also read classical poetry together.

When We Lost the Sweet Singer

"When we lost in your father the sweet singer of Israel," wrote Rev. Henry Moore to Sarah after the death of her father, "a good woman exclaimed, 'Ah! who will write poetry for us now?' Your verses will shew that the spirit is not extinct in the family."[38]

Sally had just demonstrated the Wesley spirit of versifying and her love for the Methodist preachers by writing a poem of 40 lines honoring their work and memory, and sending it to Henry Moore, the close friend and early biographer of John Wesley.

Although written in 1826, or at least dated that—35 years after John Wesley's death and 38 years after her father's death—the verses reveal the Methodist heart of Sarah. She had tenderly attended her father, the Methodist music man, during his final days, and it seems probable that she wrote the lines years before passing them to Henry Moore.

Lines to the Memory of the
First Methodist Preachers

While heroes claim the palm, and poets sing
The Sapient statesman and the patriot king;
While beauty, genius, wit, by turns demand
The sculptor's labour and the painter's hand;
While wondering crowds loud acclamations raise,
And earth reverberates with the favourite's praise:
Shall nobler Christians, in the Christian age,
Have no memorial in affection's page?
Shall ceaseless vigils, persecutions, strife,
The sacrifice of ease, of health, of life,
Have no distinction grateful—no record?[39]

Sally Wesley, daughter of the Methodist music man, died in Bristol on September 19, 1828. Even in death she showed her likeness to Uncle John by murmuring very frequently lines beloved of him, and written by father Charles:

I the chief of sinners am,
But Jesus died for me![40]

Sally was a Methodist, and her class ticket, dated for June 1828, was in her pocket. But whoso relies on the blood of Jesus Christ has a deeper assurance.

She lies buried among the bodies of five little ones who long preceded her, and that of her mother, then not long in the Father's house.

9

Tuned Up!

STRANGE ARE THE WAYS OF PROVIDENCE. It was John Wesley who first came to be really interested in hymns, John who first compiled a collection of hymns, and John who edited and published the Methodist hymnbook. That first compilation contained hymns by John, and none from the pen of Charles. On the other hand, Charles was, in the opinion of some, a much better preacher than John, in the sense of fire, eloquence, and the power to persuade men to repent and believe. Charles has been favorably compared with George Whitefield, who, incidentally, had been introduced by Charles to the Methodists.

After Charles Wesley's conversion, two of his favorite expressions became "my great Deliverer" and "my great Redeemer":

> How shall I equal triumphs raise
> Or sing my great Deliverer's praise?[1]

> O for a thousand tongues to sing
> My great Redeemer's praise![2]

His life is marked by deliverance—physical, vocational, and spiritual.

There is the source of these rivers of praise and devotion, and from this source began immediately to flow the great hymns that have blessed the world. Almost at once, he wrote a hymn of the new life, reflecting also Luther's comment on Paul's word "for me":

> O Filial Deity,
> Accept my newborn cry;
> See the travail of Thy soul,
>   Saviour, and be satisfied;
> Take me now, possess me whole,
>   Who for me, for me, hast died.[3]

In that most remarkable and painstakingly thorough work, *Representative Verse of Charles Wesley*, Frank Baker wrote:

Although the beginnings of his capacity for the making of memorable verses must be sought in his classical training, the name of Charles Wesley could hardly have been known and loved in millions of homes across two centuries and five continents without the quickening of his talent through a spiritual impetus. For any great poetry to be written there must be both consummate craftsmanship and a powerful urge. Without the spiritual urge that was born at Whitsuntide 1738 and which continued through varying phases to his life's end, Charles would have been more and less successful as a poet . . . This did not happen, however, and it is impossible to prove that it would have happened. In the event his talents as a poet were both enriched and engulfed by his discovery of a rapturous personal religion.[4]

In Christian poetry or preaching, it is "the overflow of heart that gives lips full speech." Charles Wesley, the Methodist music maker, readily and eloquently expresses this plentitude in his renderings of Ps. 45:1-2.

> My heart is full of Christ and longs
> Its glorious matter to declare!
> Of Him I make my loftiest songs;
> I cannot from His praise forbear;
> My ready tongue makes haste to sing
> The glories of my heavenly King.[5]

The hymn is a moving presentation of the entire psalm, and it helps us zero in on Charles Wesley's center of gravity, which is the living Christ in the written Word of God. His hymns are Bible-based, Bible-impregnated, and—more often than not—tapestries of biblical truth and tale. But they are not Bible-centered; rather, they are Christ-centered. From that May morning of his newborn soul, Charles's whole life and work echoed Zinzendorf's words: "I have one passion—it is He!"

Prior to May 21, 1738, as we have seen, there was very little for Charles Wesley to sing about. He had written some scraps of verse, but they were arid, lifeless things. Of those years he later wrote:

> For ten long legal years I lay
> A hopeless but reluctant prey
> To pride and lust and hell . . .

and

> Baffled by twice ten thousand foils,
> I ceased to struggle in the toils
> And yielded to a just despair.[6]

But on May 21, 1738, Christ changed all that. Like Bunyan's weary Pilgrim, Charles Wesley stood in spirit before the Cross; like Pilgrim's load, Charles's burden rolled off and away as the cords cracked; and like that worthy, Charles gave three leaps for joy and went on his way, singing

> *What a place this is!*
> *Must here be the beginning of my bliss?*[7]

The cross of Christ was Charles Wesley's tuning fork. His life has that new song of Psalm 40; his life has a lilt:

> *New songs do now his lips employ*
> *And dances his glad heart for joy!*[8]

There were scarcely enough exclamation points in Charles's inkpot to express his rapture. It is not the meters that make Wesley's hymns what they are; rather it is the *marvel*—the sheer wonder, rapture, and marvel—and his astonishment at incredible mercy and grace. Henceforth his language is ever that of adoring gratitude geared to grateful service.

The cascades of devotion and praise that poured from apparently inexhaustible springs in the soul and mind of Charles Wesley were let loose by an act of God on May 21, 1738.

Earlier in this book, we let Charles speak for himself about his divine deliverance. At this point, we can latch onto that crisis and allow him to sing *the* hymn:

> Towards ten my brother was brought in triumph by a troop of friends and declared "I believe!" We sang the hymn with great joy and parted.[9]

It was a tableau worthy of the brush of an evangelical Raphael. Indeed, the scene has been imaginatively portrayed in gorgeous stained glass in a beautiful window in Wesley's Chapel, City Road, London. There they stand, twin converts and brothers doubly linked. Charles, who was ill at the time, is dressed in his dressing gown. John wears his Episcopal garb and holds the manuscript open before him. Angels with open scroll sing above the pair, and Mr. Bray, with his wife or a friend, stands transfixed with amazement in the background. A smaller bottom panel shows Charles Wesley, the hymnist, seated at his desk with poised quill and open Bible, ready to pour more of his praise onto the paper before him. A light gleams on his countenance; it is the radiance of an inner wonder.

Thus the brothers sing. And what is the hymn they lift unitedly to heaven? The question has been frequently debated, but with all respect to other opinions, the present writer finds no solid reason for departing from the firm belief of most scholars and of the compilers of the Methodist hymnals of Great Britain and of America. The hymn they sang was that beginning

> *Where shall my wondering soul begin?*
> *How shall I all to heaven aspire?* . . .[10]

And here is the hymn, in which Charles Wesley stands like a wide-eyed child of wonder on the fringes of the greatest wonderland of all—the amazing grace of God. For a Christian is, by definition, a child of wonder and a man amazed. This conversion hymn is crammed with adoring wonder; the whole soul of Charles Wesley seems to melt in liquid fire. As F. W. Boreham would put it, the whole amazing business is largely an occasion for the hatpins of marvel and the button-hooks of astonishment. It is all exclamation and bewildered enquiry:

> *Where shall my wondering soul begin?*
> *How shall I all to heaven aspire?*
> *A slave redeemed from death and sin!*
> *A brand plucked from eternal fire!*
> *How shall I equal triumphs raise*
> *Or sing my great Deliverer's praise?*[11]

Then came the devil to tempt him. Is it not all too good to be true? And, even if it is true, is he not a very proud man to suppose that the Almighty required his doggerel?

Then came Mr. Bray, the "poor mechanic who knew nothing but Christ," and urged him to take up his pen again and praise the Lord. So he continued,

> *And shall I slight my Father's love?*
> *Or barely fear His gifts to own?*
> *Unmindful of His favours prove?*
> *Shall I, the hallowed cross to shun,*
> *Refuse His righteousness to impart,*
> *By hiding it within my heart?*

The answer to that question is:

> *No! though the ancient dragon rage,*
> *And call forth all his hosts of war,*
> *Though earth's self-righteous sons engage,*
> *Them and their god alike I dare;*
> *Jesus, the sinner's friend, proclaim;*
> *Jesus, to sinners still the same.*

> Outcasts of men, to you I call,
>   Harlots and publicans and thieves!
> He spreads His arms to embrace you all;
>   Sinners alone His grace receives;
> No need of Him the righteous have;
> He came the lost to seek and save.
>
> Come, O my guilty brethren, Come,
>   Groaning beneath your load of sin,
> His bleeding heart shall make you room,
>   His open side shall take you in;
> He calls you now, invites you home;
> Come, O my guilty brethren, come![12]

This is the great day! But a few days later, a more reasoned hymn is written. It, too, is a thrilling and moving thing, full of amazement and rejoicing. Though it lacks the "first fine careless rapture" of the conversion hymn, how magnificently it describes the "release in Christ"! Many writers see in it Peter's escape from prison, and so it seems especially in verse 4. But surely its thought is more akin to Paul's experience.

> And can it be that I should gain
>   An interest in the Saviour's blood?
> Died He for me, who caused His pain?
>   For me, who Him to death pursued?
> Amazing love! how can it be
> That Thou, my God, shouldst die _for me?_

The third verse captures Paul's fine passage in Philippians 2:

> He left His Father's throne above;
>   So free, so infinite His grace!
> Emptied Himself of all but love,
>   And bled for Adam's helpless race.
> 'Tis mercy all, immense and free,
> For O, my God, it found out me!

For the biblical background to verse 4, you may choose between Acts 12 and Acts 16:

MY FAVORITE!

> Long my imprisoned spirit lay,
>   Fast bound in sin and nature's night.
> Thine eye diffused a quick'ning ray.
>   I woke; the dungeon flamed with light!
> My chains fell off, my heart was free;
> I rose, went forth, and followed Thee.

Verse 5 is undoubtedly based on Romans 5:

> *No condemnation now I dread;*
> *Jesus, and all in Him, is mine!*
> *Alive in Him, my living Head,*
> *And clothed in righteousness divine,*
> *Bold I approach th' eternal throne*
> *And claim the crown, through Christ, my own.*[13]

Year after year Charles Wesley will pour out his glad anniversary of the heart, more and still more of wonder. More and still more of his all-but-irresistible appeals to men and women to come as he came and to come while he sings.

Thus, then, did Charles Wesley, the singing cavalier of God, set out on his pilgrimage. Henceforth in the streets of the cities and towns of Britain, as on the village greens and gutters, he would summon all mankind to the glorious banquet of God.

> *For you and for me*
> *He prayed on the tree;*
> *The prayer is accepted, the sinner is free!*
> *That sinner am I*
> *Who on Jesus rely*
> *And come for a pardon God cannot deny!*

How unspeakable is life in Jesus!

> *True pleasures abound*
> *In the rapturous sound,*
> *And whoever hath found it hath paradise found!*
> *My Jesus to know*
> *And feel His blood flow,*
> *'Tis life everlasting, 'tis heaven below!*[14]

Charles Wesley's joyous song helped his brother John to sing also. In this true pleasure that abounds in the grateful heart, the brothers are one in a manner more impressive than that in any other particular.

In a work all too frequently overlooked in the study of hymnody, Dimond wrote,

> An instructive contrast may be observed between the pages of the private Oxford diaries, and the manuscript hymnbook which was [John] Wesley's constant companion on his evangelistic tours. The diary is a dreary account of the hopeless pursuit of a mechanical morality. There is little of rejoicing in any of the records before 1738. After [John] Wesley's conversion, a new feature appears in the collections of hymns that he published from time to time. There is

added a section entitled "Hymns for Believers Rejoicing." Among the pages showing signs of most frequent use in Wesley's private manuscript volume are those where he found

> "Now I have found the ground wherein
> Sure my soul's anchor may remain."[15]

Dimond's conclusion, while referring directly to the transformation in John, is even more applicable to Charles:

> The emotional and intellectual aspects of the conversion are inseparable. The conception of God as the absolute law-giver and judge, had been replaced by a conception of God as in Christ the Redeemer and Saviour of His children . . . at his conversion this unvailing conflict gave place to reconciliation, the center of which was a gracious personal relationship mediated through faith in Jesus Christ.[16]

≡10

The Spirit, the Word, and New Life

The Holy Ghost, when we partake,
To all that ask is freely given;
And lo! on this great truth we stake
Our present and eternal heaven.[1]

The Spirit—God in Action

Previous to that memorable Pentecost Sunday in 1738, when Charles Wesley's new life began, he had not versified much on the Holy Spirit. It was on that day and in that deed that the Holy Spirit lifted the floodgate of praise and poetry on Wesley's soul. On that day songster and song were released. It is therefore no surprise that the Spirit should become the theme and His work the subject of so very many of the hymns. On that day staunchly orthodox Trinitarian belief was set ablaze. Until that day there was neither force nor fire in Charles's work, but thereafter everything was for him as for Pascal, "Fire! Fire! All is fire!" The dogma of the Person became the dynamic of a passion. Henceforth the Holy Spirit was immanent and all-pervasive in singer and song.

O Thou who camest from above,
The pure celestial fire to impart:
Kindle a flame of sacred love
On the mean altar of my heart.
There let it for Thy glory burn,
With inextinguishable blaze
And trembling to its source return
In humble prayer and fervent praise![2]

That is a commentary on the spirit and work of Charles Wesley. He was the songster of the Spirit, an Orpheus among the theologians. To

131

him, the Spirit of God is God in action, and when the Spirit acts, the entire Godhead is in action. It is therefore insufficient to confine study to that remarkable volume jointly published by the brothers Wesley in 1746, namely, *Hymns of Petition and Thanksgiving for the Promise of the Father*.

If we would grasp the Wesleys' teaching on the Holy Spirit, we must first of all realize that their teaching impregnates every aspect and area of Christian doctrine and experience. It is especially concentrated in Charles's hymns on the Trinity and those of Christian experience:

> *When'er our day of Pentecost*
> *Is fully come, we surely know*
> *The Father, Son, and Holy Ghost,*
> *Is manifest below:*
> *The Son doth in the Father dwell,*
> *The Father in His Son imparts,*
> *His Spirit of joy unspeakable,*
> *And live forever in our hearts.*[3]

We should be ready to meet the Holy Spirit at every corner and crossing, for He permeates the poet's thinking processes. Charles Wesley's creativity is energized by the Holy Spirit, his grasp and his transmission of God's truth is dependent on the Holy Spirit; he knew and rejoiced in this, and wrote his songs for the greater glory of God. Charles Wesley seldom if ever loses that "overflow of heart that gives the lips full speech." The power of his pen and his facility of speech are ever dedicated to the ceaseless praise of the Three-Personed God who is ever, always, and totally at work in the world of nature, grace, and personal experience—especially the experience of sanctified humanity.

> *Spirit immense, eternal mind,*
> *Thou the souls of lost mankind*
> *Dost with benignest influence move;*
> *Pleas'd to restore the ruin'd race*
> *And new create a world of grace*
> *In all the image of Thy love.*[4]

Thus the Spirit who created and filled His creation with the power and glory of the Creator is the Architect, Author, and Occupant of the new creation. The Holy Spirit is the Source and the Force of all creation, old and new.

> *Author of every work Divine,*
> *Who dost through both creations shine,*
> *   The God of nature and of grace,*
> *Thy glorious steps in all we see,*
> *And wisdom attribute to Thee,*
> *   And power, and majesty, and praise.*[5]

In the thinking of the man with the dancing heart, every facet, fact, experience, and expression of God's truth zeroes in on the most glorious of all truths, the reality of the personhood and constant operation of the Holy Spirit of God, for in the Spirit of Truth is the fountain and flow of all truth. Charles Wesley hears and sees the Spirit everywhere in creation, Scripture, grace, and experience. Every available symbol is conscripted into service. As an example, take the penultimate stanza of the final hymn in his Pentecost collection. The hymn beginning

> *Away with our fears,*
> *Our trouble and tears,*
> *The Spirit is come . . .*

reaches far back into the Old Testament for its symbolism:

> *The Presence Divine*
> *Doth inwardly shine,*
> *The Shekinah rests,*
> *On all our assemblies, and glows in our breasts.*
> *By day and by night*
> *The pillar of light*
> *Our steps shall attend,*
> *And convoy us safe to our prosperous end.*[6]

As Bishop Roy H. Short has written,

> Charles Wesley put into unforgettable song, not only what he and his brother preached, but also what Methodists most assuredly believed. The great dominant notes of Methodist beliefs and emphasis across the years are all in the Wesley hymns. The essential message and witness of Methodism find continuous and vivid expression in their moving lines . . . The purpose of the hymns which Charles Wesley wrote was first of all to give expression to the gladness which he and his fellow Methodists felt in their souls . . . Furthermore [they] gave welcome opportunity for testimony. The Wesley hymns also serve the purpose of exhortation. In singing them the congregation often joins the preacher in urging sinners to repent and believe the gospel, as well as in urging believers to go on to perfection.[7]

In this meaningful paragraph Bishop Short has rather strangely omitted one of the greatest values and purposes of the man with the dancing heart, which was to set out clearly the theology behind the Methodist message. As has so often been said, John Wesley saw this aspect of his brother's hymns as probably the most important of their purposes and uses. John Kirk wrote many years ago:

> All the doctrines relating to the Divine nature and manifestations; the Person, work, and glory of the Son of God and the Eternal Spirit; man's original condition, fall, and recovery; the blessed attainments of the Christian life, and the fadeless glories of the final heaven,—in one word, all the great verities of revealed theology and religion are expounded and pressed home upon the conscience with a precision, fullness, and energy which nothing can surpass.[8]

It is apparent that God answered the petition of the songster of the Spirit offered in terms of John 16:13-15:

> *Spirit of Truth descend,*
> *And with Thy Church abide,*
> *Our Guardian to the end,*
> *Our sure unerring Guide:*
> *Us into the whole counsel lead*
> *Of God revealed below,*
> *And teach us all the truth we need*
> *To life eternal know.*[9]

But all we need to know is in the Scriptures of Truth, and the Spirit of Truth who inspired Scripture will interpret Scripture and seal His work on our hearts:

> *To all our souls apply*
> *The doctrine of our Lord,*
> *Our conscience certify,*
> *And witness with the word.*[10]

The Word

"The Bible in solution" is one description of Charles Wesley's hymns. Henry Bett wrote:

> Both the brothers must have had a most profound, exact, and extensive acquaintance with the Scriptures. Indeed, it is only a close study of the Bible on our part that can reveal to us the extent of their intimacy with it. There can hardly be a single paragraph anywhere in the Scriptures that is not somewhere reflected in the writings of the Wesleys. The hymns in many cases are a mere mosaic of Biblical allusions.[11]

Is that exaggeration, overstatement, or fact? Many attempts have been made to compile a concordance to Charles Wesley's biblical references and allusions. That is a mountainous task. For example, the small pocket edition of the hymns, issued in 1876, although measuring only 5½" x 4" x ¾", has eight pages crammed with lists of Scripture references contained in that edition alone. These are laid out in biblical sequence, in the smallest of type, and number approximately 700 direct references. We should remember also that the volumes of *Hymns on Select Passages of Scripture* must in large part be added, and that there are hundreds of biblical images, allusions, and references woven into multiplied scores of hymns and poems not contained in the official hymnals of Methodism or of any other communion. John Wesley was right on target when he claimed that the *Hymns for the Use of the People Called Methodists* illustrate "both by Scripture and reason . . . all the important truths of our holy religion."

The hymnbook was for generations of Methodists the practical commentary on the Bible, the road map to heaven, the iron rations of the pilgrim, the weapon of warfare, and the *didachē* of faith, experience, and behavior. From the hymnbook they learned their theology and how to express it, for the hymnbook both expounded and expressed their evangelical faith.

And there were not only these uses but also the inherent value of the hymns for inspirational power, for private and public worship, and for evangelism.

The Scriptures and the Songster

Charles Wesley's method of handling Scripture is important to the study of his hymns. There are innumerable instances in which a verse or a word defies every attempt to locate it, and when—as Hildebrandt has said—the only safe rule is "if in doubt, it is Scriptural." He continues, "Every line is really 'a short hymn on selected passages of the Holy Scriptures.'" A summary list of key texts recurring throughout the collection would serve for the summa of Charles Wesley's theology, which demand our careful study, though cited in a footnote. They are the most important thing in this whole "little body of experimental and practical divinity," and it would be quite fatal to ignore them. Let no one cry "fundamentalism"; the prime source of Wesley's theology is here, and all other antecedents or influences are secondary.

Charles's prodigious biblical knowledge, and his jaw-dropping knack of recall, have bred awe even among those having an intricate and detailed familiarity with the Bible and with the hymns. Writer after writer reflects incredulity that any man could ever acquire such intimacy with God's Word written, and have so stocked his mind and soul with it, as to have left us "the Bible in solution," such an eloquent "tapestry of Scripture."[12]

Consider a brief example of writing from a Scripture-saturated mind:

> By four we came to a land of rest; for the brethren of Birstal [sic] have stopped the mouths of gainsayers, and fairly overcome evil with good. At present, peace is in all their borders. The little foxes that spoil the vineyard, or rather, the wild boars out of the wood that root it up, have no more place among them.[13]

Sixty words, of which 40 are quoted from Scripture! And the quotation is from Charles's daily journal! It is even more so in the hymns.

When Scripture Sings

One of the many instances of Charles Wesley's knowledge and use of Scripture can be seen in his handling of Deut. 6:6-7 in a hymn that well deserves a revival of its former popularity:

> *When quiet in my house I sit,*
> *Thy Book be my companion still;*
> *My joy Thy sayings to repeat,*
> *Talk o'er the records of Thy will,*
> *And search the oracles divine*
> *Til every heartfelt word is mine.*
>
> *O may the gracious words divine*
> *Subject of all my converse be!*
> *So will the Lord His follower join,*
> *And walk and talk Himself with me;*
> *So shall my heart His Presence prove,*
> *And burn with everlasting love.*
>
> *Oft as I lay me down to rest*
> *O may the reconciling Word*
> *Sweetly compose my weary breast!*
> *While on the bosom of my Lord*
> *I sink in blissful dreams away,*
> *And visions of eternal day.*

Rising to sing my Saviour's praise,
Thee may I publish all day long;
And let Thy precious word of grace
Flow from my heart and fill my tongue;
Fill all my soul with purest love,
And join me to the Church above.[14]

These verses were actually the last four of Wesley's poetic exposition of the passage, on which he had written six verses. Big brother John stripped the exposition of the opening two verses and thus created the hymn. "This hymn," wrote Waterhouse, "is surely one of the most beautiful and intimate that Wesley ever penned . . . There are all too few people today for whom this hymn describes their own practice of devotion, and discretion should be used in the choice of this hymn in general congregational worship."[15]

The Holy Spirit—Interpreter of the Word

Charles Wesley's concept of the inspiration and interpretation of Scripture is capsulized for us conveniently in his hymns:

Come, Holy Ghost, for moved by Thee
The prophets wrote and spoke:
Unlock the truth, Thyself the key,
Unseal the sacred book.[16]

Only He who moved the holy men of old to record what is written in the Book can ever be the true and reliable Interpreter of what was recorded.

God through Himself we then shall know,
If Thou within us shine:
And sound with all Thy saints below,
The depths of love divine.[17]

These verses are part of a hymn that was one of three written for singing or praying before the reading of Scripture. The spirit of all three hymns is that which motivated John in his famous *Preface to the Standard Sermons:*

God has written it down in a book! Oh! give me that book! At any price give me the book of God! I have it . . . I sit down alone: only God is here. In His presence I open, I read this book . . . Does anything appear dark or intricate? I lift up my heart to the Father of Light . . . "Lord—Thou hast said 'If any be willing to do Thy will he shall know.' I am willing to do; let me know."[18]

Back to the Source! To which Charles adds,

> Come, Holy Ghost, our hearts inspire,
>   Let us Thy influence prove;
> Source of the old Prophetick Fire,
>   Fountain of Life and Love.[19]

Light will come only from and through the Spirit of Light. He who dispelled the primeval night, saying, "Let there be light: and there was light" (Gen. 1:3), alone can let the light break from the Holy Book. Therefore Charles prays,

> Expand Thy wings, celestial Dove,
>   Brood o'er our nature's night;
> On our disordered spirits move,
>   And let there now be light!

The Inspirer is the Interpreter:

> Spirit of Faith, come down,
>   Reveal the things of God;
> And make to us the Godhead known . . .

> Whate'er the ancient prophets spoke,
>   Concerning Thee, O Christ, make known.
> Sole subject of the sacred Book,
>   Thou fillest all, and Thou alone;
> Yet there our Lord we cannot see
> Unless Thy Spirit lend the key.[20]

Saving Faith and New Life

> Spirit of Faith, come down,
>   Reveal the things of God;
> And make to us the Godhead known,
>   And witness with the Blood:
> 'Tis Thine the Blood to apply,
>   And give us eyes to see
> Who did for every sinner die
>   Hath surely died for me.[21]

This is one of the most impressive and expressive of all Charles Wesley's *Hymns of Petition and Thanksgiving for the Promise of the Father*. As Timothy Smith has suggested, the hymn should be read and studied in association with brother John's "two great sermons on the text in Eph. 2:8, 'By grace are ye saved through faith.'" John's note on Eph. 2:8 says:

This text lays the axe to the very root of spiritual pride, and all glorying in ourselves. Therefore St. Paul, foreseeing the backwardness of mankind to receive it, yet knowing the absolute necessity of its being received, again asserts the very same truth, v. 8, in the very same words.

And on verse 8 he notes beautifully:

> Grace, without any respect to human worthiness, confers the glorious gift. Faith, with an empty hand, and without any pretence to personal desert, receives the heavenly blessing.[22]

That is strongly but beautifully said. As G. Croft Cell expresses the point,

> Wesley regarded any qualification or limitation of the idea of divine grace by a reference to the human subject as so much poison to the Christian consciousness. It is the Wesleyan doctrine that man is by nature absolutely void of all spiritual life and that an operation of the Spirit of God by a power equivalent to that which raises the dead is indispensably necessary to the lowest degree of Christian faith.[23]

Both brothers are adamant on the priority of grace as the gift and work of the Holy Spirit of God. "Pardon is applied to the soul by a divine faith, wrought by the Holy Ghost," wrote John.

> "There is one faith"; which is the free gift of God, and is the ground of their hope. This is not barely the faith of a heathen: namely, a belief that "there is a God" and that he is gracious and just, and, consequently, "a rewarder of them that diligently seek Him." Neither is it barely the faith of a devil; though this goes much farther than the former . . . But it is the faith of St. Thomas, teaching him to say with holy boldness, "My Lord, and my God!" It is the faith which enables every true Christian believer to testify with St. Paul, "The life which I now live, I live by faith in the Son of God, who loved me, and gave himself for me."[24]

Saving faith, then, is that splendid free gift of God, given through His Holy Spirit on those who are utterly undeserving and unworthy of it. It is "not perceivable by eyes of flesh, or by any of our natural senses or faculties." It is rather the unearned, unpurchasable, free gift of naked grace.

> *No man can truly say,*
>   *That Jesus is the Lord,*
> *Unless Thou take the veil away,*
>   *And breathe the living word.*
> *Then . . . only then we feel*
>   *Our interest in His blood,*
> *And cry with joy unspeakable*
>   *Thou art my Lord, my God!*[25]

Only the Holy Spirit can work the miracle of grace. All we can do is to look to Him alone and receive His glorious gift:

> *Inspire the living faith*
> *(Which whosoe'er receives*
> *The witness in himself he hath,*
> *And consciously believes).*[26]

It is all by the Spirit of Grace! From the first dawning of grace in the soul to entrance into the Eternal City.

> *Spirit of Grace, we bless Thy name,*
> *Thy works and offices proclaim,*
> *Thy fruits, and properties, and powers:*
> *Thou dost with kind, intendering care*
> *The godless heart of man prepare,*
> *That God may yet again be ours . . .*
>
> *Thou dost the first good thought inspire,*
> *The first faint spark of pure desire*
> *Is kindled by Thy gracious breath;*
> *By Thee made conscious of his fall,*
> *The sinner hears Thy sudden call*
> *And starts out of the sleep of death.*[27]

And so it is in all Christian experience. The Holy Spirit is God in Christ in continuing action. In all mortification of the flesh; in daily dying to self and living to Christ; in all worship and service and intercession; in all conquest and triumph; in all the peace and joy of sonship; in all these and in much more the work is the Spirit's and the glory is God's, until—as He wills—we receive the bliss of heaven, earnest of which we now receive!

> *Firstfruits of yonder land above,*
> *Celestial joy, seraphic love,*
> *To us, to us in Thee is given:*
> *And all that to the Spirit sow,*
> *Shall of the Spirit reap, and know*
> *The ripest happiness of heaven.*[28]

The Sanctifying Spirit

Paul the apostle wrote to the Roman Christians that "the law of the Spirit of life in Christ Jesus hath made me free from the law of sin and death. For what the law could not do, in that it was weak through the flesh, God [has done] . . . that the righteousness of the law might be fulfilled in us, who walk not after the flesh, but after the Spirit" (8:2-4).

Charles Wesley wrote,

> *To make an end of sin,*
> *   And Satan's works destroy,*
> *He brings His kingdom in,*
> *   Peace, righteousness, and joy;*
> *The Holy Ghost to man is given;*
> *Rejoice in God sent down from heaven.*
>
> *The cleansing blood t'apply,*
> *   The heavenly life display,*
> *And wholly sanctify,*
> *   And seal us to that day.*
> *The Holy Ghost to man is given,*
> *Rejoice in God sent down from heaven!*[29]

The Spirit of holiness is both Giver and Gift. Charles would have us seek the Giver rather than the Gift, the Worker with whom the work is sure; for the Spirit is always the sanctifying Spirit, ever applying the virtue and power of the atonement of Christ: "The gift without the giver is bare," so it is said. Without the Spirit of holiness, not even the desire for holiness would remain, therefore seek the Blesser for himself, for not having Him we have nothing but a vacuum in the soul. And every Christian receives the Holy Spirit—

> *Our God to us His Spirit gave,*
> *   And dwells in us, we know;*
> *The witness in ourselves we have,*
> *   And all His fruits we show.*[30]

To both brothers, the new birth was precisely the door of religion, the entrance into the sanctified life. It is the beginning of sanctification:

> The new birth is not the same with sanctification. This indeed is taken for granted by many . . . This is a part of sanctification, not the whole; it is the gate to it, the entrance into it. When we are born again, then our sanctification begins, our inward and outward sanctification begins; and thenceforth we are gradually to "grow up in Him who is our head" . . . The same relation which there is between our natural birth and our growth, there is also between our new birth and our sanctification.[31]

Charles expressed this principle in his own way:

> *Thou art my daily Bread,*
> *O Christ Thou art my Head!*
> *Motion, virtue, strength, to me,*
>   *Me Thy living member flow;*
> *Nourish'd I, and fed, by Thee,*
>   *Up to Thee in all things grow.*[32]

In all of this the brothers are at one, and both are in general accord with evangelical Reformed belief. But the paths of Reformed belief and Wesleyan opinion soon begin to diverge. The Wesleys come to see that salvation from all sin, by the love of God filling our hearts, is a really crucial matter that must be settled somewhere along the pathway of spiritual progress. Thus, as John wrote in the *Large Minutes,* "Strongly and explicitly exhort all believers 'to go on unto perfection.' That we may all speak the same thing."[33]

=11
The Hymns in Experience and Doctrine

*T*HE TRUE EMBODIMENT of the theology of the Methodist movement is that little book titled *Hymns for the Use of the People Called Methodists,* and more particularly the hymns of Charles Wesley contained therein. John Wesley was regarded as the spiritual father of the Methodists, and his writings, together with those of John Fletcher and the hymns of Charles, supplies the criteria of doctrine.[1]

Hymn singing was a part of life for the Wesleys long before "the change which God works" in both brothers in May 1738. It had been John's practice to sing hymns four or five times daily, a practice that continued after the Aldersgate experience. He included hymn singing as an indispensable element of group or society worship. In Georgia he was summoned before the grand jury to answer charges including:

1. "Inverting the order and method of our liturgy";
2. "Changing the versions of Psalms publicly authorised to be sung in church";
3. "Introducing into Church and service at the Altar compositions of psalms and hymns not inspected or authorized by any proper judicature."[2]

John Wesley's first published hymnbook was the *Charlestown Collection* of 1737, the first hymnbook compiled specifically for Anglican congregations. Winfred Douglas wrote that this little book of 70 hymns was "the first real Anglican Hymnal."[3] Nothing of Charles's work is included, the heavenly Muse not yet having attuned the soul of the younger brother; but when the fire of the Spirit fell on Charles on May 21, 1738, the music of the Spirit came with the fire.

Charles Wesley is the most prolific, poetic, powerful, and evangelical hymn writer of the English-speaking Christian Church. His

hymns, so solidly based in the letter and spirit of Scripture, and so devotedly Christ-centered and objective, are without peer in our language. Their inestimable worth, both in proclaiming and in expounding the gospel, was realized fully by John, who saw these hymns not
only as the expression of Christian experience but also as an invalu-
able teaching tool. Whaling wrote that John Wesley,

> when he became the freely acknowledged leader of the Methodist
> revival turned this into his cherished role of spiritual director . . . In
> a way but to the same end, Charles became chief Psalmist of the
> movement, and it was no accident that the Methodist people
> learned at least as much doctrine from Charles' hymns as they did
> from John's preaching. What is crucial is that it was the same doc-
> trine![4]

High estimate is made of Charles Wesley's poetry by writers of various traditions; and while it is usually the more popular hymns that
catch the limelight, it is true that the judgment can be extended also to
the lesser-known hymns. As Rattenbury says,

> It would be possible today to publish hundreds of his forgotten
> hymns which, if their authorship were unrecognised, would be
> hailed as exceptionally fine, and if wedded to melodious tunes
> would certainly become popular.[5]

Such glowing tributes are easy to document, not only from Methodist sources but also from others not likely to be swayed by denomi-
national pride. Bernard Manning, the Congregational layman, for example, paid his high tribute in terms now familiar to all lovers and
students of Wesley hymns:

> You may think my language about the hymns extravagant:
> therefore I repeat it in stronger terms. This little book[6] ranks in
> Christian literature with the Psalms, the Book of Common Prayer,
> the Canon of the Mass. In its own way, it is perfect, unapproach-
> able, elemental in its perfection. You cannot alter it except to mar it:
> it is a work of supreme devotional art by a religious genius. You
> may compare it with Leonard's "Last Supper" or King's Chapel;
> and, as Blackstone said of the English Constitution, the proper atti-
> tude to take to it is this: we must venerate where we are presently
> not able to comprehend.[7]

From the Roman Catholic camp, John Todd wrote:

> The hymns are of overwhelming importance. They were the
> perfect complement to John's preaching. By their means, the tradi-
> tional Christian doctrines cut through into the hearts of the ordinary
> people, gripping their lives, drawing them into an experience of the
> meaning of the Cross, making them real followers of Christ . . . by
> and large Charles is the faithful interpreter of his brother's thought,

and indeed of Christian tradition, as much so that his hymns are sung in Catholic as well as in Anglican and Methodist places of worship.[8]

There is no greater tribute to Charles Wesley's holy genius than that written by Wesleyanism's great 19th-century theologian, Richard Watson, in his review of the life of John Wesley by the Rev. Henry Moore, which was published in London in 1824.

It is clear that Watson is enamored of Charles Wesley at least as much as he is of John Wesley. The eulogy is rather lengthy, but it does summarize the immense range, depth, and influence of Charles Wesley and his hymns. It also faithfully reflects the sanctified pride felt by the Methodists of the 19th century in the holy genius of the man with the dancing heart. Watson wrote:

> In the commendation of the great excellence of the Family Hymn-Book, we agree with the author; but it is, we think, in the large Hymn-Book in use in all our congregations, that we are to look for the noblest monument of Mr. Charles Wesley's hallowed genius; and it is that which gives him an everlasting claim upon the gratitude of the body at large. We think it, indeed, a singular providence that two men should be raised up, so connected, so accomplished, and each with those peculiar gifts which fitted them so eminently to be the instruments of reviving the spirit of true religion, and of establishing its influence in the judgments and the hearts of men; one, the distinguished teacher; the other, the sweet singer of Israel, whose varied and copious strains embody, in clear, nervous, and beautiful verse, all the principles and all the emotion of a deep-seated piety—the entire recovery of his image, and the triumphant anticipations of his glory. Of hymns of prayer and praise, many had been written by others, and some had written them well; but never before had all that passes in almost every heart which is the subject of a work of God, varied as that "mighty working" is in different individuals, been expressed in such compositions; in which every feeling flows forth in appropriate words, that seem to leave nothing, in the hearts of any, untold to God; nothing unformed into a devotional act; and which, therefore, on all experimental subjects especially, become so fit and edifying a medium of private and public worship. Had that talent been less eminent, we should at this day have been doomed to sing, as part of our devotions, strains less ennobling, less nervous, and, consequently, less beneficially influential.[9]

Writing about the same time as Watson was John Kirk, most famous for his biography of Susanna Wesley.[10] Kirk declared:

> This great change was the turning point of Charles Wesley's whole life. He now bounded along his course of duty as a giant re-

freshed with new wine, rejoicing as a strong man to run a race. His poetry, losing its mystic touch and gloomy shade, became thoroughly evangelical: greater power attended his preaching and his whole life vindicated the Pentecostal Sabbath of May the 21st 1738, as the day of his conversion.[11]

While acknowledging Charles Wesley's shortcomings and flaws, Kirk claims for the poet:

> Truly, when the Divine afflatus was upon him, "or even he was aware his soul made him like the chariots of Ammi-nadib" for swiftness. His "heart indited a good matter," and when he "spoke to the things touching the King" his tongue was as "the pen of a ready writer."
>
> Hence his lines are not like "petrefactions, glittering, and hard, and cold, formed by a slow but certain process in the laboratory of abstract thought," but "like flowers springing spontaneously from a kindly soil, fresh and fragrant, and blooming in open day."[12]

And yet, we must not suppose that Charles relied upon his astonishing facility of speech or his power with words. It was his way to submit his writings to very careful revision, often amending, sometimes altering, but always carefully revising his work and endeavoring not to offer the Lord a costless gift.

"It is the hymns which are characteristic of the 18th-century Evangelical Revival which illustrate most richly the wide-ranging category of hymnody in which the experience of the work of God within the human soul is emphasized." So wrote Norman Goldhawk, who continued:

> While a description of the work of the Holy Spirit within Christian experience is to some extent common to all periods of hymnody, it is to Charles Wesley that the crown for such an undertaking must be awarded . . . [He] concentrated in the main upon man's turning to God, and the work of divine grace within the experience of the individual and in the fellowship of believers. Every facet of the Christian's pilgrimage is described, from the earliest promptings of prevenient grace towards conscious salvation through justification by faith, and its development to final sanctification in heaven, the whole process being accompanied by portrayals of the various aspects of the work of the Spirit.[13]

Charles Wesley is preeminently the songster of the Spirit. Hymns definitive and hymns exultant crowd his pages: he applies his heaven-born gift systematically and charismatically, sometimes analyzing, more often expounding, but always adoring the ever-blessed, ever-present Holy Spirit. True it is that his *Hymns of Petition and Thanksgiving for the Promise of the Father* gathered many of the Pentecost hymns usefully together,[14] but a great many incidental and marginal references to the person and the work of the Holy Spirit meet us in hymns not specifically written for that purpose. For example, the well-loved hymn "Love Divine, All Loves Excelling" includes the tender plea:

> Breathe, O breathe Thy loving Spirit
> Into every troubled breast.

But the hymn is part of the collection for those "that seek and those that have Redemption in the blood of Jesus Christ," published in London a year later than the collection of hymns on the promise of the Father. And there are many such instances.

The work of Charles Wesley extends also to the great Christian festivals. In these, rapture and sorrow follow each other like shadows across an English meadow. His Christian hymns such as "Hark! the Herald Angels Sing" bring the soul to her feet with a cheer, even in our more tame but more understandable modern presentation. For how many moderns would understand

> Hark! how all the welkin rings:
> Glory to the King of kings!

For many a Christian, the celebration of Easter would seem deficient without

> Christ, the Lord, is ris'n today.
> Alleluia!

And the celebration of Communion is powerfully enriched by

> And can it be that I should gain
> An interest in the Saviour's blood?

These hymns and many others are here presented to demonstrate the incredible scope and variety of Charles Wesley's spiritual gifts and poetic genius.

To celebrate the 250th anniversary of the birth of the man with the dancing heart, the office of the *Methodist Recorder* published a very fine issue. The anniversary number carries a moving little poem from the pen of that redoubtable Methodist, Maldwyn Edwards:

> Prophet speaking to all time
>   Ageless accents in your song:
> God's word caught within your rhyme,
>   God's fire lighting on your tongue.
>
> Let that song in thunder come
>   To the deafened ears of man:
> Show once more the soul's true home,
>   Raise our hearts to God again.[15]

For all the two and a half centuries that have rolled past since the Divine Maestro tuned the soul of Charles Wesley, his prophetic voice still sounds loud and clear, winsomely but imperatively, calling on all men everywhere to turn, repent, and be converted.

The Man with the Dancing Heart

Commenting on Paul's words in Col. 3:16, Bishop Handley Moule wrote:

> Full inspired sanction is given here on the one hand to the culti-
> vation of God's gifts of poetic and musical form, in the entire con-
> viction that they ARE His gifts, and meant by Him for a purpose.
> On the other hand the Apostle lays it solemnly upon us to see that
> these rich resources as used "in spirit and in truth." The great pur-
> pose of the holy melody, next to its being "unto the Lord," is to be
> the "instruction and admonition of one another."[16]

Charles Wesley is one in spirit with those first Christians who expressed their faith—and the faith once delivered to the saints—in
Christ-exalting words and music.

In times when there is a growing tendency to regard congregational praise as some sort of preliminary or interlude in the more serious matter of worship and preaching, it would be well to rub shoulders with this man with the dancing heart. His Christ-centered
singing might provide a welcome replacement for so many modern
hymns and songs that are like sinking ships laden to the Plimsoll line
with cargoes of moanings. For our actual personal faith is more clearly
expressed in the hymns we choose to sing than in the creeds drawn
up with scrupulous care by professional theologians using word
tweezers. As Gregory wrote,

> A good hymn is one of the most effective means ever devised
> of pressing on men's minds the vital truths of the Christian religion.
> If it be said that the people do not want doctrinal hymns and will
> not sing them, that is simply so much evidence of a decay of faith. It
> is not objected that people will listen to theology in sermons but not
> in hymns: the objection if there be one, is to theology in any definite
> form at all; and this springs from the offence of Christianity itself . . .
> We preach God Incarnate, Christ crucified, risen and present to
> save; and in this proclamation of good tidings our hymns exercise a
> unique power which stamps them with the authentic seal of the
> Holy Spirit.[17]

John Richard Green, the historian, wrote:

> Charles Wesley . . . came to add sweetness to this sudden and
> startling light . . . His hymns expressed the fiery conviction of its
> converts in lines so chaste and beautiful that its more extravagant

features disappeared. The wild throes of hysteria and enthusiasm passed into the passion for hymn-singing, and a new musical impulse was aroused in the people which gradually changed the face of public devotion in England.[18]

The man with the dancing heart! His hymns long ago ceased to belong exclusively to the people called Methodists. They belong to all of us. They do most emphatically belong to those who—taking a whole Christ for their salvation, a whole Bible for their staff, the whole world as their parish, and the whole salvation of the whole person as their objective—seek to declare the whole gospel to every man.

But these hymns are not merely good poetry with a toe-tapping tempo that sets the heart dancing, or in softer tones expresses its mourning. History and experience alike have justified the claims that big brother John made in that famous *Preface:*

> I desire men of taste to judge, (for these are the only competent judges) whether there be not in some of the following hymns the true spirit of poetry, such as cannot be acquired by art labour, but must be the gift of nature . . . By labour a man may become a tolerable imitator of Spencer, Shakespeare, or Milton . . . but unless he be BORN a poet he will never attain the genuine spirit of poetry.[19]

But still it is the affairs of the holy heart that are the focus of poet Charles and editor John alike. Toward the end of the famous preface, brother John writes:

> That which is of infinitely more moment than the spirit of poetry is the spirit of piety. And I trust all persons of real judgment will find this breathing through the whole collection. It is in this view chiefly that I would recommend it to every reader, as a means of raising or quickening the spirit of devotion; of confirming his faith; of enlivening his hope; and of kindling and increasing his love to God and man. When Poetry thus keeps its place as the handmaid of Piety, it shall attain, not a poor perishable wreath, but a crown that fadeth not away.[20]

The theologian, the litterateur, and the earnest seeker after holiness all echo John's thrusting questions:

> In what other publication of this kind have you so distinct and full an account of Scriptural Christianity? Such a declaration of the heights and depths of religion, speculative and practical? So strong cautions against the most plausible errors; particularly those that are now most prevalent? and so clear directions for making your calling and election sure; for perfecting holiness in the fear of God?[21]

New Singer, New Song

I repeat, the fact is that the fountain of those torrents of song that burst from the soul of Charles Wesley was undoubtedly his evangelical conversion. The text for such an assertion might well be

> *In the heavenly Lamb*
> *Thrice happy I am;*
> *And my heart it doth dance at the sound of His Name!*

✳   ✳   ✳

> *The remnant of days*
> *I spend to His praise*
> *Who died the whole world to redeem;*
> *Be they many or few*
> *My days are His due,*
> *And they all are devoted to Him!*[22]

The poems that Charles wrote before that glorious May 21, 1738, are not to be compared with the glory that followed, as we might expect.

From that May morning of his soul, Charles was the man of the dancing and the burning heart:

> *New songs do now his lips employ*
> *And dances his glad heart for joy!*[23]

May 21, 1738, was an evening never to be forgotten, the great divide of Wesley's life: all the world, it seems, was a new place. Days of darkness will still come over him, and sorrow's path he will sometimes tread; but the glory of that hour will remain forever. Later he will sing, in the very words of Scripture, the Magna Charta of his new life in Christ Jesus:

Jesus, the first and last,	Rev. 1:8
On Thee my soul is cast;	Ps. 55:22
Thou didst the work begin	Phil. 1:6
By blotting out my sin.	Ps. 51:1
Thou wilt the root remove	Matt. 15:13
And perfect me in love.	1 John 4:12
Yet when the work is done,	John 17:4
The work is but begun;	Phil. 1:6
Partaker of Thy grace,	Phil. 1:7; 1 Pet. 5:1
I long to see Thy face;	Rev. 22:4
The first I prove below,	1 Cor. 13:12
The last I die to know.	1 Cor. 13:12[24]

The Man with the Sharing Heart

If, as we have often heard said, "it is the overflowing heart that give the lips full speech," then that person is not an evangelist who does not feel the sweet burden of compassion and the expansive love of Christ in his heart.

Charles Wesley was an evangelist of the Pauline type. The love of Christ constrained him. He was a man with a caring and, therefore, a sharing heart. Just as Charles had once been a beggar seeking the Bread of Life, the thought and sight of every other hungry heart goaded him to tell the world where to find bread, to take them by the hand and lead them to the Father's house where there is "bread enough and to spare" (Luke 15:17).

Charles Wesley was a true evangelist, able to leave the 99 and seek the lost up and down the wild countryside of England, Wales, and Ireland, finding often that the lost sheep were as wild as cornered wolves. He was a man of "calmly fervent zeal" whose "heart full of Christ" joined with his heavenly disposition and ready tongue to share the Good News with all men. The most striking phrase of his *Journal* must surely be, "I offered them Christ"; and the words that focus his soul's vocation must be

> 'Tis all my business here below
> To cry "Behold the Lamb!"[25]

How divinely successful Charles Wesley was in seeking and finding the lost! "Harlots and publicans and thieves: ministers, scholars, soldiers: some of the so-called upper classes but mostly those of the forgotten multitudes of Britain were brought to 'that open side.'"[26] One might almost write a history of the Revival from the hymns of Charles Wesley. Here we read the sort of men and women who turned to God. They were mostly poor and despised by the society of the day, treated with contempt and often with disgust. The Duchess of Buckingham once wrote to Lady Huntingdon regarding the Wesleys and Whitefield, complaining:

> Their doctrines are most repulsive and strongly tinctured with impertinence and disrespect to their superiors. It is monstrous to be told that you have a heart as sinful as the common wretches that crawl on the earth. This is highly insulting and I wonder that your ladyship should relish any sentiment so much at variance with high rank and good breeding.[27]

Yet these "common wretches" were lifted by grace and came to walk the earth with the dignity that becomes the children of God. In Wesley's hymns we may read both of the judgment of the world upon His converts and of the dignity of those who, discounted by the world, have nevertheless found favor with the Almighty.

> Ye simple souls that stray
>   Far from the path of peace,
> That lonely unfrequented way
>   To life and happiness,
> Why will ye folly love,
>   And throng the downward road,
> And hate the wisdom from above
>   And mock the sons of God? . . .
>
> Riches unsearchable
>   In Jesu's love we know:
> And pleasures springing from the well
>   Of life, our souls o'erflow;
> The Spirit we receive
>   Of wisdom, grace, and power;
> And always sorrowful we live,
>   Rejoicing evermore.
>
> On all the kings of earth
>   With pity we look down,
> And claim in virtue of our birth,
>   A never-fading crown.[28]

Search them out! Bring them in! Build them up! Send them out to bring others in! There you have Charles Wesley's philosophy of evangelism, and it sounds rather like "Let him that heareth say, Come" (Rev. 22:17).

The Sweep of Charles Wesley's Message

To the man with the dancing heart, one great reason for singing was the wide sweep of the mercy and love of God. "For me—for all" —that is the majestic scope of the gospel of grace: "Sufficient, sovereign, saving grace."

In that gracious awakening, the Wesleys saw with wonder how God the Spirit gathered in people of all sorts, all ages, and every condition. These "common wretches" found their place with the "uncommon wretches" in the kingdom of God.

> Help us Thy mercy to extol,
>   Immense, unfathomed, unconfined;
> To praise the Lamb who died for all,
>   The general Saviour of mankind.

> *Thy undistinguishing regard*
> *Was cast on Adam's fallen race;*
> *For all Thou hast in Christ prepared*
> *Sufficient, sovereign, saving grace.*[29]

The message of the evangelist accentuated limitless grace. The promise of his conversion hymn breathed and thundered through hundreds of later poems. In the gracious awakenings he everywhere saw the work of an "undistinguishing regard" for the salvation of all men.

The story of that blessed revival of spiritual religion in 18th-century England can be told in song and was so told by the man with the dancing heart:

> *See how great a flame aspires,*
> *Kindled by a spark of grace!*
> *Jesu's love the nations fires,*
> *Sets the kingdoms on a blaze.*
> *To bring fire on earth He came;*
> *Kindled in some hearts it is;*
> *O that all might catch the flame,*
> *All partake the glorious bliss!*
>
> *When He first the work begun,*
> *Small and feeble was His day:*
> *Now the word doth swiftly run,*
> *Now it wins its widening way;*
> *More and more it spreads and grows*
> *Ever mighty to prevail;*
> *Sin's strongholds it now o'erthrows,*
> *Shakes the trembling gates of hell.*
>
> *Sons of God, your Saviour praise!*
> *He the door hath opened wide;*
> *He hath given the word of grace,*
> *Jesu's word is glorified;*
> *Jesus, mighty to redeem,*
> *He alone the work hath wrought;*
> *Worthy is the work of Him,*
> *Him who spake a world from nought.*

Saw ye not the cloud arise,
    Little as a human hand?
Now it spreads along the skies,
    Hangs o'er all the thirsty land:
Lo! the promise of a shower
    Drops already from above;
But the Lord will shortly pour
    All the Spirit of His love![30]

Come—All the World!

No message of limited grace could have reached and won such people as Wesley found everywhere and made of them such a people: "children of God through faith in Christ Jesus"—the people called Methodists. The raw material was unpromising, but the product was magnificent. Such a work of transformation called for a gospel broad as humanity, high as the throne of God, deeper than hell, stronger than Satan, and infinitely more abundant than sin. Charles Wesley preached such a gospel.

The universal sweep and unashamed catholicity of Charles Wesley's gospel was firmly based in Scripture and verified in his experience and that of thousands of converts all over the land. He reasoned that the mercy and the love that had found him out and taken him in was

So wide it never passed by one
Or it had passed by me![31]

He is sure that any man, every man, and all men may repent and be converted. *Charles was agreed with John that "just as wide as sin extends, the propitiation extends also."*

This was Charles Wesley's Arminianism. It was positive, persuasive, jubilant: with mind convinced and heart on fire, he lifted up his voice with strength to invite all and sundry to see and to know their sins forgiven.

His Mercy's Whole Design

Charles Wesley must not be classified simply as an Arminian. As Gordon Rupp put it,

> The intricate theological dissertations of the Dutch Arminius, the mediating theology of the Arminian divines of the Church of England, had nothing in them to set the Thames or the Zuider Zee on fire. But Evangelical Arminianism is the return to the plan of salvation for all men, to what Charles Wesley called "His mercy's whole design."[32]

Charles Wesley was an evangelical Arminian standing in the evangelical line of the English Puritans, not that of the Cambridge Platonists. His Arminianism was Arminianism on fire. All through his glorious hymns on God's everlasting love rings the constant refrain, like the recurring theme of a classical symphony, "Pure universal love Thou art!" This is the characteristic emphasis of the Wesley hymns. They are, as he called them, *Hymns of God's Universal Love.* Indicative and exemplary of these many hymns is one beloved of experts in English literature as of Wesleyan preachers. It has been described as the finest lyric in the English language; even Isaac Watts coveted the honor of having written it. The poet takes the experience of Jacob wrestling with the angel and presents it as the story of the agony and joy of every truly repentant and eventually justified sinner:

> *Come, O Thou Traveller unknown,*
> *Whom still I hold but cannot see!*
> *My company before is gone,*
> *And I am left alone with Thee;*
> *With Thee all night I mean to stay,*
> *And wrestle till the break of day.*
>
> *I need not tell Thee who I am,*
> *My misery and sin declare;*
> *Thyself hast called me by Thy name,*
> *Look on Thy hands and read it there!*
> *But who, I ask Thee, Who art Thou?*
> *Tell me Thy name, and tell me now! . . .*
>
> *'Tis Love! 'Tis Love! Thou diedst for me!*
> *I hear Thy whisper in my heart!*
> *The morning breaks! The shadows flee!*
> *Pure **universal love** Thou art!*
> *To ME . . . to ALL . . . Thy bowels move;*
> *Thy nature and Thy name is love!*[33]

Of this poem, which runs to 14 six-line verses, Watts said, "That single poem, Wrestling Jacob, is worth all the verses I myself have written."[34]

It has captured the hearts and minds of many Christians in similar manner. James Montgomery, the Moravian songster, said of it and of the poet:

> With consummate art he has carried on the action of a lyric drama; every turn in the conflict with the mysterious Being with whom Jacob wrestles all night being marked with precision by the varying language of the speaker, accompanied by intense, increasing inter-

est, till the rapturous moment of discovery when he prevails and exclaims, "I know Thee, Savior, who Thou art."[35]

But although, as Mary Champness put it, this work is "splendid as a poem, it is not a good hymn for public worship, as the words are difficult to sing."[36]

The hymn that can with greater precision be called really declarative of Charles Wesley's evangelical Arminianism is titled "The Universal Love of Christ," a magnificent hymn of 10 verses, including

> *Let earth and heaven agree*
> > *Angels and men be joined;*
> *To celebrate with me*
> > *The Saviour of mankind!*
> *T'adore the all-atoning Lamb*
> *And bless the sound of Jesu's name!*
>
> *Jesus, transporting sound!*
> > *The joy of earth and heaven!*
> *No other help is found;*
> > *No other name is given*
> *By which we can salvation have,*
> *But Jesus came the world to save!*
>
> *For me and all mankind*
> > *The Lamb of God was slain;*
> *The Lamb His life resigned*
> > *For every soul of man!*
> *Loving to all He none passed by,*
> *He would not have one sinner die!*
>
> *O for a trumpet voice*
> > *On all the world to call!*
> *To bid their hearts rejoice*
> > *In Him Who died for all!*
> *For all my Lord was crucified!*
> *For all—for all—my Saviour died!*[37]

However, the hymn generally designated "The Arminian Hymn" is 17 verses in length, the first 8 of which are a rousing statement of the gospel of all-embracing universal love, and the remaining 9 a further satirical exposure of the preaching of limited grace based on a limited atonement.

> *Father, whose <u>everlasting love,</u>*
> *Thy only Son for sinners gave,*
> *Whose grace to ALL did <u>freely</u> move,*
> *And sent Him down a WORLD to save.*[38]

See the empathy of Charles Wesley with Moses and with Paul (Exod. 32:32 and Rom. 9:3). The rest of the hymn was presented earlier in this book.[39] Excluded from the 1964 *Hymnbook of the Methodist Church in America*, "The Arminian Hymn" has nevertheless held its place in the various Methodist hymnbooks in Britain, howbeit usually condensed to five or six verses drawn from the first eight written by Charles. The hymn abounds in such terms as "all," "died for all," "a world to save," "the general Saviour of mankind," "undistinguishing regard," "all ye ends of earth," etc., and concludes with the arresting truth

> *For those that <u>will not come to Him</u>*
> *The ransom of His death was paid.*[40]

Charles Wesley felt that he had no good news for anyone if he did not have good news for everyone. The selfless spirit of Moses and of Paul breathed in his soul:

> *Lo! all my hopes I here resign*
> *If all may not find grace with me!*[41]

It is all gathered up poignantly in a hymn woven like a beautiful tapestry:

> *O let me kiss Thy bleeding feet*
> *And bathe and wash them with my tears;*
> *The story of Thy love repeat*
> *In <u>every drooping sinner's ears;</u>*
> *That ALL may hear the quickening sound*
> *Since I, e'en I, have mercy found!*
>
> *O let Thy love my heart constrain,*
> *Thy love for <u>every</u> sinner free;*
> *That <u>every</u> fallen soul of man*
> *May taste the grace that found out me!*
> *That <u>all mankind</u> with me may prove*
> *Thy sovereign, everlasting love.*[42]

For me, for you, for all.

 The immense sweep and scope of Charles Wesley's gospel will almost certainly raise thoughts about universalism. But we must also remember that although the world is invited by him to the gospel feast, he bids them come personally and individually.

> *Come all the world*
> *Come sinner thou . . .*[43]

The universal call has its concomitant in Wesley's insistent and persistent appeal to each individual to respond personally and to surrender to the all-embracing and all-redeeming love of God in Jesus Christ. This love reaches all because it reaches each. God loved the world in order that whosoever will believe shall be saved. Thus the man with the dancing heart never tired of personalizing the universal gospel:

> *To me, to all Thy mercies move*
> *Thy nature and Thy Name is love!*
>
> *For you and for me He prayed on the tree;*
> *The prayer is accepted, the sinner is free!*[44]

Every man has his own peculiar personal place in the universal love of God in Christ Jesus; He loves each as though there were but one to love. But each person must respond directly and personally to that love once for all displayed in the sacrifice of God's only begotten Son. Poured out lavishly on all the world, God's love is undistinguishing:

> *His soul was once an offering made*
> *For every soul of man!*[45]

But each person must put his will and his heart into his response. Luther's counsel, which had been so crucial to Charles Wesley, was echoed and reechoed in Wesley's call to others. "FOR ME!" he said, "say it over and over again! for ME, for ME!"

> *Me He loved, the Son of God!*
> *For me! for ME, He died!*[46]

Any accusation of universalism in these hymns is overwhelmingly obliterated by the poet's emphasis on personal faith, choice, and commitment.

> *God, who all your lives hath strove,*
> *Woo'd you to embrace His love . . .*
> *Why, ye long sought sinners, why*
> *Will ye grieve your God, and die?*
>
> *You, of reason's powers possess'd,*
> *You, with will and memory blest,*
> *You, with finer sense endued,*
> *Creatures capable of God . . .*

> *You, whom He ordained to be*
> *Transcripts of the Trinity . . .*
> *Why will you forever die?*[47]

Because the hindrances to living faith are not in our heads (arising from lack of evidences) but in our hearts (arising from a lack of willingness to believe), Charles Wesley holds us to that point.

> *Your willing heart and ear incline,*
> *My words believingly receive;*
> *Quickened your souls by faith divine*
> *An everlasting life shall live.*[48]

The Singer on the Sidewalk

There is providential significance in the fact that, in the earlier part of the memorable month of May 1738, Charles Wesley was deeply immersed in a devotional reading of the evangelical prophet Isaiah. Nine days before his conversion, Charles wrote,

> Fri., May 12, I waked in the same blessed temper, hungry and thirsty after God. I began Isaiah, and seemed to see that to me were the promises made, and would be fulfilled, for that Christ loved me.[49]

On the afternoon of the same day, he read a portion from the same book to a small company of friends:

> We were all much encouraged to pursue the glorious prize held out to us by the evangelical Prophet.[50]

Isaiah was a great guide and comforter to Charles Wesley.

> I found much comfort both in prayer and in the word, my eyes being opened more and more to discern and lay hold on the promises. I longed to find Christ, that I might show Him to all mankind; that I might praise, that I might love him.[51]

About this time Wesley wrote a hymn that reveals the strong influence of the evangelical prophet and heralds the coming of the singer's day of grace:

> *The day, the Gospel day draws near,*
> *When sinners shall their voices raise,*
> *Sing the new song with heart sincere,*
> *Triumphant in the land of praise.*

> *Glory to God! they all shall cry:*
> *Who is so great a God as ours?*
> *Why have a city strong and high?*
> *Salvation is for walls and towers.*

> Salvation to our souls brought in,
>   Salvation from our guilty stains,
> Salvation from the power of sin,
>   Salvation from its last remains.[52]

This is the first hymn in that two-volume set published by Charles in Bristol in 1749 without consulting John, and it is the first in a series of hymns based on the teaching of the evangelical prophet. The series concludes with the significant verse:

> They now the holy people named,
>   Their glorious title shall express,
> From all iniquity redeemed,
>   Filled with the Lord their righteousness.
>
> A chosen, saved, peculiar race,
>   Sion, with all thy sons thou art,
> Elect through sanctifying grace,
>   Perfect in love, and pure in heart.[53]

True it may be that, in these hymns written in early May 1738, we do not feel the rapture and review soon to vibrate in later songs; but the truth and promise of the gospel of grace is there powerfully and clearly—redemption for the whole wide world and Christian perfection—those twin foci of the Wesley gospel. The passion of the prophet Isaiah as it passes into the soul of Charles Wesley, and so soon to be baptized into Christ, is already becoming evident, that spirit of the evangelist that will soon throb and pulse through almost all that he will write.

Charles Wesley is the evangelical prophet of the Great Awakening, both its harbinger and its portrayer. He is its authentic voice. In him evangelism is not a program but a passion, a heavenly disposition constraining the soul. It is seen and felt in many a hymn. From the hour of his conversion, Charles Wesley became a voice: the voice of one crying in the streets and in the fields, by the seashore and by the mine shaft, to rich and poor, high and low:

> The mercy I feel to others I show
> I set to my seal that Jesus is true;
> Ye all may find mercy who come at His call
> O come to my Saviour, His grace is for all!
>
> O let me commend my Saviour to you,
> The publican's Friend and Advocate too;
> For you He is pleading His merits and death,
> With God interceding for sinners beneath.[54]

It was a true Wesleyan spirit that moved the Bristol Methodists to place the fascinating statue of Charles Wesley in the *courtyard* of their New Room, his back to the stable and church, his face to the passing throng, his hand—with the Bible in it—stretched out persuasively, standing "as though he pleaded with men," and on the statue's base the theme song of his life: "O let me commend my Saviour to you!" In the first month of his new life in Christ this evangelical prophet of England—moved by the words of Isaiah—wrote:

> *Arm of the Lord, awake, awake!*
> *Thine own immortal strength put on!*
> *With terror clothed, hell's kingdom shake,*
> *And cast Thy foes with fury down!*[55]

The evangelist's challenge carries the gospel call. Whenever the enemy rages, he rages in vain, and the gates of hell tremble at the Spirit's onslaught. The "foes" in St. Ives found out that:

> They swore bitterly I should not preach there again; which I disproved, by immediately telling them Christ died for all. Several times they lifted their hands and clubs to strike me; but a stronger arm restrained them. They beat and dragged the women about, particularly one of a great age, and trampled on them without mercy. The longer they stayed, and the more they raged, the more power I found from above. I bade the people stand still and see the salvation of God; resolving to continue with them, and see the end. In about an hour the word came, "Hitherto shalt thou come, and no farther." The ruffians fell to quarrelling among themselves, broke the Town-Clerk's (their captain's) head and drove one another out of the room.
>
> Having kept the field, we gave thanks for the victory; and in prayer the Spirit of glory rested upon us.[56]

To celebrate this victory, Wesley wrote:

> *Worship and thanks and blessing*
> *And strength ascribe to Jesus.*
> *Jesus alone*
> *Defends His own*
> *When earth and hell oppress us.*
>
> *Jesus with joy we witness*
> *Almighty to deliver;*
> *Our seals set to,*
> *That God is true*
> *And reigns a King forever.*[57]

This was no cloistered virtue; this was not the call of the professional evangelist from the comfort of an upholstered pulpit to a foe conspicuous by its absence. Wesley was seeking the lost as his Master did in the beginning of the Gospel. He found them, brought them in, and folded them, just as the Master did, for they were "the sheep for whom their Shepherd died." Down Kingswood way, where the god-less colliers lived on the animal level, drunken and sensual, the evangelist called them home to God and then gave them hymns of their very own. Wesley's predecessor, John the Baptist, had said, "God is able of these stones to raise up children unto Abraham" (Matt. 3:9). The 18th-century voice of the Master's servant sang:

> The people that in darkness lay,
>   In sin and error's deadly shade,
> Have seen a glorious gospel day,
>   In Jesus's lovely face displayed.
>
> Thou only Lord the work hast done
>   And bared Thine arm in all our sight;
> Hast made the reprobates Thine own
>   And claimed the outcasts as Thy right.[58]

But whether consorting with outcasts or preaching in fashionable churches, whether on the village greens or on the corner of High Street and Main, always it is the sweet wooing and haunting note and then the trumpet call of the gospel:

> All ye that pass by
> To Jesus draw nigh.
> To you is it nothing that Jesus should die?[59]

Sometimes the answer is "Nothing! . . . Nothing at all!" but the invitation is insistent.

> Come sinners to the Gospel feast!
> Let every soul be Jesus's guest;
> Ye need not one be left behind
> For God hath bidden all mankind!
>
> Sent by my Lord on you I call!
> The invitation is to all!
> Come ALL THE WORLD, Come sinner thou!
> All things in Christ are ready now!

But always there are those who say, "I pray thee have me excused" (Luke 14:18-19). These the singing cavalier anticipates and makes ready his answer:

> Excused from coming to a feast!
> Excused from being Jesus's guest!
> From knowing now your sins forgiven!
> From tasting here the joys of heaven!

And back to his Lord goes the commissioned messenger to complain that the invited guests are unwilling to attend, and hears the words:

> *Invite the rich and great no more,*
> *But preach the Gospel to the poor.*
> *Search every land and every street,*
> *And bring in all the souls you meet!*
>
> *Tell them their sins are all forgiven;*
> *Tell EVERY CREATURE UNDER HEAVEN*
> *I died to save them from all sin,*
> *And force the vagrants to come in!*

And thus doubly assured he goes out again with

> *Ye vagrant souls, on you I call;*
> *O that my voice could reach you all!*
> *Ye all may now be justified;*
> *Ye all may live, for Christ hath died!*
>
> *His love is mighty to compel;*
> *His conquering love consent to feel;*
> *Yield to His love's resistless power,*
> *And fight against your God no more!*
>
> *This is the time; no more delay!*
> *This is the acceptable day!*
> *Come in this moment at His call,*
> *And live for Him who died for all!*[60]

What could be more wistful yet more forceful and persuasive than

> *Weary souls that wander wide*
> *   From the central point of bliss;*
> *Turn to Jesus crucified*
> *   Fly to those dear wounds of His;*
> *Sink into the purple flood,*
> *Rise into the life of God.*[61]

To Charles Wesley, the hymns of the gospel must be sound scriptural sense. He does not betray the Bible; indeed, as someone has said, "The Bible is here in solution." Whole passages are pressed into evangelistic service as great Scripture portions are launched on wings of praise. The evangelical prophet of the Old Testament provides the Methodist evangelist with many notes of the eternal gospel. Take, for example, Isa. 55:1-3:

> *Ho! everyone that thirsts draw nigh!*
> *'Tis God invites the fallen race;*
> *Mercy and free salvation buy;*
> *Buy wine and milk and Gospel grace!*
>
> *Nothing ye in exchange shall give;*
> *Leave all you have and are behind;*
> *Freely the gift of God receive,*
> *Pardon and peace in Jesus find.*

The call continues through nine more verses of winsome preaching of the evangel, reaching its peak in

> *Your willing heart and ear incline,*
> *My words believingly receive;*
> *Quickened your souls by faith divine*
> *An everlasting life shall live.*[62]

Erik Routley wrote insightfully that

> there is in the hymns of Wesley a quality of thought and of poetic power which commands the attention, engages the affection, and in the end informs the thought and speech. . . . For it happened that the Methodist hymnody was founded by a man who combined with a revivalist enthusiasm two cooling and moderating disciplines— that of poetry and that of Biblical Theology. . . . The discipline of the Bible is always there.[63]

Charles Haddon Spurgeon has been quoted as asserting that the best way to defend the Bible is to let it loose. Under God, Charles Wesley does just that. For biblical content and evangelistic fervor wedded to sound Christian doctrine, there is nothing in all Christendom like these hymns of the man with the dancing heart. Even in the exegetically enlighted 20th century, Charles Wesley will let the Bible loose if we will allow him to do so. He can help us make it come alive and real as we press the claims of Christ on the "weary souls" who still "wander wide from the central point of bliss."

=12

Entire Sanctification, Holiness, and Perfect Love

*T*HE WESLEY BROTHERS had their differences of opinion both as to the nature and the time of what John described as "that grand depositum that God has lodged with the people called Methodists," namely "perfect love" or "entire sanctification," or "Christian perfection." By this last term John meant "the humble, gentle, patient love of God and our neighbor, ruling our tempers, words, and actions," and believed that such a condition could be initiated in an instantaneous act of the Holy Spirit.

One question was: when could such a work be done, in this life or at death? This was a matter that troubled more than a few of John Wesley's preachers, and at one point at least had threatened to disrupt the progress of the great Revival. It was probably the main reason why John devoted entire conferences of the preachers to the question. The issue was so serious that John wrote five letters to various London newspaper editors. Published between 1760 and 1766, these letters were "apologia" for Wesley's understanding and teaching on sanctification and Christian perfection.

Wesley had a possible separation on his hands as some radical Methodist preachers began to make fanatical statements and radical claims in the area of Christian perfection. These teachings by some of the preachers such as Maxfield, Bell, and Owen are condensed for us in a letter from John Wesley to Maxfield. John wrote:

> I dislike your supposing man may be perfect as an angel; that he can be absolutely perfect; that he can be infallible, or above being tempted; or that the moment he is pure in heart he cannot fall from it.[1]

Some of these preachers were actually making these claims, notably Maxfield with his strange notions of perfection, and Bell with what Wesley dubbed his "enthusiasm" for eschatology—especially his insistence on setting a date for the end of the world, an event he predicted for February 28, 1763. But the main trouble was the time of entire sanctification, and the dispute had been growing since the mid-1740s, as is verified by John Wesley's minutes of the Fourth Annual Methodist Conference in June 1749. On a number of points there was agreement:

1. Everyone must be entirely sanctified in the moment, instant, and article of death.

2. That before that tremendous moment, every believer should press toward perfection.

3. That the preachers exhort all believers to do so.

But the big question was whether Christians should expect to be saved from all sin *before* the instant of death. John said yes but Charles was far from saying so.

From the late 1740s, Charles Wesley appears increasingly hesitant about regarding or at least asserting entire sanctification as a crisis experience in the life of the believer, that is, as a specific punctiliar action of the Holy Spirit. He creates the impression that only in the very instant and article of death will God entirely sanctify the Christian soul. It is a case of

> 'Til death Thy endless mercies seal,
> And make the sacrifice complete.[2]

Despite all his prayers, pleas, and praises, we are left wondering why no specific answer to the question is forthcoming from Charles. Indeed, on the contrary, he seems to veer not only toward the gradual work of sanctification but also, probably because of that, toward seeing the work effected at death. Let us be clear, however: Charles was not in any doubt whatsoever about the necessity of holiness for entry into heaven, nor did he doubt that God desires and wills that holiness:

> He wills that I should holy be:
> What can withstand His will?[3]

Nor does Charles ever doubt that such holiness is possible, desirable, and available through the atonement of Christ, and thus must be bestowed in grace:

> If Thou hast power and will to save,
> Saved to the utmost I shall be![4]

But the former confidence of the early years of the Revival is now qualified. Whereas once he would and did assert

In all the confidence of hope,
I claim this blessing now![5]

hasty and spurious profession of the blessing by some Methodists, and the pitfalls he thought he saw, appear to have caused Charles to modify his approach, and the big question became the "when?" of the Spirit's work in this respect. Such was the very issue of the Fourth Annual Methodist Conference.

Charles would have been satisfied, I believe, had John been content not to hedge his concept of Christian perfection with so many possibilities of imperfection. On the other hand, it seemed to John that Charles was actually "setting perfection too high," so high indeed as effectually to make it absolutely unobtainable in this life. Perhaps the chief difficulty was terminological and definitive, although John never lacked words and definitions!

For whatever cause, the brothers did have their differences along this line. As John wrote to Charles,

> Of *that perfection* which I believe, I can boldly preach because I think I see 500 witnesses to it. Of that perfection which you preach, you do not think you see any witnesses at all. . . . there is no such perfection here as you describe—at least I never met with an instance of it; and I doubt I ever shall. Therefore I still think that to set perfection so high is effectually to renounce it.[6]

> I ask, once for all, Shall we defend this Perfection, or give it up? You all agree to defend it, meaning thereby (as we did from the beginning), salvation from all sin, by the love of God and man filling our heart. The Papists say, "This cannot be attained till we have been refined by the fire of purgatory." The Calvinists say, "Nay, it will be attained as soon as the soul and body part." The old Methodists say, "It may be attained before we die: A moment after is too late." Is it so or not? You are all agreed, we may be saved from all sin before death. The substance then is settled; but, as to the circumstance, is the change gradual or instantaneous? It is both the one and the other. From the moment we are justified, there may be a gradual sanctification, a growing in grace, a daily advance in the knowledge of love of God. And if sin cease before death, there must, in the nature of the thing, be an instantaneous change; there must be a last moment wherein it does exist, and a first moment wherein it does not exist. . . . Certainly we must insist on the gradual change, and that earnestly and continually. And are there not reasons why we should insist on the instantaneous also? . . . should we not encourage all believers to expect it? . . . They are "saved by hope," by this hope of a total change, with a gradually increasing salvation. Destroy his hope, and that salvation stands still, or,

rather, decreases daily. Therefore whoever would advance the gradual change in believers should strongly insist on the instantaneous.[7]

These extracts from the writings of John set out the heart of his
teaching on the distinctions that must be made between beginning,
continuing, and entire sanctification. In preaching and writing on the
theme, John constantly used the hymns of Charles to explain, illustrate, and apply his meaning. A high percentage of the hymns selected
by John for this purpose were written and published in the hymnbook
of 1742. Indeed, Charles's most striking hymns on the subject seem to
have been written between 1738 and 1742, but his 1749 book *Hymns
and Sacred Poems,* published in two volumes, does contain a number of
hymns on sanctification. For example, there are 20 hymns in the cycle
he heads "Waiting for Full Redemption":

> *What is the reason of my hope,*
> > *My hope to live and sin no more?*
> *After His likeness to wake up,*
> > *And God in spirit and truth adore,*
> *To serve Him as the hosts above*
> *In perfect peace, and perfect love?*[8]

His one and only hope lies in the sanctifying blood of Jesus and in
the will and written promise of the Lord:

> *Faith in the blood of Christ I have;*
> > *He freely loved and died for me:*
> *Sinners He came from sin to save,*
> > *From all, from all iniquity;*
> *Without the camp He deigned to die,*
> *Us by His blood to sanctify.*

> *His blood shall sanctify throughout*
> > *My spirit, soul, and body <u>here:</u>*
> *Because He died I cannot doubt,*
> > *Because He died I cannot fear;*
> *His blood shall make me pure within,*
> *His blood shall cleanse me from all sin.*

> *He wills that I should holy be,*
> > *He promises to make me clean,*
> *His oath confirms the sure decree;*
> > *The remnant and the root of sin*
> *The God of truth hath sworn to slay*
> *And take its being all away.*

Such thorough purifying of the being of the poet he sees, then, to be the purpose and intention of God in the atonement of Christ, as declared in Scripture.

> God hath ordain'd that I should see
>   In perfect holiness His face,
> Retrieve His image here, and be,
>   Forever sanctified by grace;
> His truth, and power, and mercy join,
> The will, and word, and oath Divine.
>
> Here then my foot of faith stands sure,
>   And earth, and hell in vain deny;
> I shall be pure as God is pure,
>   Holy as God is holy I,
> Perfect as God is perfect, rise,
> And take my mansion in the skies.[9]

Thus does Charles describe the ground of the hope of full sanctification in this life. But this series of hymns reflects that hope from various angles.

> My plague I know shall all be healed!
> A perfect soundness faith shall give,
>   A perfect holiness below;
> Jesu, I in Thy blood believe,
>   Thy blood shall wash me white as snow.
>
> But Thou canst perfect me in love,
> Canst perfect me in love today.
> I cannot plead for sin's remains,
> When Thou hast said, "Ye shall be clean."
>
> If Thou hast power and will to save,
>   Saved to the utmost I shall be,
> The fulness of the Godhead have;
>   For all the Godhead is in Thee.[10]

Among the 20 hymns in "Hymns for those that wait for full salvation," I find not one that does not seek, ask for, or describe entire sanctification in present instantaneous terms. Further, in the 16 headed "The Same. For any who think they have already attained," I find the same teaching, though salted with counsels of caution, it is true, and occasionally guarded by strong criticism of those who oppose it, but nevertheless strongly and persistently maintained all the way from

> We would not our own souls deceive
> Or fondly rest in grace begun . . .[11]

to

> Partake on earth the heavenly bliss,
> And pure and holy be,
> And perfect as the Father is,
> And one with God in Thee.[12]

In the joint publications of the brothers, as well as in publications approved by each, agreement on these lines is evident. There are no fewer than 56 stanzas of the hymns of Charles used by John in his *Plain Account of Christian Perfection* to support and to apply his meaning. These are from hymns published in the period 1739-59, but since John's final revision of the little classic was made in 1777, it seems clear that he continued to use and thus to approve his brother's hymns on the subject.[13]

As we noted earlier, however, in 1749 Charles published two volumes of poems without his brother's knowledge. Of these John wrote:

> As I did not see these before they were published, there were some things in them which I did not approve of. But I quite approved of the main of the hymns of this head; a few verses of which are subjoined.[14]

The "few" number 19 altogether! A second edition was published in 1752 with the approval of John.

Summing up John Wesley's use of his brother's hymns, Rattenbury wrote:

> So John Wesley took his brother's hymns, which expressed his own evangelical doctrine in vivid verse, as his declaration of what theology, speculative and practical, the Methodists believed. . . . Charles Wesley's evangelical hymns gave noble expression to the doctrines which were his goodly heritage as well as to those of the quickening experiences of the Methodist Revival.[15]

All of which is very true and very impressive. And yet! And yet!

To Charles Wesley, Christian perfection was so perfect as to be incapable of further perfecting. A perfection requiring perfecting made little appeal to him.

> Thy only love do I require,
> Nothing in earth beneath desire
>   Nothing in heaven above!
> Let earth and heaven and all things go,
> Give me Thy only love to know,
>   Give me Thy only love![16]

This soul craving, this obsession for more and more love for his Savior, grew stronger as Charles grew older, hence his "setting perfection too high" became increasingly prevalent in his hymns and in his preaching.

> Unless the stony Thou remove,
>   Unless Thou show me who Thou art,
> 'Tis quite impossible to love
>   The Lord my God with all my heart.

> Come, then, Jehovah crucified,
>   The God supreme in Christ revealed,
> And through Thy sacred blood applied,
>   My soul shall feel its pardon sealed.

> Restore me to my first estate,
>   Renew me, Saviour, from above;
> And sin I perfectly shall hate,
>   And Thee I perfectly shall love.[17]

Charles did succeed in distinguishing between purity on the one hand and ongoing growth to maturity of love on the other. To him, true holiness consisted, as with John, in perfection of love. His lofty ideal of perfect love, held so deeply and passionately, is after all realizable only when the soul awakes in His likeness. It is therefore quite consistent that not long before his death our poet should write:

> Me to that great salvation keep,
>   That when Thy nature I partake,
> I in Thy arms may fall asleep,
>   And in Thy glorious presence wake.[18]

The hunger for absolutely perfect love and total likeness to Christ, and for a heart and mind and habit like His—this was the ever-supreme desire and quest of his life.

When Charles confessed the great change of May 21, 1738, part of his confession was that he "rejoiced in hope of loving Christ." Thereafter he was one of those described by the prophet as "prisoners of hope." It was not a confining but a releasing hope. It was to Charles "a blessed hope of perfect love," a "glorious hope of perfect love." Only the ever-growing and deepening passion for Christ, and a holy love for all for whom his Jesus died, could and did keep him at the demanding work of the evangelist and pastor, and move his soul to torrents of holy praise and prayer. From that day in May 1738, when he "rejoiced in hope of loving Christ," through that day 11 years later when he prayed

O Love Divine, how sweet Thou art!
When shall I find my longing heart
  All taken up by Thee?
I thirst, and faint, and die to prove,
The greatness of redeeming love,
  The love of Christ to me. . . .
For love I sigh, for love I pine,
This only portion, Lord, be mine,
  Be mine this better part . . .

and on through his life as evangelist supreme, and then as pastor, Charles Wesley was controlled and driven by one great, supreme desire—more and yet more of love.

Enlarge, enflame, and fill my heart,
  With boundless charity divine;
So shall I all my strength exert,
  And love them with a love like Thine,
And lead them to Thy open side—
The sheep for whom their Shepherd died![19]

Is there any real difference between such a love and John's familiar definition of Christian perfection as "perfect love"? John asked his preachers, "What is Christian perfection?" He answered his own question with

The loving God with all our heart, mind, soul, and strength. This implies, that no wrong temper, none contrary to love, remains in the soul; and that all the thoughts, words and actions, are governed by pure love.[20]

Further, while this writer firmly believes that John Wesley did indeed give personal witness to the experience of entire sanctification, the matter as to whether or not he did so has been as seriously discussed as brother Charles's interpretation of it. The differences of opinion between the brothers is more emphatic toward their later years; but even then and right to the end of life, Charles continued to insist that to be perfect in love, the believer must be freed from all sin. To Charles, the whole purpose of God in the gospel of Christ is that the image of God be restored to believers and the whole life be filled and controlled by perfect love poured into our hearts by the Holy Ghost:

Perfect love which God supplies
Is perfect holiness.[21]

In 1762 Charles Wesley published those two volumes titled *Short Hymns on Select Passages of the Holy Scripture.* In his preface, he wrote:

Several of the hymns are intended to prove, and several to guard, the doctrine of Christian Perfection. I durst not publish the one without the other. In the latter sort I use some severity: not against particular persons, but against Enthusiasts and Antinomians, who, by not living up to their profession, give abundant occasion to them that seek it, and cause the truth to be evil spoken of.[22]

In his "Advertisement," Jackson noted this and commented:

On the subject of Christian Perfection, the Author intimates in the preface that he might have something unwelcome to say in the course of his work; and accordingly we find several passages in which the doctrine usually held by the Methodists appears to be contradicted, if not ridiculed. Perhaps if a formal and complete statement of his views had been asked for, or published, they would not have been found materially different from those of his brother; but as he dealt with the subject in fragments, and as the several texts then before him seemed to dictate, there is sometimes an apparent want of harmony between them. The time, too, was unfavorable to calmness, as the doctrine had been greatly discredited by the indiscretions of some professors, and the absolute fanaticism of others.

The different dispositions of the two brothers were remarkably exemplified in their mode of dealing with the subject in these circumstances. Charles was indignant at the folly and inconsistency which he witnessed, and lashed the delinquents without mercy. His brother John knew that some of the deluded ones were quite sincere. . . . His patience, condescension, gentleness, and forbearance are very conspicuous at this juncture, both in his dealings with his brother, and with those to whom his brother's caustic remarks were intended to apply, and show him to have been a most accomplished guide of souls, and a true follower of the Good Shepherd.[23]

> Must we not walk before we run,
>   And run before we fly,
> From strength to strength go humbly on,
>   And labour up the sky?

> The children walk in Christ, improve
>   To youths, and run their race,
> The fathers soar with perfect love,
>   And see Him face to face.[24]

13

Visible Words: Charles Wesley and the Sacraments

*I*N ENDEAVORING TO WRITE about the sacrament of the Lord's Supper, we are overwhelmed by the sense of unworthiness and awe. As Robert J. Paul wrote,

> No writer can plumb the depths or ascend the heights of the Sacrament that stands at the center of Christian worship. All our deepest insights and most enlightened perceptions are but flashes from the surface of its meaning. One is aware of so much more that should have been said.[1]

For the sacrament of the Lord's Supper is the word of the Cross made visible, and who can ever begin to comprehend, far less communicate, this "mystery of godliness" before which even angels and archangels, cherubim and seraphim can only bow in speechless wonder and awe? We can do no more, nor can we rely on anything less, than the manifest pardoning love of God, perhaps even in the words of Charles Wesley:

> *Father, hear the blood of Jesus*
> *Speaking in Thine ears above;*
> *From the wrath and curse release us,*
> *Manifest Thy pardoning love.*[2]

Before the wondrous Cross, all expressions of Christian thought are but opinions. The Calvinist Watts and the Arminian Charles Wesley express themselves in almost indivisible terms:

> *Love so amazing, so divine,*
> *Demands my soul, my life, my all.*

> *Amazing love! How can it be*
> *That Thou, my God, shouldst die for me?*[3]

Whereas the Calvinist Whitefield might choose to limit salvation to a fixed number of elect, and Charles and John Wesley see salvation as wide as mankind and as high as the heavens, they were each as passionate as the others in proclaiming the word of the Cross. And to all of them, the sacrament of Communion was the redeeming word of the Cross made visible.

> In this expressive bread I see
> The wheat by man cut down for me,
>   And beat, and bruised, and ground:
> The heavy plagues, and pains, and blows,
> Which Jesus suffered from His foes,
>   Are in this emblem found.
>
> The bread dried up and burnt with fire
> Presents the Father's vengeful ire,
>   Which my Redeemer bore:
> Into His bones the fire He sent
> Till all the flaming darts were spent
>   And Justice asked no more.
> He suffers to reverse our doom;
> And lo! my Lord is here become
>   The Bread of life to me.[4]

Hymns on the Lord's Supper

In the 18th century, attendance at the Lord's Supper had seriously declined within the Church of England, and it was the Methodists who revived the use of it. The Oxford Holy Club members communicated every Sunday and every holy day, closely observing every rule and rubric of the church. It was largely because of this that they received the nicknames they did. To incredulous observers, they were Methodists, of course, but also Sacramentarians. Although the former mode prevailed, the insight of the latter persisted. The views of the Wesleys altered little if at all throughout their lives. John's diaries and his sermons, especially that on "Constant Communion," are clear witness to that, and Charles's hymns and the use John made of them indicate the same belief and spirit in the younger brother.

John's Views on the Lord's Supper

Twelve years or more before his evangelical conversion, John had a conversation with his young friends at Stanton Harcourt rectory on the nature of the sacrament and on observing it. "Much harm," said he, "is done by exaggerating the venerableness of it. Proposing it as an object of fear rather than love deters multitudes from receiving it." The Wesleys possessed a godly, wholesome, and reverential awe for the sacrament of the Lord's Supper. On the outward voyage to Georgia, John read about 20 books aboard ship. Only one of these was not an ecclesiastical or liturgical volume. Included in the list were a number of strong books on the Communion service, its nature and practice, by five nonjurors and three Roman Catholics.

These works influenced Wesley's rejection of transubstantiation but strengthened his belief that the bread and wine are consecrated into the sacramental body of Christ by the effectual but secret operation of the Holy Spirit, and that by that same Holy Spirit believers are enabled to eat and to drink "discerning the Lord's body" (1 Cor. 11:29). The books he read show us where his sympathies lie. In later years he reprinted eight of them wholly or in part.

One action that John came to regret deeply and sorrowfully was that in Georgia he turned away from the Communion table his godly friend Bolzius, a German pastor, because he had been baptized by a minister who was not episcopally ordained.[5]

In 1732 John wrote his powerful sermon "On the Duty of Constant Communion," in which he shows that true believers will "commune" as often as they possibly can, neglecting neither preparation, opportunity, nor attendance at this means of grace. It is a duty and a privilege, not a routine or a chore. This sermon Wesley abbreviated and published toward the end of his life.

In that same year John received a letter from Susanna on the same subject. Susanna wrote:

> February 21, 1732.
>
> The young gentleman you mentioned seems to me to be in the right concerning the real presence of Christ in the sacraments. I own I never understood by the "real presence" more than what he has elegantly expressed that "the divine nature of Christ is then eminently present to impart by the operation of his Holy Spirit the benefits of his death to worthy receivers." And surely the divine presence of our Lord thus applying the virtue and merits of the great atonement to each true believer makes the consecrated bread more than a sign of Christ's body; since by his so doing, we receive not only the sign, but with it the thing signified, all the benefits of his incarnation and passion! But still, however this divine institution may seem to others, to me it is full of mystery. Who can account for the operation of God's Holy Spirit or define the manner of his working upon the spirit in man, either when he enlightens the understanding or excites and confirms the will and regulates and calms the passions without impairing man's liberty?[6]

In replying to Susanna's letter, John affirmed his substantial agreement with these views, all of which are rather strikingly characteristic of reformed Anglicanism. As Parris says of them,

> Wesley's doctrine of the Lord's Supper is thoroughly Anglican, and not "High" even as that position was represented by the hon. Jurors, with whom he had so much else in common . . . it is true . . . that Wesley in his open avowal of this position is closer to Reformed teaching, and at the opposite pole to the ultra-high position of his own, and particularly of later days, that might be inferred from his "ritualistic concerns."[7]

The Wesley brothers were powerfully influenced by their understanding and presentation of the Lord's Supper by the writings of a certain Dr. Daniel Brevint. This gentleman was a fellow of Jesus College, Oxford, pastor of a French Protestant congregation in Normandy, and later dean of Lincoln. During Brevint's residence in Paris, he was prevailed upon by the princesses of Turenne and Bauillon to write for them a devotional handbook to the Lord's Supper unencumbered by terminological subtleties. In response, he produced a work titled *The Christian Sacrament and Sacrifice.*

Brevint had earlier written a lengthy treatise explaining the intricate subject of the Roman mass for the enlightenment of "Reformed and Un-reformed Christians." The treatise on the Lord's Supper was published in Oxford in 1679, that on the Roman mass in the same city a little before then, in 1672.

Although the Wesley brothers were probably acquainted with the earlier work, it was the later one that held their attention as they studied and presented the subject of the Lord's Supper and the problems created for them first of all by the sacramental laxity of their contemporary Anglicanism, and then by the resistance of the Anglican clergy to administering the sacrament to the multitudes of common people converted in the Revival.

Charles Adds to "Hymns on the Lord's Supper"

By far the most interesting and influential publication of the brothers with relation to the Lord's Supper is that of 166 *Hymns on the Lord's Supper.*[8] This was published in 1745 in the name of both "John and Charles Wesley: Presbyters of the Church of England." The publication became quite popular and went into 11 editions during the next 80 years. John extracted the gist of Brevint's material and used it as a preface to this hymnbook. Brevint's outline of contents carries eight sections, but the hymnbook omits the first of these, although John includes it in his summary. Hence, excluding the first item, Charles Wesley's outline is substantially that of Brevint and provides the framework around which the hymns are built.

I make a simple selection to demonstrate the points, and with abbreviation.

I. The Nature of the Sacrament as *a Memorial of the Sufferings and Death of Christ*

> *Receive us then, Thou pardoning God;*
> *Partakers of His flesh and blood*
> *   Grant that we now may be;*
> *The Spirit's attesting seal impart,*
> *And speak to every sinner's heart:*
> *   The Saviour died for Thee.*[9]

II. As *a Sign and a Means of Grace*

> *Author of our salvation, Thee*
> *   With lowly thankful hearts we praise,*
> *Author of this great mystery,*
> *   Figure and means of saving grace.*
>
> *We see the blood that seals our peace,*
> *   Thy pardoning mercy we receive:*
> *The bread doth visibly express*
> *   The strength through which our spirits live.*[10]

III. As *a Sign and a Pledge of Heaven*

> *Come let us join with one accord*
> *Who shared the supper of the Lord,*
> *   Our Lord and Master's praise to sing;*
> *Nourish'd on earth with living bread,*
> *We now are at His table fed,*
> *   But wait to see our heavenly King;*
>
> *To see the great Invisible*
> *Without a sacramental veil,*
> *   With all His robes of glory on,*
> *In rapturous joy and love and praise*
> *Him to behold with open face,*
> *   High on His everlasting throne!*[11]

IV. As it implies *a Sacrifice*

> *Father, behold Thy dying Son!*
> *Even now He lays our ransom down,*
> *   Even now declares our sins forgiven;*
> *His flesh is rent, the living way*
> *Is open'd to eternal day,*
> *   And lo, through Him we pass to heaven!*[12]

V. Concerning *the Sacrifice of Our Persons*

> *God of all-redeeming grace,*
> *   By Thy pardoning love compell'd;*
> *Up to Thee our souls we raise,*
> *   Up to Thee our bodies yield.*

> Just it is, and good, and right
>   That we should be wholly Thine,
> In Thy only will delight
>   In Thy blessed service join.[13]

VI. *After the Sacrament*

> How happy are Thy servants, Lord,
>   Who thus remember Thee!
> What tongue can tell our sweet accord,
>   Our perfect harmony?
>
> Shout all our Elder Brethren,
>   While we record the story
> Of Him that came
> And suffer'd shame
>   To carry us to glory! . . .
>
> Himself, and all His fulness,
>   Who gives to the believer;
> And by this Bread
> Whoe'er are fed
>   Shall live with God forever.[14]

But the mystery and the marvel of the whole splendid truth remains over the soul of the man with the dancing heart. This is focused in hymn no. 57:

> Who shall say how bread and wine
> God into man conveys!
> How the bread His flesh imparts,
>   How the wine transmits His blood,
> Fills His faithful people's hearts
> With all the life of God![15]

Or, less mystically perhaps, in hymn no. 92:

> It doth not appear,
> His manner of working; but Jesus is here![16]

The hymns are pervaded with the sense and experience of the spiritual presence of the Lord in the Sacrament, precisely because it is a specially appointed means of grace. Charles Wesley's religious experience was much too full and developed for such an error to be made. For example,

> Fasting He doth, and hearing bless,
>   And prayer can much prevail,
> Good vessels all to draw the grace
>   Out of salvation's well.

> *But none, like this mysterious rite*
> *Which dying mercy gave,*
> *Can draw forth all His promised might*
> *And all His will to save.*[17]

It seems little wonder, therefore, that the brothers Wesley encouraged frequent Communion so strongly. And yet they steered well clear of all suggestions of transubstantiation or taints of the Roman mass. As John put it, "We freely own that Christ is to be adored in the Lord's Supper; but that the elements are to be adored we deny."[18]

John's free rendering of Brevint's words seem fitting to round off this line of thought:

> I dare appear before the Lord, with all my sins and my sorrows. It is just also that I should appear with these few blessings. Having received them of Thy hand, now do I offer them to Thee again. Forgive, I beseech Thee, my sins, deliver me from my sorrows, and accept of this my sacrifice; or rather look, in my behalf, on that only true Sacrifice, the sacrifice of Thy well-beloved Son, proceeding from Thee, to die for me. O let Him come unto me now, as the only-begotten of the Father, full of grace and truth.[19]

Finally, in these beautiful hymns Charles Wesley helps us to realize the oneness of God's people in heaven and on earth. The communion of saints is a shining, bright reality:

> *Angels in fix'd amazement*
> *Around our altars hover,*
> *With eager gaze*
> *Adore the grace*
> *Of our Eternal Lover.*[20]

And again:

> *One with the living Bread Divine*
> *Which now by faith we eat,*
> *Our hearts, and minds, and spirits join,*
> *And all in Jesus meet.*
>
> *So dear the tie where souls agree*
> *In Jesu's dying love:*
> *Then only can it closer be,*
> *When all are join'd above.*[21]
>
> *Part of His host has cross'd the flood,*
> *And part is crossing now!*[22]

One host!

Keeping the Feast

Because to the Wesleys the sacrament of the Lord's Supper was "the grand channel whereby the grace of His Spirit was conveyed to the souls of all the children of God," they were most empathic and insistent on the observance of it, even to the extent of withholding the society ticket of a willful absentee. Affirmatively, instructions were:

> Lose no opportunity of receiving the sacrament. All who have neglected this have suffered loss; most of them are as dead as stones: therefore be you constant herein, not only for example, but for the sake of your own souls.[23]

Themselves assiduous in their celebration, the brothers consistently and constantly urged like behavior and spirit upon the Methodists. They were to attend the parish church and to partake of the Lord's Supper even if or when the local minister was hostile. Thus, in the wake of the mighty converting sweep of the Holy Spirit all over the country, local ministers found themselves confronted with almost unbelievable crowds of communicants. This was often a great embarrassment to the ministers, many of whom not only were simply unsympathetic to the converts but were themselves unconverted men performing as a rite and ritual what was to the Methodists a living channel of divine grace.

Eventually John Wesley had to alter his stance. His people and preachers had minds of their own, although they were usually willing to accept John's directives and obey them. John presently conceded the possibility of the Methodists not being edified by attendance at Communion in the parish church, especially

1. When the minister is a notoriously wicked man

2. When he preaches Arian or other equally pernicious doctrine

3. When there are not churches in the town sufficient to contain the people

4. When there is no church at all within two or three miles[24]

Hence John Wesley opened the exit door from the Church of England, even if for the time being the opening was but a crack. The concession also laid the first paving stone toward Methodist ordination. To quote Parris,

> It was, in fact, because the Methodist people were deprived of the Sacraments, in America, in Scotland, and finally in parts of England, that Wesley was moved to ordain men to perform these functions.[25]

With regard to Charles, on no account whatsoever, and not for any reason, would he accept any measure that in his opinion could lead to separation from the Church of England. He was a thoroughly convinced and committed Anglican and intended to remain so. Further, he was equally determined that the Methodists, too, would continue within that communion. Therefore, while Charles was equally as strong as John on the observance of Communion, he opposed even the slightest move toward celebration and ordination that might even hint at separation. He fought separatist tendencies with might and main. He walked out of the Annual Conference of 1755 angrily, declaring that if the societies separated from the Church of England, they would separate from him! Nevertheless, although Charles would not and did not adopt John's stance toward the Church of England, and although the Methodists necessarily followed John's policy leading to separation, we may adjudge that Charles's opinion and stance was a providential restraint on John at a time when hurried and irregular action would or could have had serious consequences. As Edwards observes,

> His brother's restraining hand was providential. It delayed the separation long enough for Methodism to become a Church and not a sect, and it enabled Methodists in the next century to value their close links with the Church of England and the inheritance which had come through that association.[26]

So, although Charles opposed anything that would weaken the ties of the Methodists with the Anglicans, he did exert an influence from Bristol and from London, as well as in Conference, that surely shows him undeserving of Harrison's vindictive assertion:

> John's main aim was to find the will of God and do it, and his spirit was sensitive to new impressions. He was growing to the end. Charles became fossilized after he ceased to travel.[27]

Conclusion from Harrison's line of reasoning: "Charles was out of the will of God as a pastor and insensitive to new impressions"—not a good conclusion even for a worshiper of John Wesley.

Baptism

John

On the matter of baptism, it is much more difficult to understand John than Charles. It is natural to suppose that, as priests of the Church of England, they would be equally committed to the beliefs and practices of that communion. And in many ways they are, but not all; and some points are expressed rather differently. At one time John appears to teach baptismal regeneration; at another point this seems obscure. And then again we become convinced that he does not believe any such thing:

This greatest confusion, as his interpreters see it, is caused by Wesley himself in certain statements concerning the inter-relationships of Baptism and the New Birth, or, as some see it, the lack of such relationship. The judgments of Wesley scholars differ, from concluding that Wesley rejects baptismal regeneration, to claiming that his judgments are confused and even contradictory to holding that he never repudiated baptismal regeneration at all.[28]

The conclusion at which we arrive so far as John is concerned will be strongly swayed by our understanding of his distinction between infant and adult baptism. He seems to teach two forms of regeneration, one referring to infants for whom baptism signifies that in innocence they belong to the family of God, and another referring to adults who, having reached accountability, must repent and believe the gospel (which babies cannot do) in order to be born again "as little children." Hence Christian education of little children is very important in Wesley's understanding of infant baptism:

> Scripture, reason, and experience jointly testify that, inasmuch as the corruption of nature is earlier than our instructions can be, we should take all pains and care to counteract this corruption as early as possible. The bias of nature is set the wrong way: Education is designed to set it right. This, by the grace of God, is to turn the bias from self-will, pride, anger, revenge, and the love of the world, to resignation, lowliness, meekness, and the love of God.[29]

To Wesley infant baptism indicated not the cure for original sin but the cleansing away of the guilt of original sin; thereafter the person becomes accountable and must bear his own accrued guilt. In the personal case of John Wesley, he felt that he had not sinned away the benefit of infant baptism until he was about 10 years of age.

Yet John seems clear and firm that there is no such thing as baptismal regeneration for adults, however close the relationship may be between baptism and regeneration. In a reply to Vicar Potter, John wrote:

> Of the new birth you say, "The terms of being regenerated, of being born again, of being born of God, are often used to express the works of gospel righteousness." I cannot allow this. I know not that they are ever so used in Scripture to express any outward work at all. They always express an inward work of the Spirit, whereof baptism is the outward sign . . .
>
> You proceed: "Our holy Church doth teach us that . . . by the laver of regeneration in baptism we are received into the number of the children of God . . . This is the first part of the new birth." What is the first part of the new birth? Baptism? It is the outward sign of that inward and spiritual grace; but no part of it at all. It is impossi-

ble it should be. The outward sign is no more a part of the inward grace than the body is part of the soul.[30]

On this point John is even more direct and forthright in his sermon "The New Birth."[31] It is, moreover, rather strange that when making general reference to baptism, he could say that "the merits of Christ's life and death, are applied to us in baptism . . . the ordinary instrument of our justification,"[32] and yet in such an important doctrinal document as his sermon "The Scripture Way of Salvation," not even mention baptism!

Charles

Although Charles Wesley's conclusions about adult baptism were fairly similar to John's, he saw in this sacrament more of assurance of pardon and regeneration, and he captured more of the joy of it than we discover in the prosaic and analytic work of John. It is true that Charles's hymns on infant baptism show that sacrament to be occasion for praise and gladness; nevertheless his hymns for adult baptism are fuller and richer than could possibly be the case for infant baptism. There is a liberty and a joyous spirit, a sense of expectancy and promise of grace that thrills the soul. There is an absence of mere formality and the presence of a sense of release from sin and acceptance with God. There is in these hymns rapture and rhapsody.

Not only in his hymns do we feel the pulsating gladness, but also his *Journal* and his letters likewise affect us. To Bishop Butler of Bristol, Charles wrote in 1739, naming seven persons:

> My Lord,
>
> Several persons, both Quakers and Baptists, have applied to me for baptism . . . It has pleased God to make me instrumental in their conviction . . . they desire to be received into the Church by my ministry. They choose likewise to be baptized by immersion; and have engaged me to give your Lordship notice, as the Church requires.[33]

From his *Journal* on May 21, 1740, the second anniversary of his own conversion:

> I carried Bridget Armstead to Bloomsbury Church, where the Minister baptized her. She had been bred a Quaker. I was one of the witnesses. We were all in great heaviness before; but perceived that Christ was with us always in his ordinances. The Spirit infallibly bears witness on this occasion. Our youngest sister assuredly knows that she is born of water and of the Spirit.[34]

Many sections of Charles Wesley's *Journal* are replete with gratitude for the blessing of the Lord both at His table and at the baptismal service, e.g.:

> May 11th. He showered down blessings upon us at His table
> ... Sun. May 25th. Our Lord was made known to us, as he always
> is, in the breaking of bread. Let the Quaker and orthodox *dispute*
> about the ordinance: our Saviour satisfies us in a shorter way.[35]

And a few days later, on June 3, he writes:

> My morning's congregation drank in every word. I spake with
> the Society severally. When I saw them last there was scarce a justi-
> fied person among them: now fourscore testify their having experi-
> enced the pardoning love of God.
>
> I baptized an Anabaptist; and all her fears and troubles fled
> away in a moment.[36]

Neither Charles's letters nor his *Journal* are ever dull, but they are
especially thrilling when he recounts experiences of the sacraments.
Quakers, Baptists, and Anabaptists galore are baptized or received into the Communion.

"Good old M. Pearce" is baptized by immersion at four o'clock in
the morning of July 18, 1748! "Our hearts were all melting wax" at the
Kingswood sacrament. "Sisters Roberston and Nutler" just "would
not lose the sacrament," though "sorely bruised by an overturn into a
pit." One entry brackets together baptism, Lord's Supper, and love
feast!

> Sun. July 31st [1748]. I baptized a woman in Kingswood, and
> trembled at the descent of the Holy Ghost. All present were more or
> less sensible of it, especially the person baptized. We joined in the
> Lord's Supper, and had his never-failing presence. So again at our
> first lovefeast in the new room. For two hours we were sensible of
> Christ in the midst.[37]
>
> Whitsunday, May 14th [1749]. Our brother Thompson partook
> with us, and declared "he was in heaven!"[38]
>
> May 16th. A woman, in baptism, received both the outward
> visible sign, and the inward spiritual grace.[39]
>
> May 13th [1750]. I baptized Hannah, M. Gibs's maid; and the
> whole congregation with her were conscious of the descent of the
> Spirit, who bears witness with the water.[40]
>
> July 9th. I administered the sacrament to a dying believer, late-
> ly called; but now made equal to them that have borne the heat and
> burden of the day.[41]

Multiple instances could be presented. One final example:

> Sun. June 2 [1751]. I baptized Sarah and Eliz., Quaker and a
> Baptist, before a full congregation. All were moved by the descent
> of that Spirit: many wept, and trembled, and rejoiced. The persons
> baptized, most of all.[42]

"The descent of the Spirit," "Christ in the midst," "the Spirit infallibly bears witness on this occasion"—these oft-repeated phrases and many similar ones make it readily apparent that Charles Wesley's central emphasis in adult baptism was assurance, assurance of pardon and of the reception of the Holy Spirit.

In the hymns this accent is much more prominent. Charles's hymns on the Spirit linked with his hymns on baptism are like trumpet notes of Christian assurance.

Hymns on Infant Baptism

Jesus, in earth and heaven the same,
Accept a parent's vow.
To Thee, baptized into Thy name,
I bring my children now;
Thy love permits, invites, commands,
My offspring to be blessed;
Lay on them, Lord, Thy gracious hands,
And hide them in Thy breast.

To each the hallowing Spirit give
Even from their infancy;
And pure into Thy Church receive,
Whom I devote to Thee;
Committed to Thy faithful care,
Protected by Thy blood,
Preserve by Thine unceasing prayer,
And bring them all to God.[43]

These verses are extracted from Charles Wesley's *Hymns on the Four Gospels and Acts of the Apostles,* dated 1762. They constitute his poetical commentary on Matt. 19:13-15, ever a fitting and popular scripture for use at the baptism of a child. The verses are a beautiful expression of parental desire and prayer on such occasions.

Another such prayer appears as Wesley's commentary on Gen. 48:16 and closely applies the concept of that scripture thus:

The great redeeming Angel, Thee,
O Jesus, I confess;
Who hast through life delivered me,
Thou wilt my offspring bless;
Thou that hast borne my sins away,
My children's sins remove,
And bring them through the evil day,
To sing Thy praise above.

My name be on the children? No!
But mark them, Lord, with Thine,
Let all the heavenly offspring know
By characters divine;
Partakers of Thy nature make,
Partakers of Thy Son,
And then the heirs of glory take,
To Thine eternal throne.[44]

Of those hymns that bear most directly on the very occasion of infant baptism, one from the 1780 collection is more explicit:

Lord of all, with pure intent,
From their tenderest infancy,
In Thy temple we present
Whom we first received from Thee:
Through Thy well-beloved Son,
Ours acknowledged for Thine arm.

Sealed with the baptismal seal,
Purchas'd by the atoning blood,
Jesus in our children dwell,
Make their heart the house of God.
Fill Thy consecrated shrine,
Father, Son, and Spirit divine.[45]

It does seem that Charles's accents fall more heavily than John's on assurance of pardon accompanying adult baptism, and on recognition of belonging to the family of God in infant baptism. Charles is also firmer in his recognition of "a grace infused" in infant baptism, at which John has but ambiguously hinted. Charles would say that the Lord Jesus in His death took the place of all mankind; further, that in His life He identified himself with humanity at every stage, and that in this representative Christ infants are included; and in the death of the representative Christ, infants and their inherited sinfulness are included. And when we remember that the faith by which adults receive the righteousness of Christ is the gracious, unearned, unattainable free gift and work of the Holy Spirit, we can scarcely claim that the same Holy Spirit cannot thus operate in infants.

Hymns on Adult Baptisms

There is no shortage of hymns in the area of adult baptism. As we have seen, Charles's *Journal* indicates repeatedly that he regarded baptism as extremely important for all adult believers. It can be safely asserted that, like their evangelical mentors, the converts of the Wesleys had indeed "sinned away" the "virtues of infant baptism." Some of these probably lacked enlightenment as to the significance of earlier baptism, and in the flush of conversion faith felt the need and challenge of some kind of dramatic act of rebaptism. As is possible with every practice in the church, infant baptism can be poorly administered and no "follow-up" education given, with the result that rebaptism may often be sought.

However, in view of the fact that the Wesleys held so stubbornly to the idea that "baptism by other than Episcopal Administrators was no baptism at all," it is no great surprise that in the early years of the Revival the Wesleys would continue to baptize any Dissenter who pressed for it. We really do not know when they left off this practice, if indeed they did, but their reluctance to pull away from the Church of England meant increasing unwillingness to rebaptize. On the other hand, as that relationship weakened and the association became less close, Dissenters desiring Episcopal baptism would not turn for it to the Wesleys.

When the Revival ministry was powerfully under way, the Wesleys felt little hesitancy about baptizing their own converts, and even prior instruction was minimal. Their approach appears to have been Peter's: "Can any man forbid water, that these should not be baptized, which have received the Holy Ghost as well as we?" (Acts 10:47). That Charles should compose so many hymns for baptism, and so many others suitable for such use, suggests the great need of them. Some of these hymns appear in his poetic commentary on select portions of Scripture. One or two were written specifically for the baptismal service, and others are readily adaptable.

> Bid me step into the pool,
>   By repentance I obey:
> But my filthiness of soul
>   Cannot thus be purged away:
> Tears may wash my actual sin;
>   Guilt requires a stronger flood,
> Purge and make my spirit clean
>   In the fountain of Thy blood.[46]

In answer to Naaman's question, "Are not Abana and Pharpar . . . better . . . ?" (2 Kings 5:12), Charles wrote:

> No! for the Lord is not in them,
> But Jordan's consecrated stream:
> And by the means Himself ordains,
> We all may wash away our stains.
> A leprous world may be restored
>   By virtue of the gospel-word,
> Our spirit, soul, and flesh renew'd
>   In the pure river of His blood . . .
>
> Wash in the Fountain and be clean,
>   Repent and be forgiven,
> Believe and be redeem'd from sin,
>   Love and be rapt in heaven![47]

The thought of washing, cleansing, sprinkling, pouring obsesses Charles Wesley to an extent that the terminology of baptism more often than not raises in him thoughts of Calvary and atonement than of water baptism:

> Wash me, and make me thus Thine own.
>   Wash me, and mine Thou art:
> Wash me, but not my feet alone,
>   My hands, my head, my heart![48]

And sometimes it is Pentecost that is raised in his mind, but again it will be baptismal language:

> What avails the outward sign
>   Without the inward grace?
> Lord, I want Thy Spirit Divine,
>   The spark of love to raise.
> Strait'd through intense desire
>   To feel the pure baptismal flame,
> Let the Holy Spirit inspire,
>   And plunge me in Thy name.[49]

Thus does Charles Wesley's "interest in the Saviour's blood" reveal itself in very many areas and in many ways.

Of course, many hymns written when the poet had no direct approach to baptism in mind were nevertheless adaptable and used in that relation, e.g.:

> Soldiers of Christ, arise!
> And put your armour on![50]

14

Celebrating the Christian Festivals

Introduction: "In the beginning—God!"

The man with the dancing heart succeeded in making doctrine sing and dance—at least most of the time. There are other times when his poems become quite pedestrian and monotonous. Probably this is to be expected when the poetic output is so great. The most recent estimate puts Charles Wesley's production at 9,000 over a lifetime of 81 years!

When writing about the Trinity, he rises to respectable heights and sinks to monotonous levels too. Rattenbury wrote

his successes were not numerous, though one or two are good singing hymns, especially one which is not in the Trinitarian books, but in the Redemption hymns of 1747.[1]

That is the hymn beginning with

> Father, in whom we live,
> In whom we are and move,

and concluding with

> When heaven and earth are fled
> Before thy glorious face,
> Sing all the saints thy love hath made
> Thine everlasting praise![2]

Perhaps Charles was aware of his comparative failure to adequately hymn the Trinity, but he did not fail to try. He wrote three sets of hymns on the Trinity, plus a great many not included in these collections, but it would seem that his reverential awe suppressed his usual buoyancy. Our intention, however, is not to test Charles's Trinitarian orthodoxy but to catch his spirit and to join him in devoted praise.

The arid deism, Arianism, unitarianism, and Socinianism prevalent in 18th-century England were all damnable heresies to Charles Wesley. All were attacks on the evangelical Trinitarianism he held so devotedly. Therefore, some of his hymns in this area seem more dogmatic than adoring, more pugilistic than pious. In his day there was a strong drift in the direction of unitarianism, and some leading Anglican and Presbyterian divines were caught in the current; so Charles Wesley's presentation of orthodox Trinitarian doctrine was strong and positive but sometimes lacking in lilt. William Cannon wrote

> the Wesleyan Revival arose, therefore, as a positive affirmation of Scriptural Christianity in the face of the rationalistic and deistic philosophy which characterized the intellectual temper of the 18th century.[3]

The Wesleys were concerned about this militantly antievangelical philosophy, but they paid no great heed to it and went forward declaring and singing the positive message of the Bible.

Speaking of John Wesley, Cannon wrote that

> the religious skepticism engendered by deism seems to have passed him by; and even the rational appeals of Socinianism and English Arianism, which at one time had threatened his mother, never seems to have erected any barrier for her son. The forces which produced John Wesley's theology are not, therefore, to be found in the intellectual subtleties of various and conflicting modes of philosophical thought. Rather, they are to be found in the moral and spiritual endeavors of his life, in his earnest attempt to be something and to do something in and for the kingdom of God.[4]

John himself inadvertently summed up the great chasm of thought lying between him and the theorists:

> I described (in very plain terms) the real difference between what is generally called Christianity, and the true old Christianity, which under the new name of Methodism is now also everywhere spoken against.[5]

Thus John was ever ready with his apologia when it seemed called for, but chiefly he went right on preaching the word of the gospel, content to rest in the shining truth he once heard expressed by the Lutheran minister, Mr. Miller, known also to Charles. John wrote:

> From him I learned that the earnest religion that I found in so many parts of Germany is but of late date, having taken its rise from one man, August Hermann Franke! So can God, if it pleaseth Him, enable one man to revive His work throughout a whole nation.[6]

Therefore went the Wesley brothers forward; not flinching from the challenge of the sophists, not overloading the vehicle of experience, but always shaping their doctrine of God and their message of grace out of the truth of God and His grace revealed in the Bible, and neither discovered nor discoverable by men lacking the antenna of the Holy Spirit.

Hymns on the Trinity

What Charles had done with Brevint on the Eucharist he did also with William Jones of Nayland on the Trinity. He took the scriptures around which Jones had erected an impressive theology of the Trinity, and turning Jones's prose to poetry, and baptizing Jones's thought into experience, he wrote his remarkable *Hymns on the Trinity*.

The editor of the *Poetical Works* summarized Charles's method as follows:

> The poet has followed Mr. Jones's arrangement, and made a hymn or hymns on each text or set of texts adduced by him. In some respects he has excelled his original. He repeatedly asserts the doctrine of our Lord's Divine Sonship, by his omission of which Mr. Jones has much impaired his claim to be considered as teaching the *catholic doctrine* of the Trinity. And he has never lost sight of the experimental and practical bearings of that doctrine. Mr. Jones has an excellent paragraph at the conclusion of his argument, warning his readers that a sound belief without a holy life will not profit them. But our poet, true to the mission of Methodism, makes experience the connecting link between knowledge and practice, and devotes an entire section of his work to "Hymns and Prayers to the Trinity," in which the doctrine is presented in most intimate connection with his own spiritual interests, and those of his readers.[7]

Although Charles eulogizes God for His works and deeds in nature, he does not do so here. He makes no effort to present the so-called proofs of the existence of God, which are in any case unsatisfactory at their best, and plunges directly into the divinity of Christ. In his opening poem he had a rather gentle but unmistakable tilt at those so-called Christians who denied that divinity:

> *Rock of offence at first He was:*
> *And Christians stumbling at the cross*
> *Deny whom <u>Jews</u> denied:*
> *They will not know that Christ is He,*
> *Or the supreme Jehovah see*
> *In Jesus crucified.*[8]

But straightway Charles begins to identify Jesus as God and to exult in the fact. Zeroing in on two cardinal scriptures—Isa. 43:11: "I, even I, am the Lord; and BESIDE ME there is no SAVIOUR"; and 2 Pet. 3:18: "OUR LORD AND SAVIOUR JESUS CHRIST"—he wrote,

> *In Jesus's name Jehovah is found,*
> *The throne of the Lamb We worship around,*
> *Supreme adoration We pay the Most High,*
> *Who brought us salvation Himself from the sky.*[9]

Linking another pair of Scripture texts—Luke 1:76 and Matt. 11:10—he sang,

> *The prophet of the Lord most high*
> *Was sent before His face,*
> *With tidings of Jehovah nigh,*
> *And to prepare His ways:*
> *And every messenger of His*
> *Rejoices to proclaim,*
> *Jesus the great Jehovah is!*
> *Bow all to Jesus' name!*[10]

But Charles nevertheless desires us to make proper distinction between the First and the Second Members of the blessed Trinity. Citing Matt. 11:10 and Mal. 3:1, he wrote,

> *A PERSONAL distinction see*
> *Betwixt the Father and the Son!*
> *Yet is the Filial Deity*
> *With the Paternal Godhead one:*
> *A different person we confess,*
> *Jesus, whom all His saints admire,*
> *Whom all His host celestial praise,*
> *One and the same with God the Sire.*
>
> *Jehovah who in Jesus dwells*
> *His whole Divinity imparts,*
> *To souls prepared His Son reveals,*
> *And sends His Spirit into our hearts.*[11]

Further, Charles sees the unity of the Jehovah of the Old Testament with the Jesus of the New Testament in some scriptures that we might bypass in reading. Linking Ps. 78:56 with 1 Cor. 10:9, he wrote:

> Who tempted Christ, the faithless race
>   Tempted, and anger'd the Most High:
> And still we in the wilderness
>   His Spirit grieve, His wrath defy,
> Jehovah's Fellow who disown,
> And would the Filial God dethrone.
> But give us through Thy Spirit's power,
>   Jesus, a right to call Thee Lord,
> Thee, the One sovereign God, to' adore,
>   Thy Father's uncreated Word,
> The Second person of the three
> Who was from all eternity.[12]

Charles does a magnificent job when he takes up Paul's exultant expression of hope in Titus 2:13. The result is a singable poem on the Trinity:

> We wait for the returning
>   Of our great God and Saviour,
> Our dying God
> Who by His blood
>   Procured His Father's favour:
> Jesus, the true Jehovah,
>   The Man to sinners given,
> Triumphant here
> Shall soon appear,
>   And take us up to heaven.
>
> The God from everlasting,
>   Almighty to deliver,
> Around His throne
> Our songs shall own
>   The God that reigns forever.[13]

As a final example of Charles Wesley's treatment of the Christ who is God and of God who is Jesus, consider his presentation of a familiar Pauline verse, 2 Cor. 5:19:

> God was in Christ, the' eternal Sire
>   Reveal'd in His eternal Son,
> Jehovah did on earth expire,
>   For every soul of man to' atone:
> The one almighty God supreme,
>   Jehovah lavish of His blood
> Pour'd out the' inestimable stream,
>   And reconciled the world to God.

> *Thy Godhead whole was in Thy Son,*
>   *When Jesus pray'd, and gasp'd, and died:*
> *The precious ransom was laid down;*
>   *'Tis finish'd; I am justified!*
> *The Spirit of faith applies the word,*
>   *And cries Thy new-born child to Thee,*
> *Hail, holy, holy, holy Lord,*
>   *One glorious God in persons three.*[14]

And what more fitting conclusion to this so brief selection than a poem in which Charles indicates that in all this he is not unmindful of the dangers that lurk in false doctrine. He takes seriously Paul's warning in Col. 2:8-9:

> *TRUE, absolute Divinity,*
> *Jesus, we dare ascribe to Thee,*
> *Which vain philosophy denies,*
> *And baffles us with glozing lies,*
> *Thy glorious Deity blasphemes*
> *With <u>Arian</u> or <u>Socinian</u> dreams,*
> *To cast the weak believers down,*
> *And rob the children of their crown.*

> *But grounded on Thy written word,*
> *We worship our almighty Lord:*
> *In Thee, whom Thy own Spirit reveals,*
> *The fulness of the Godhead dwells:*
> *Thy person really Divine,*
> *Thy body is Jehovah's shrine,*
> *The whole substantial Deity*
> *Resides eternally in Thee.*[15]

In *Hymns on the Trinity*, there are 56 given presenting the divinity of Christ. These are not the total of Charles Wesley's hymns on this theme, for there are hundreds if not thousands of almost incidental references in many other hymns. The complete and total divinity of Jesus Christ is the polestar in Charles Wesley's theological firmament, and all other aspects of Christian truth revolve around this center of attraction.

> *Veiled in flesh the Godhead see;*
> *Hail the incarnate Deity!*[16]

Hymns Celebrating the Incarnation

I suppose it is possible for us to celebrate the great festivals of our Christian faith without the help of Charles Wesley, but it is not possible to celebrate Charles without noting his hymns for these great Christian festivals. It would seem strange were we to celebrate Christmas without singing "Hark! the herald angels sing," or Lent without "Arise, my soul, arise. Shake off thy guilty fears," and "And can it be that I should gain / An interest in the Saviour's blood?" And could we pass through Easter without singing "Christ, the Lord, is risen to-day," or Pentecost minus "Love divine, all loves excelling"?

It is close to incredible that all of these favorites, and many more, are from the hand of the man with the dancing heart. He leads us in song as we progress through the Christian year, and it becomes even more thrilling as we sing with him.

We now come directly to the pamphlet titled *Hymns for the Nativity of Our Lord*. By near unanimous opinion, this pamphlet is among Wesley's best. Whereas in the Trinitarian pamphlet he accentuates in such a manner as to leave no doubt about his faith in the divinity of the Lord Jesus Christ, in this pamphlet the accentuation expresses his belief in the real and true humanity of the Lord Jesus Christ. Published in 1745 as the second of three pamphlets, it was one of his series for the great Christian festivals, and it breathes the pure spirit of worship and adoration. Nevertheless it does not contain Wesley's most famous and popular Christmas song, "Hark! the Herald Angels Sing." That had been written six years earlier, in 1739, and has a history all its own.

Briefly put, Whitefield included that song in his Tabernacle hymns, but he changed, and we think improved upon, at least the first verse, by altering what was even then "old English" to make the hymn more comprehensible to his congregation. Charles Wesley had written

> *Hark! how all the welkin rings:*
> *Glory to the King of kings . . . ,*[17]

a couplet that Whitefield changed to

> *Hark! the herald-angels sing*
> *"Glory to the new-born King,"*[18]

and thus it has remained, although questions about the hymn were still being raised as late as 1850, a century after it was written.

The works in *Hymns for the Nativity of Our Lord* are sprinkled with vivid, arresting, and provocative phrases as well as soul-lifting and exhilarating thought. The spirit is that of adoration and wonder.

HYMN I.

Ye simple men of heart sincere,
   Shepherds who watch your flocks by night,
Start not to see an angel near,
   Nor tremble at this glorious light.

An herald from the heavenly King,
   I come your every fear to chase:
Good tidings of great joy I bring,
   Great joy to all the fallen race!

To you is born on this glad day
   A Saviour, by our host adored;
Our God in Bethlehem survey,
   Make haste to worship Christ the Lord.

By this the Saviour of mankind,
   The' incarnate God, shall be display'd,
The Babe ye wrapp'd in swathes shall find
   And humbly in a manger laid.[19]

HYMN IV.

Glory be to God on high,
   And peace on earth descend;
God comes down: He bows the sky,
   And shows Himself our Friend!
God th' invisible appears,
   God, the blest, the great I AM,
Sojourns in this vale of tears,
   And Jesus is His name.

Stand amazed, ye heavens, at this!
   See the Lord of earth and skies!
Humbled to the dust He is,
   And in a manger lies!

Knees and hearts to Him we bow,
   Of our flesh, and of our bone,
Jesus is our brother now,
   And God is all our own![20]

HYMN V.

Let earth and heaven combine,
Angels and men agree,
To praise in songs Divine
Th'incarnate Deity,
Our God contracted to a span,
Incomprehensibly made man.

See in that Infant's face
The depths of Deity,
And labour while ye gaze
To sound the mystery;
In vain; ye angels, gaze no more,
But fall, and silently adore.

He deigns in flesh to appear,
Widest extremes to join,
To bring our vileness near,
And make us all Divine;
And we the life of God shall know,
For God is manifest below.

Made perfect first in love,
And sanctified by grace,
We shall from earth remove,
And see His glorious face;
His love shall then be fully show'd,
And man shall all be lost in God.[21]

HYMN VIII.

Away with our fears!
The Godhead appears
In Christ reconciled,
The Father of Mercies in Jesus the Child.

He comes from above,
In manifest love,
The Desire of our eyes,
The meek Lamb of God in a manger He lies.

Then let us believe,
And gladly receive
The tidings they bring,
Who publish to sinners their Saviour and King.

And while we are here
Our King shall appear,
His Spirit impart,
And form His full image of love in our heart.[22]

HYMN X.

Come, Thou long-expected Jesus,
    Born to set Thy people free,
From our fears and sins release us,
    Let us find our rest in Thee:
Israel's strength and consolation,
    Hope of all the earth Thou art,
Dear Desire of every nation,
    Joy of every longing heart.

Born Thy people to deliver,
    Born a child and yet a king,
Born to reign in us forever,
    Now Thy gracious kingdom bring:
By Thy own eternal Spirit
    Rule in all our hearts alone,
By Thy all-sufficient merit
    Raise us to Thy glorious throne.[23]

HYMN XVI.

O mercy Divine,
How couldst Thou incline,
My God, to become such an infant as *mine?*

What a wonder of grace,
The Ancient of Days
Is found in the likeness of *Adam's* frail race!

Our God, ever blest,
With oxen doth rest,
Is nursed by His creature, and hangs at the breast.

The shepherds behold
Him promised of old
By angels attended, by prophets foretold.

The wise men adore,
And bring Him their store,
The rich are permitted to follow the poor.

To the inn they repair,
To see the young Heir;
The inn is a palace, for Jesus is there.

Like Him would I be,
My Master I see
In a stable; a stable shall satisfy me.[24]

HYMN XVIII.

All glory to God in the sky,
    And peace upon earth be restored!
O Jesus, exalted on high,
    Appear, our omnipotent Lord!
Who, meanly in <u>*Bethlehem*</u> *born,*
    Didst stoop to redeem a lost race,
Once more to Thy creatures return,
    And reign in Thy kingdom of grace.[25]

Atonement

If God loves us to the extent declared in Scripture, it follows that the Atonement has its source in that love. It thus became impossible that the Father should stand impassively by while the Son brought about the salvation and the reconciliation of the human family.

The New Testament does not emphasize that Jesus showed His love for us by dying for us (although that is true also). The emphasis of the New Testament is rather that "*God* so loved the world, that *he* gave *his* only begotten Son" (John 3:16, emphases added). It is God's love that is in action in the Atonement: the Heavenly Father suffers in and with His Son. To say that God the Father suffers does not diminish in any way His majesty, power, or glory. Rather it indicates the supreme evidence and revelation of divine love; and that love has dimensions beyond imagining, and wondrous strategies of its own for dealing with the sin and sins of all humankind.

To Charles Wesley there is always "the mystery of godliness," the impenetrable fact that it is God himself who is born at Bethlehem, walks incognito in Galilee, dies on Calvary, and rises victorious from the tomb in Joseph's garden.

Charles Wesley does not sell himself fully on any one neat little theory of atonement. The cradle and the Cross shadow each other in the hymns, and the crown of glory shines over the empty tomb. To Charles, the resurrection of Jesus Christ is the indestructible hinge on which swings the whole glorious matter of atonement and the eternal priesthood of Christ.

The Resurrection is the event and the means that ensures the continuing ministry of Christ. The Atonement is both finished and unfinished. The Atonement split open the veil; Christ entered the holy of holies and—in Hebrew religious terms—sprinkled His blood on the high altar, and it became the mercy seat of the gospel. The Resurrection from among the dead is the bridge into the yet-unfinished work of Christ in which He authenticates and applies the power and virtue of His blood spilled on Calvary. Charles refuses, if indeed it ever occurred to him that it could happen, to separate in any manner or degree Christ the Reconciler and Christ the High Priest. The Lamb is the Priest and continues the ministry of reconciliation through mediation.

To Wesley, the Resurrection not only was a triumphant conclusion but also crowns Christ's once-for-all sacrifice with eternal glory. This aspect of things prompted Gustav Aulen to write:

> The classic idea has never wholly died out; it was too deeply rooted in the classical formulae of Christianity to be completely lost. It appears from time to time in the hymnody of a Wesley in England or a Grundtvig in Denmark.[26]

Certainly the paradoxical reality of Victor-Victim and Christus Victor is strongly present in Wesley hymns. The wounds of Christ are the badges of His triumph:

> *The dear tokens of His passion*
> *Still His dazzling body bears,*
> *Cause of endless exultation*
> *To adoring worshippers!*
> *With what rapture gaze we*
> *On those glorious scars![27]*

The prayer of all who would be reconciled with God is "Look on Thy hands and read it there!" The conviction that possessed Charles Wesley has possessed Christian men from the beginning and is the life principle of the Church—that Jesus Christ overcame evil, death, and the devil and is alive forever at God's right hand in heavenly places. Christ really was victorious and really is King of Kings and Lord of Lords. This *is* the faith; it is not an appendage tacked on to complete the story. That victory means that salvation is the ongoing work of the Spirit of the living Christ in every believing heart.

The Resurrection is embraced in the Atonement. As Paul says, "[He] was delivered for our offences, and was raised again for our justification" (Rom. 4:25). The Resurrection spells the continuing ministry of Christ; it is the bridge into the holy of holies, where the crucified Christ reigns as Priest and King.

For Charles Wesley, this thought dominates every theory of atonement.

> The example of Charles Wesley shows that such divergent outlooks can—and indeed must—be combined if we are to do justice to the New Testament and to attain to a mature understanding of Christian theology.[28]

Charles was in step with the New Testament preachers. They do not stay with one theory of atonement. It may be that in some places we get one major concept, only to be swallowed elsewhere by another; but the fact is like an unimaginably magnificent jewel of many facets, turning slowly in the bright light of revelation. To the New Testament writers and to Charles Wesley, the Atonement is like the vast ocean, forever the same yet never the same, unchanging yet ever changing to the eye of the beholder.

John Eadie of Scotland wrote

> our redemption is a work at once of price and power—of expiation and of conquest. On the cross the purchase was made, and on the cross the victory was gained. The blood which wipes out the sentence against us was there shed, and the death which was the death-blow of Satan's kingdom was there endured.[29]

In like manner Charles Wesley mingles all the great concepts of atonement. He uses them all but gravitates in them toward the classical conclusion—the conquest of all our foes on the Cross by Christ and confirmed, demonstrated, and proclaimed in three worlds in His resurrection and ascension to the right hand of power.

Colin Williams was of the opinion that "the classical theory is given less emphasis in John Wesley,"[30] but to Charles Wesley it is the unavoidable summation and meaning of them all. John's words are appropriate:

> The Gospel (that is, good news for guilty sinners) means the whole revelation made to men by Jesus Christ . . . the substance of all is . . . "God so loved the world that He gave His only begotten Son, to the end we might not perish, but have everlasting life."[31]

Tag that with a formula, and you have labeled the Atonement. To conceptualize Charles Wesley on the Atonement, you must compound the nativity, ministry, death, resurrection, ascension, enthronement, and heavenly priesthood of God the Son. The absolute triumph of the Son of God is the big thing with the man of the dancing heart. The shattered shackles of Satan, the purging power of the blood of Jesus, new life from the dead, hearing for the deaf, sight for the blind, leaping lameness, light in the darkness, union with God, heaven on earth

—all go together in a glorious jumble of jubilation reflecting the rays of power pouring from the prism of atonement.

"For me"—"For you!"

The substitutionary truth of the Atonement also has profound importance to the man with the dancing heart. There are indeed many writers who hold it to be the dominant element in his concept of the Atonement, and that he strongly and consistently employs it is beyond doubt—a fact illustrating his freedom of thought.

> Died He *for me,* who caused His pain?
>
> That Thou, my God, shouldst die *for me?*
>
> Friend of sinners, spotless Lamb,
> Thy blood was shed *for me!*
>
> O Jesus my hope, *for me* offered up,
> Who with clamor pursued Thee to Calvary's top!
>
> Sinners, ye may love Him too.
>
> O God of all grace, Thy goodness we praise;
> Thy Son Thou hast given, to die in our place.
> He came from above, Our curse to remove,
> He hath loved, He hath loved us, because He would love.
>
> Love moved Him to die, And on this we rely.
> He hath loved, He hath loved us, we cannot tell why;
> But this we can tell, He hath loved us so well
> As to lay down His life to redeem us from hell.
>
> My pardon I claim; For a sinner I am,
> A sinner believing in Jesus's name.
> He purchased the grace Which now I embrace.
> O Father, Thou knowest He hath died in my place.[32]

This substitutionary and vicarious nature of the death of Christ is indeed a very great and precious truth to Charles Wesley. It especially inspires his love and devotion and breaks out in a countless number of hymns. Perhaps the most moving of these is the following, in which Charles's staggering ability to paint word pictures creates a tapestry of Calvary:

> Would Jesus have the sinner die?
>   Why hangs He then on yonder tree?
> What means that strange expiring cry?
>   Sinner, He prays for you and me;
> "Forgive them, Father, O forgive,
> They know not that by Me they live!" . . .
>
> O let me kiss Thy bleeding feet,
>   And bathe and wash them with my tears;
> The story of Thy love repeat
>   In every drooping sinner's ears;
> That all may hear the quickening sound,
> Since I, e'en I, have mercy found.

A familiar verse from a more familiar hymn exhorts us,

> See all your sins on Jesus laid:
>   The Lamb of God was slain,
> His soul was once an offering made
>   For every soul of man.[33]

This momentous truth of the substitutionary nature of the death of Jesus, once for all, is extended into the heavenly ministry of Christ and into the life of every believer:

> Thy blood which pleaded on the cross,
>   Prevalent still for sinners cries;
> It speaks; and it hath gain'd my cause
>   And bought my mansion in the skies.[34]

There is ongoing virtue, power, and significance to the blood of Jesus "shed for rebels, shed for sinners, shed for me!"

> Save me, through faith in Jesu's[35] blood,
>   That blood which He for all did shed;
> For me, for me, Thou know'st it flowed,
>   For me, for me, Thou hear'st it plead;
> Assure me now my soul is Thine,
> And all Thou art in Christ is mine![36]

In a hymn for "mourners convinced of sin," and once greatly used in society meetings, this continuing significance is made very plain:

> Jesus the Lamb of God hath bled,
>   He bore our sins upon the tree;
> Beneath our curse He bowed His head;
> 'Tis finished! He hath died for me!

See where before the throne He stands
  And pours the all-prevailing prayer;
Points to His side, and lifts His hands,
  And shows that I am graven there.

He ever lives for me to pray;
  He prays that I with Him may reign;
Amen to what my Lord doth say;
  Jesus, Thou canst not pray in vain.[37]

Easter Hymns

Charles Wesley's emphasis on Christus Victor coupled with his deep understanding of Christ as substitute meant that he held the Passion whole. There is no real separation of Cross, empty tomb, and the occupied throne in the heavenly places. When he sings of the victorious Christ, he means Christ crucified, buried, risen, ascended, and reigning. Thus he will leap at one bound in thought directly from Calvary to the heavenly throne of Christ the Priest-King.

Rejoice, the Lord is King;
  Your Lord and King adore!
Rejoice, give thanks, and sing,
  And triumph evermore.
Lift up your heart; Lift up your voice,
Rejoice; again I say: rejoice!

Jesus, the Saviour, reigns,
  The God of truth and love.
When He had purged our stains,
  He took His seat above . . .

His kingdom cannot fail;
  He rules o'er earth and heav'n,
The keys of death and hell
  Are to our Jesus giv'n . . .

He all His foes shall quell,
  Shall all our sins destroy,
And every bosom swell
  With pure seraphic joy!
Lift up your heart; Lift up your voice,
Rejoice; again I say: rejoice![38]

For this hymn G. F. Handel wrote the exultant tune "Gopsal" and took justifiable pride in this composition.

Beyond reasonable doubt, however, Charles Wesley's most familiar and popular Easter hymn is one that appeared as early as 1739
with the title "Hymn for Easter Day." It was first published in those
two volumes that Charles produced on his own, to John's slight annoyance. In all the verses there is the normal Wesley dependence on
the words of Scripture. In verse 3 the thought seems to have been
sparked by a phrase from big brother Samuel:

> *In vain the stone, the watch, the seal*
> > *Forbid an early rise*
> *To Him who burst the gates of Hell,*
> > *And open'd paradise.*

Verse 6 is probably based on a thought borrowed from the poet
Young:

> *Triumphant King of Glory! Soul of bliss!*
> *What a stupendous turn of fate is this!*[39]

but on the other hand it may be Wesley's use of Ps. 24:8. Note how
Calvary, Easter, and Ascension are all included; and how futile and
vain were all human obstacles to the Resurrection. Note also how
Christ's resurrection implies that of the believer, and His ascension an
unshakable assurance of eternal life: "ours the cross, the grave, the
skies!"

> *Christ the Lord is ris'n today,*
> *Sons of men and angels say!*
> *Raise your joys and triumphs high,*
> *Sing ye heavens, Thou earth reply!*
>
> *Love's redeeming work is done;*
> *Fought the fight, the battle won:*
> *Lo! The sun's eclipse is o'er,*
> *Lo! he sets in blood no more!*
>
> *Vain the stone, the watch, the seal,*
> *Christ hath burst the gates of hell!*
> *Death in vain forbids His rise,*
> *Christ hath open'd Paradise!*
>
> *Lives again our glorious King!*
> *Where, O death, is now thy sting?*
> *Once He died, our souls to save;*
> *Where's thy victory, boasting grave?*

Soar we now where Christ hath led,
Following our exalted head:
Made like Him, like Him we rise;
Ours the cross, the grave, the skies!

King of glory! Soul of bliss!
Everlasting life is this,
Thee to know, Thy power to prove;
Thus to sing and thus to love.[40]

These triumphant and exultant trumpet notes of faith ought never to be divorced from Handel's glorious music and should use the "Al-le-lu-ia!" sometimes appended to every thought in the hymn.

One of the most beautiful and rich examples of Wesley's way of interpreting Calvary through the focus of Easter and Ascension is:

Lamb of God whose bleeding love,
    We now recall to mind,
Send the answer from above,
    And let us mercy find;
Think on us, who think on Thee;
    And every struggling soul release;
O remember Calvary,
    And bid us go in peace!

By thine agonizing pain
    And bloody sweat, we pray,
By thy dying love to man,
    Take all our sins away:
Burst our bonds, and set us free;
    From all iniquity release;
O remember Calvary,
    And bid us go in peace! . . .

Never will we hence depart,
    Till Thou our wants relieve,
Write forgiveness on our heart
    And all thine image give!
Still our souls shall cry to Thee,
    Till perfected in holiness,
O remember Calvary,
    And bid us go in peace![41]

Behold the Man!

In this writer's opinion, Charles Wesley's greatest, most pro-found, and most moving commentary on Christ's crucifixion, resur-rection, ascension, and heavenly ministry is the hymn so well loved and often used:

> Arise, my soul, arise.
>   Shake off thy guilty fears.
> The bleeding Sacrifice
>   In my behalf appears.
> Before the throne my Surety stands;
> My name is written on His hands.
>
> He ever lives above
>   For me to intercede
> His all-redeeming love,
>   His precious blood to plead.
> His blood atoned for all our race,
> And sprinkles now the throne of grace.
>
> Five bleeding wounds He bears,
>   Received on Calvary.
> They pour effectual prayers;
>   They strongly plead for me.
> "Forgive him, O forgive," they cry,
> "Nor let that ransomed sinner die."
>
> The Father hears Him pray,
>   His dear Anointed One;
> He cannot turn away
>   The presence of His Son.
> His Spirit answers to the blood,
> And tells me I am born of God.
>
> My God is reconciled;
>   His pard'ning voice I hear.
> He owns me for His child;
>   I can no longer fear.
> With confidence I now draw nigh,
> And, "Father, Abba, Father," cry.[42]

This powerful and beautiful hymn, about the influence of which many arresting stories are told, appeared first in the 1742 publication of *Hymns and Sacred Poems* under the heading "Behold the Man!" sug-gesting scriptures such as Lam. 1:12; Isa. 49:16; and Heb. 4:15-16.

Jesus Christ is alive forevermore. He lives above, that is, in the immediate presence of the eternal God in that heaven that once He left. And there His passion is the central fact and theme. There is historical continuity of the glorious Lord Jesus Christ with the life and death and resurrection of the Jesus of history. He carried His humanity with the marks of His humiliation into the heaven of heavens to the very throne of God. He is Prophet, and Priest, and King.

Jesus is gone up on high,
Takes His seat above the sky;
Shout the angel choirs aloud,
Echoing to the trump of God. . . .

Power is all to Jesus given,
Power o'er hell, and earth, and heaven!
Power He now to us imparts;
Praise Him with believing hearts.[43]

In his rendering of Psalm 24, Charles gives full vent to his praise of the risen and ascended Christ as He enters "the heavenly courts above, covered with meritorious scars":

Our Lord is risen from the dead,
Our Jesus is gone up on high;
The powers of hell are captive led,
Dragged to the portals of the sky.
There His triumphal chariot waits,
And angels chant the solemn lay;
"Lift up your heads, ye heavenly gates,
Ye everlasting doors, give way!"
"Who is this King of glory, who?"
"The Lord that all His foes o'ercame,
The world, sin, death, and hell o'erthrew,
And Jesus is the Conqueror's name."[44]

The magnificent picture of the ascended Christ as "He took His seat above" is emphasized repeatedly by Charles as he presents the Prophet, Priest, and King gathering up in himself all the authority, all the virtue, and all the rights of His threefold office.

Trusting in our Lord alone,
A great High-priest we have!
Jesus, God's eternal Son,
Omnipotent to save,
With the virtue of His blood,
Ascending to the holiest place,
Pass'd the heavenly courts, and stood
Before His Father's face.

> *There He ever lives to plead*
>   *His suffering people's cause,*
> *Let us then pursue our Head,*
>   *And bear His daily cross,*
> *Hold our pure profession fast,*
>   *And faithful unto death remain:*
> *Then the end of faith at last,*
>   *The crown of life we gain.*[45]

The glorious Christ is not only Intercessor but also Giver of the Holy Spirit, by whom His presence and ministry is continued without break or hindrance on the earth. The apostle Peter proclaimed this truth on Pentecost Day. Charles Wesley sings,

> *Our Advocate there*
> *By His blood and His prayer*
> *The Gift hath obtained;*
> *For us He hath pray'd, and the Comforter gain'd:*
> *Our glorified Head,*
> *His Spirit hath shed,*
> *With His people to stay,*
> *And never again will He take Him away.*[46]

The Holy Spirit is Christ's other Self; the Spirit in us is Christ in us:

> *The purchased Comforter is given,*
> *For Jesus is returned to heaven,*
>   *To claim and then THE GRACE impart:*
> *Our day of Pentecost is come*
> *And God vouchsafes to fix His home*
>   *In every poor expecting heart.*[47]

Rattenbury notes with a little misgiving this near-identity of Christ Jesus and the Holy Spirit in the Pentecost hymns of Charles Wesley:

> In Charles Wesley's deepest moods, although they were obviously those in which he was most in communion with the Holy Ghost, he addresses his intimate companion as his Saviour Christ. . . . In these hymns the second and third persons of the Trinity seem to be indistinguishable.[48]

But is this a cause for misgiving? After all, the Holy Spirit *is* the other Self of Christ, and frequently it is difficult to distinguish each from the other in the New Testament writings. Any distinction and separation we may make is purely for our own purpose and convenience or that of our theology.

Whene'er our day of Pentecost
Is fully come, we surely know
The Father, Son, and Holy Ghost
Our God, is manifest below:
The Son doth in the Father dwell,
The Father in His Son imparts
His Spirit of Joy unspeakable,
And lives forever in our hearts.[49]

The student will do well to have beside him Timothy Smith's little gem, *The Pentecost Hymns of John and Charles Wesley* (Kansas City: Beacon Hill Press of Kansas City, 1982), which is a pocket-size reprint of the Wesley publications of 1739-45, *Hymns of Petition and Thanksgiving for the Promise of the Father*, with profitable and insightful notes and introduction by Smith.

But not all of Charles Wesley's hymns on and for the Holy Spirit are contained in that collection—not by far. Indeed, some of his finest are not in it. For example, probably no other Wesley hymn is more popular and in more consistent general use throughout the entire Christian Church than the profound hymn of praise and petition for the Holy Spirit, which is not included in that collection:

Love Divine, all Loves excelling,
Joy of heaven to Earth come down,
Fix in us Thy humble Dwelling,
All thy faithful mercies crown;
Jesus, Thou art all Compassion,
Pure, unbounded Love Thou art,
Visit us with thy Salvation,
Enter every trembling heart.

Breathe, O breathe thy loving Spirit
Into every troubled breast,
Let us all in Thee inherit,
Let us find that Second Rest:
Take away our Power of Sinning,
Alpha and Omega be,
End of Faith as its Beginning,
Set our hearts at liberty.

Come, Almighty to deliver,
Let us all thy life receive,
Suddenly return, and never,
Never more thy Temples leave.
Thee we would be always blessing,
Serve Thee as thy Hosts above.
Pray, and praise Thee without ceasing,
Glory in thy perfect Love.

Finish then thy New Creation,
Pure and sinless let us be,
Let us see thy great Salvation
Perfectly restor'd in Thee;
Changed from Glory into Glory
Till in Heaven we take our place,
Till we cast our crowns before Thee
Lost in Wonder, Love, and Praise.[50]

It is not unlikely that Wesley's original idea was derived from Dryden's poem "King Arthur," in which the poet writes,

Fairest Isle, all Isles excelling,
Seat of pleasures and of loves;
Venus here will choose her dwelling
And forsake her Cyprian groves.[51]

Charles Wesley's hymn again reveals that astonishing familiarity with Scripture that characterizes all of his hymns. A minimal list of biblical references in "Love Divine" would include the following: Ps. 84:4; Mal. 3:1; Matt. 11:28-29; John 14:23; 20:22; Rom. 8:21; 1 Cor. 3:16; 2 Cor. 3:18; 6:16; Heb. 4:9-10; Rev. 4:10-11; and 21:3.[52]

The Work of the Holy Spirit

The Holy Spirit is the Executive of the Godhead. His office and work in the world and in believers would demand an entire and large book to show it as Charles Wesley presents it in hundreds of places and implies it in hundreds more. However, a survey of this Wesley theme must necessarily indicate the following 12 facets of His ministry in the unbelieving world and in Christians:

1. To pursue, awaken, and convict sinners

The Spirit of the Lord my God
(Spirit of Power, and Health, and Love)
The Father hath on Christ bestow'd
And sent him from his throne above . . .

To minister his pardoning grace
And every sin-sick soul to heal . . .

'Tis his the drooping soul to raise,
   To rescue all by sin oppressed,
To clothe them with the robes of praise,
   And give their weary spirits rest:

To help their grov'ling unbelief,
   Beauty for ashes to confer,
The oil of joy for abject grief
   Triumphant joy for sad despair.[53]

2. To move sinful men to faith and to assist them to believe

Spirit of Faith, come down,
   Reveal the things of God;
And make to us the Godhead known,
   And witness with the blood:
'Tis Thine the blood to' apply,
   And give us eyes to see
Who did for every sinner die
   Hath surely died for me.[54]

God, who all your lives hath strove,
Woo'd you to embrace his love . . .
Why, ye long-sought sinners, why
Will ye grieve your God, and die?[55]

And these are the words of the Spirit, according to Charles Wesley. The Spirit is appealing to all men, even to those who make pretense of faith:

You, who call the Saviour Lord,
You, who read His written Word,
And will you unfaithful prove,
Trample on His richest love?
Jesus asks the reason, why,
Why will you resolve to die?[56]

The appeal is ever strong, but sweet and plain:

Sinners, turn, why will you die?
God, the Spirit, asks you why . . .
Will you grieve your God and die?[57]

It is to Charles incredible that anyone anywhere should slight the Father's love, the Son's sacrifice, the Spirit's call to full salvation here and life eternal; to him that, too, "passes knowledge." The hymn just quoted poses the same question "Why?" from

> *God your Maker asks you, "Why?"*
> *God your Saviour asks you, "Why?"*
> *God the Spirit asks you, "Why?"*[58]

and then the heavyhearted evangelist himself asks, "Why?"

> *Dead already, dead within,*
> *Spiritually dead in sin:*
> *Dead to God, while here you breathe,*
> *Pant ye after second death?*
> *Will you still in sin remain,*
> *Greedy of eternal pain?*
> *O, ye dying sinner, Why,*
> *Why will you forever die?*[59]

The hymn is a long one and is divided into three hymns, or at least into three numbers in the 1780 book. The spirit is one of grieving poignancy, and the appeal is multisided and persistent. The final question of the entire piece could hardly be more appealingly pressing:

> *Can you doubt if God is love?*
> *If to all His bowels move?*
> *Will you not His* <u>Word</u> *receive?*
> *Will you not His* <u>oath</u> *believe?*
> *See! The suffering God appears!*
> *Jesus weeps; believe his tears!*
> *Mingled with his blood they cry,*
> *"Why will you resolve to die?"*[60]

For it is not God's will that anyone should perish. "What more can He say than to you He hath said?" If any person perishes after having heard the gospel clearly, it is only because that person has "resolved," made up his mind to reject the Christ of the Cross and turn a deaf ear to the call of the Holy Spirit.

3. To give assurance of salvation

> *His Spirit answers to the Blood,*
> *And tells me I am born of God.*[61]

Once again it must be noted that, specific hymns on assurance apart, there are multiplied scores of references, statements, allusions, and associated ideas that should be studied to gain a more or less complete concept of Charles Wesley's all-pervasive presentation of assurance. He had long been rather agitated by the fact that he was a stranger to any real assurance. It was not until May 21, 1738, that real light and hope began to rise on his horizon. Peter Böhler's doctrine and obvious enjoyment of the assurance of faith was attractive, and in the period of sickness that came on him in the spring of 1738, he was longing for the "surety that my sins are forgiven."

In his *Journal* for April 28, Charles entered:

> In the morning Dr. Cokburn came to see me; and a better physician, Peter Böhler. . . . He stood by my bedside, and prayed over me, that now at least I might see the divine intention, in this and my late illness. I immediately thought it might be that I should again consider Böhler's doctrine of faith; examine myself whether I was in the faith; and if I was not, never cease seeking and longing after it, till I attained it.[62]

After recording that he had received the sacrament from Mr. Piers, Charles wrote:

> Now I have demonstration against the Moravian doctrine that a man cannot have peace without assurance of his pardon. I now have peace, yet cannot say of a surety that my sins are forgiven.[63]

But less than a month later, Charles is marveling at what he terms a foretaste of heaven:

> *O, how shall I the goodness tell,*
> *Father, which Thou to me hast show'd?*
> *That I, a child of wrath and hell,*
> *I should be called a child of God!*
> *Should know, should feel my sins forgiven,*
> *Blest with this antepast of heaven!*[64]

Charles Wesley's assurance might readily be shown by collating hymns such as

> *My God I am Thine,*
> *What a comfort divine,*
> *What a blessing to <u>know</u> that my Jesus is mine!*[65]

or

> *How happy are they*
> *Who the Saviour obey,*
> *   And have laid up their treasure above,*
> *Tongue cannot express*
> *The sweet Comfort and Peace*
> *   Of a Soul in its earliest Love.*
>
> *That Comfort was mine,*
> *When the Favour Divine*
> *   I first found in the Blood of the Lamb.*[66]

and many more of the same.

Five "universals" form the vertebrae of the theology of the Wesley brothers. These are:
1. All men need salvation.
2. All men may be saved.
3. All men may know themselves saved.
4. All men should witness to their salvation.
5. All men may perfect holiness in the fear of the Lord.[67]

The doctrine and experience of assurance centers around nos. 3 and 4. Neither of these was new to Christian theology, but the fogs of medieval scholasticism and mysticism had obscured them from experience; and now, being expressed with such confidence and joy by the Wesleys and the early Methodist people, they fell on the incredulous ears of the 18th century with all the explosive power of a fresh discovery. Thus their teaching on assurance, or the witness of the Holy Spirit, may properly be designated one of the two unique contributions of the Wesleys to the progress of Christian doctrine. Although not strictly equivalent, we use the terms "witness of the Spirit" and "assurance" interchangeably.

What a transformation was wrought in John Wesley from May 24, 1738, forward! That very point became part of the authorized interpretations and standards of Wesleyan doctrine we call Wesley's *Sermons* and *Explanatory Notes upon the New Testament*. Wesley came to define the matter in these words:

> An inward impression on the soul, whereby the Spirit of God directly witnesses to my spirit, that I am a child of God; that Jesus Christ hath loved me, and given Himself for me; and that all my sins are blotted out; and I, even I, am reconciled to God. It is a testimony distinct from that of the believer's own spirit, or the testimony of a good conscience.[68]

He came to that conviction on May 24, 1738. Writing of the "change" God worked in him, he said,

> I felt I did trust in Christ, Christ alone for salvation; and an assurance was given me that He had taken away *my* sins, even *mine*, and saved *me* from the law of sin and death.[69]

To turn from the familiar words of John to the testimony of Charles is to feel the truth begin to dance. To Charles also the inward witness was "the strongest proof of Christianity," as he had heard his dying father say. In Charles also the change that God worked was revolutionary.

Leslie Church put it pithily and pertinently: "The early Methodists were not taught a theological system, they had caught a spiritual experience."[70] To a very high degree, Charles Wesley made that experience highly contagious. The experience vibrates throughout his verses, not only those in which he is of set purpose presenting assurance, not only those where the specific terms occur, but all along the line, even when least expected. The verse just quoted is from the conversion hymn, but just a few weeks later he wrote the ever-popular number, "And can it be, that I should gain . . . ?" and, as with so many others of the hymns, the sheer ecstasy of liberty echoes in line after line.

As well tell the erstwhile blind man of John 9, upon whose new eyes a whole colorful new creation has burst, that it really isn't true and he cannot know that it is; as well tell old Legion that he is but imagining that the manacles no longer dangle and rattle from wrists and ankles; as well tell Peter that he is still asleep and dreaming about rushing to Mary's house; as well do all of these as tell Charles Wesley that his assurance of forgiveness and freedom is an empty dream!

That glorious hymn had more verses than we get to sing nowadays. Charles wrote six verses, but editors frequently reduce the number to three or four. The fifth verse underscores the inward witness:

> Still the small inward voice I hear,
>   That whispers all my sins forgiven;
> Still the atoning blood is near,
>   That quenched the wrath of hostile heaven;
> I _feel_ the life His wounds impart;
> I _feel_ the Saviour in my heart![71]

It appears that the pronouns "me," "my," and "mine" and the verbs "know" and "feel" are the strong red cords of personal assurance woven into the Wesley hymnody.

It breaks through so often that about the most we can do is let Charles loose to shout it out!

> What we ourselves have felt and seen
>   With confidence we tell,
> And publish to the sons of men,
>   The signs infallible.[72]

Assurance and the witness of the Spirit, direct and indirect—this is the warp and woof of Wesley's hymns, the foundational fact of his experience. This it was that gave the ring of authority to the songs and sermons of the man with the dancing heart. This is what imparted that near-cavalier bearing to him when faced by hostile mobs and by obstinately prejudiced parsons and police. In his evangelism there is that authoritative certainty without which proclamation feebly fails, and with which the preacher is powerfully persuasive. For it is clear that, as has been said, "The religion we can have without knowing we can lose without missing!" But the faith we have and know we have becomes the accent of undeniable authority.

Of course, John Wesley had his own way of putting it: his question-and-answer method; his exegetical and expositional method; even his "earnest appeal" and "plain account." But Charles's hymnic expression is infinitely more convincing, expressive, and persuasive. This truth is indeed caught rather than taught.

Not that John ignored the potential of hymnic expression to communicate the doctrine and experience of assurance. His superb translation from the German of Paulus Gerhardt, Johann Rothe, and Gerhardt Tersteegen are sufficient evidence that John nobly employed song medium. And he makes strong translations from French and Spanish, strong enough to be more forceful than some of the originals. But he lacks the verve, the dance, the life, and the liveliness of Charles.

However, it is quite wrong to give the impression that Charles spread only the contagion of assurance; he also expounded it, even analyzed it. He led the Methodist worshipers to the heart of the doctrine of the witness of the Spirit. Probably very few sermons have done this so efficiently, and certainly no hymn has done it more adequately, than the analytical hymn beginning, "How can a sinner know his sins on earth forgiven?" a hymn that has been expounded over and over again and still leaves us with the feeling that we have not really mined its seams of biblical truth. The hymn is well worthy of the commendation John expressed on the theological comprehensiveness of the hymnbook.

This remarkable hymn is really the first of a series of five hymns under the title of "The Marks of Faith." Originally all five hymns, written in the same meter, consisted of eight lines to each verse, but this hymn has often been subdivided and abbreviated by various editors to facilitate its congregational use.

Some of the later verses are rather mischievous in import, and perhaps the editors may be justly excused for regarding them as unsingable. For example, in hymn 2, verse 2, Charles wrote:

> Redeem'd from all his woes,
>   Out of his dungeon freed,
> Ask, how the prisoner knows
>   That he is free indeed.
> How can he tell the gloom of night
>   From the meridian blaze?
> Or I discern the glorious light
>   That streams from Jesu's face?[73]

From hymn 3, verse 4, we have,

> *Wherefore from us depart,*
> *And to each other tell*
> *"We cannot on our heart*
> *The written pardon feel."*
> *A stranger to the living Bread*
> *Ye may beguile and cheat,*
> *But us you never can persuade*
> *That honey is not sweet.*[74]

The first hymn of the five is, then, Wesley's classic piece on this subject. Step by step, Charles expresses the doctrine and experience of assurance of salvation through the witness of the Holy Spirit: the direct witness; the indirect witness; the witness as the earnest of heaven and the pledge of future bliss; the witness of belonging to the family of God; the witness of a daily life obedient to the will of God and to the commands of Christ; and the witness of a guided life. Verse 1 asks the fundamental question: how can we actually *know* that we have been forgiven for all our sins? By what means can a heavenly event be shown clearly on earth?

> *How can a sinner know?*
> *His sins on earth forgiven?*
> *How can my Saviour show*
> *My name inscribed in heaven?*[75]

First of all, we inwardly know by the impact of the Holy Spirit on our own spirit and consciousness. Although clear and convincing and beyond doubt to the recipient, it is something that is indefinable: an impression of divine origin, the direct touch of God's Holy Spirit, "strong, and permanent, and clear."

> *We who in Christ believe*
> *That He for us hath died,*
> *His unknown peace receive,*
> *And feel His blood applied;*
> *Exults for joy our rising soul,*
> *Disburden'd of her load,*
> *And swells, unutterably full*
> *Of glory and of God.*[76]

It is peace, joy, and glory. And it is a baptism of holy love and courage.

> His love, surpassing far
>   The love of all beneath,
> We find within, and dare
>   The pointless darts of death.

"Pointless," mind you, for the sharpness and the sting of death has been drawn:

> Stronger than death, or sin, or hell,
>   The mystic power we prove,
> And conquerors of the world we dwell
>   In heaven, who dwell in love.[77]

For the witness given by the Holy Spirit is both "pledge" and "earnest," that is, it is a piece of heaven on the way there. As Paul said, "Eye hath not seen, nor ear heard, neither have entered into the heart of man, the things which God hath prepared for them that love him. BUT God hath revealed them unto us by his Spirit" (1 Cor. 2:9-10, emphasis added).

> The pledge of _future_ bliss
>   He _now_ to us imparts,
> His gracious Spirit _is_
>   The earnest in our hearts:
> We antedate the joys above,
>   We taste the eternal powers,
> And _know_ that all those heights of love
>   And all those heavens are ours.

But meanwhile, until "Christ, who is our life, shall appear" (Col. 3:4), the Spirit has stamped on our souls the seal of divine ownership:

> Till He our life reveal,
>   We rest in Christ secure:
> His Spirit is _the seal,_
>   Which made our pardon sure:
> Our sins His blood hath blotted out,
>   And sign'd our soul's release:
> And can we of His favours doubt,
>   Whose blood declares us His?[78]

Is it not possible, however, and a terrible possibility, that we may be deceived, led astray by our own emotions, self-deceived? Is this direct witness a really safe test? There are divine counterbalances and directives: red lights of warning, and green lights of guidance. "Let no one presume to rest in some supposed witness of the Spirit divorced from the fruit of the Spirit."

We by His Spirit prove
And know the things of God,
The things which of His love
He hath on us bestowed:
Our God to us His Spirit gave
And dwells in us, we know,
The witness in ourselves we have,
And all His fruits we show.[79]

What are these "fruits of the Spirit" that prove His indubitable presence in the heart? They are Christlikeness, self-sacrifice, a transformed mind, but chiefly a life of obedience under divine guidance and lived to the glory of God:

The meek and lowly heart,
Which in our Saviour was
He doth to us impart
And signs us with His cross:
Our nature's course is turn'd, our mind
Transformed in all its powers,
And both the witnesses are join'd,
The Spirit of God with ours.[80]

However, it is ultimately obedience that proves belonging. As the essence of original sin was "one man's disobedience" (Rom. 5:19), so obedience is the essence of holiness; and holiness is, simply put, the life-style that pleases God.

Whate'er our pardoning Lord
Commands, we gladly do,
And guided by His word
We all His steps pursue.
His glory is our whole design,
We live our God to please,
And rise with filial fear Divine
To perfect holiness.[81]

This, in 64 lines, is Charles Wesley's doctrine of assurance and the witness of the Spirit. John used many more words, faceted the truth from many angles, but he said no more than Charles did in this remarkable hymn. Perhaps it is necessary to abbreviate it for singing by modern congregations trained in and accustomed to the "first and last verses" habit, but it is a very great pity!

In our era when countless numbers of people, many professing Christians among them, are struggling for identity and confidence, the hymns of Charles Wesley properly used could become a sheet anchor

to the soul, and this hymn in particular. Shredding it may help preserve brevity of worship, but it is no service to the Christian congregation.

Converted at Newgate jail under the preaching of John Wesley,
Silas Told received in an instant the Spirit's witness in his head and in
his heart.

Of these things and this aspect of truth, Charles Wesley has a
very great deal to say. Life in the Spirit is the indubitable evidence of
the Spirit's life in the Christian. It is proof incontrovertible:

> Jesus, plant Thy Spirit in me,
> Then the fruit shall show the tree,
> Every grace its Author prove,
> Rising from the root of love.[82]
>
> Holy Lamb, who Thee confess,
> Followers of Thy holiness,
> Thee they ever keep in view,
> Ever ask: What shall we do?
> Governed by Thy only will,
> All Thy words we would fulfill,
> Would in all Thy footsteps go,
> Walk as Jesus walked below.
> Works of love on man bestow'd,
> Secret intercourse with God.
>
> Such our whole employment be,
> Works of faith and charity;
> Vessels, instruments of grace,
> Pass we thus our happy days
> 'Twixt the mount and multitude,
> Doing or receiving good;
> Glad to pray and labour on,
> Till our earthly course is run,
> Till we, on the sacred tree,
> Bow the head and die like Thee.[83]

This most impressive and expressive hymn appears in the 1747
collection of *Hymns for the Use of Families, and on Various Occasions*, a
publication that ever has been regarded very highly.

Benjamin Gregory, statesman and leader of Methodism in the late
19th and early 20th centuries, wrote concerning it:

> It breathes the tranquil fervour of the completest consecration.
> Each successive clause embodies a clear idea in a bar of music. Each
> verse is perfect itself. Each line fits in like the cubes of an exquisite

mosaic pavement. There is not a loose thread, there is no rough edging. The balance of rhythm, and the antithesis or parallelism of idea, are equally exact. Lines and verses seem "knit together in love."[84]

Not only does the hymn illustrate poetic "balance" and "rhythm," but also it expresses most beautifully that "life in the Spirit" is a beautiful balance and rhythm between private and personal communion with God and loving care, concern, and service to men. The person who indeed does "keep in step with the Spirit" (Gal. 5:25, NIV) is living the balanced and rhythmic life, for such a life is really and actually lived "'Twixt the mount and multitude." As Rattenbury indicates, this hymn "concentrates in 32 lines what is true and possible in the imitation of Christ."[85]

> *Thy bright example I pursue,*
> *To Thee in all things rise;*
> *And all I think, or speak, or do,*
> *Is one great sacrifice.*
>
> *Careless through outward cares I go,*
> *From all distractions free:*
> *My hands are but engaged below,*
> *My heart is still with Thee.*[86]

No hymn of Wesley's, however, seems to me more fully to express this principle of balance and rhythm in the Spirit-filled life, both in doctrine and in experience, than that beginning:

> *Jesu, shall I never be*
> *Firmly grounded upon Thee?*

Headed "Phil. 2:5," the hymn introduces Paul's profound but familiar teaching on the mind of the humbled and exalted Christ: "Let this mind be in you, which was also in Christ Jesus." Verses 5 through 13 especially expound the subject positively, presenting the "mind of Jesus" adjectivally:

V. 5: Jesu's is a quiet mind.

V. 6: Jesu's is a gentle mind.

V. 7: Jesu's is a patient mind.

V. 8: Jesu's is a noble mind.

V. 9: Jesu's is a spotless mind.

V. 10: Jesu's is a loving mind.

V. 11: Jesu's is a thankful mind.

V. 12: Jesu's is a constant mind.

V. 13: Jesu's is a perfect mind.[87]

These verses are framed around almost 20 New Testament verses, each used to expound and apply Phil. 2:5 ff., and the entire poem ably presents the balanced life of walking in step with the Holy Spirit.

By way of summary, we can say that to Charles Wesley all truly Christian people are by the Holy Spirit being sanctified in intention, motive, and action. They are also being led into truth and the discerning of truth according to the mind and will of the Spirit of God, guiding them in all the affairs of daily service and commitment. They do indeed live in the fulcrum balance of two worlds. This is the life of "keep[ing] in step with the Spirit" balanced "'twixt the mount and multitude."

Hymns on the Last Things

Many of the "eschatological" hymns of Charles Wesley were prompted by the parallels he drew between the events of his day and the apocalyptic words and pictures of the Hebrew prophets and the New Testament prophecies. We in turn can even more readily see parallels between these biblical descriptions and the events of the 20th century. This fact seems to make those hymns in some ways more relevant to us than to Wesley's contemporaries.

The atmosphere in Wesley's society was one of foreboding, of fear and apprehensiveness of impending disaster, if not of doom. The old European order was crumbling. Science was beginning to scratch at the surface of the complex universe. Weapons of warfare showed signs of sinister developments. England seemed caught at the geographical center of actual and possible bloodshed. The apocalyptic horsemen were riding, and a great many common people thought they could hear the clattering hooves. Rebellion from the Scottish north and war in Europe, which threatened invasion from France, suggested more terrible things to come. Vacillating politicians, press-gangs in the streets, open revolution in the American colonies—it all hung like a funeral pall over England. A depraved lower class doping itself with alcohol, while the so-called upper classes—very far down on their uppers—appeared in many instances to be living things up while they could and paying little or no heed to dangers threatening the nation. England tottered like a drunken man on the edge of a precipice.

In such an atmosphere, the Wesleys had first of all to rouse a largely decadent generation, calling upon it to flee from the impending wrath of a holy, righteous, long-suffering God. The brothers declared that all that stood between that generation and divine judgment was the incredible patience of the Heavenly Father. Earthquakes, plagues, desolations of war, and the havocs of revolution—through all God was thundering His message: He is not simply "love"; He is *holy* love.

Is there much to choose between that generation and ours? Has not the piercing of nature's secrets in the earth and in the stellar heavens already begun to pull back the apocalyptic curtains?

Charles Wesley's gospel was alive with the most positive and powerful accents of divine love, and grace, and pardon, and promise of life on earth and heaven at the end of it. But he was far too honest an ambassador and watchman to foster false hopes. His evangel had in it strong notes of inevitable holy judgment; his trumpet could and did blow the solemn note also. His was "a gladly solemn sound."

Earthquakes, disasters, thunders, electric storms, invasion threats, and many another contemporary happenings were conscripted by Charles as aids to persuasion:

> He comes! He comes! the Judge severe!
> The seventh trumpet speaks Him near;
> His lightnings flash; His thunders roll:
> How welcome to the faithful soul.

and again,

> The great Archangel's trump shall sound
> (While twice ten thousand thunders roar)
> Tear up the graves, and cleave the ground,
> And make the greedy sea restore.[88]

It is noteworthy that, in the words of F. L. Wiseman, writing over 50 years ago in the *Methodist Recorder* (March 31, 1933, p. 11), "In no particular does the Methodist Hymnbook of today differ more widely from its great predecessor of 1780 than in its treatment of death and judgment to come." The situation has not altered; indeed, from our viewpoint it has worsened. If we add to death and judgment the doctrine of the return of Jesus Christ, the hymnbooks of the 20th-century Methodists are strangely deficient. The present hymnbook of Methodists in the United States reflects the uncertainty and tentativeness of the people called Methodists on the issue of last things.

Beginning with the British Methodist Hymnbook of 1904, there seem to be strong editorial tendencies to abandon the apologetic nature of the early hymnbook. Whereas John Wesley structured the 1780 hymnbook around the pilgrimage motif—save that it commences, not with a pilgrim already fleeing from the wrath to come, but further back—the modern editors apparently see things much differently. To the Wesleys, the last things—death-judgment-heaven-hell—were powerful realities and constituted equally powerful tools of persuasion in convincing unbelievers to turn from the evil of their ways, find peace and joy in believing, and make a start on the narrow way of life leading to eternal happiness in heaven. They spoke, sang, and wrote of these realities in awe, but not with tongue in cheek! Modern Methodist editorial committees seem to look on these things with doctrinaire attitudes of mild interest.

Thus the "Last Things" have been removed from the persuasive at the beginning of the earlier hymnals and appear only as phrases in the Apostles' and Nicene creeds. No doubt modern Methodists have their own reasons for this departure, but there is no denying the power and effectiveness of John Wesley's use of Charles's hymns on Last Things in the opening, rather than the closing, section of the hymnbook.

Part First:

Section I   Exhorting sinners to return to God.

      II   Describing, 1. The pleasantness of religion
                           2. The goodness of God
                           3. Death
                           4. Judgment
                           5. Heaven
                           6. Hell

     III   Prayer for a blessing.[89]

While Wesley did not include a specific section on the Return of Jesus Christ, the New Testament teaching on it was given place as part of the persuasive argument in evangelism:

> *Hearken to the solemn Voice,*
>   *The awful midnight cry!*
> *Waiting souls, rejoice! rejoice!*
>   *And see the Bridegroom nigh:*
>
> *Lo! He comes to keep His word;*
>   *Light and joy His looks impart:*
> *Go ye forth to meet your Lord,*
>   *And meet Him in your heart.*[90]

This hymn was included in the 1876 and 1904 British hymnals but dropped by the editors of the present hymnal. Other examples abound, for Charles Wesley wrote many hymns on the Return of Christ and Last Things, but we have to tooth-comb the post-1904 books to detect any.

However, one hymn that has kept its place is Charles Wesley's poetic interpretation of Rev. 1:7:

> *Lo! He comes with clouds descending,*
>   *Once for favor'd sinners slain . . .*[91]

Death

Charles Wesley's hymns and parts of his *Journal* abundantly justify the claim of brother John that "our people die well." From time to time, each brother had reason to say so. They had witnessed the confidence and assurance of their father as he crossed the river of death. "When I am released," commanded mother Susanna, "sing a hymn of praise to God." John died with a hymn on his lips—"I'll praise my Maker while I've breath"—and Charles was still writing hymns on his deathbed. In his *Journal*, Charles records an interview with a doctor he met at the bedside of a dying Methodist woman, a Mrs. Hooper. The doctor had told her there was little hope of recovery but reported,

> She had no dread upon her spirits. Most people die from fear of dying; but I never met such people as yours. They are none of them afraid of death; but calm, patient, resigned to the last.[92]

And then, turning toward the patient, he said, "Madam, be not cast down." "Sir," she replied smiling, "I shall never be cast down!"[93]

Charles Wesley himself was ever ready to die. It seems to the reader of some of the hymns that he was almost envious of the dying inasmuch as the face of the Lord Jesus would, he was persuaded, await Him on the other side of the veil, and he lived with "Faith's warm finger thro' the veil!"

Neither disillusionment with the present world nor morbid curiosity about the next, but the jubilant expectation of being "lost in wonder, love, and praise" lay behind these seemingly morbid words:

> *Ah, lovely appearance of death*
> *What sight upon earth is so fair?*
> *Not all the gay pageants that breathe*
> *Can with a dead body compare:*
> *With solemn delight I survey*
> *The corpse, when the spirit is fled,*
> *In love with the beautiful clay,*
> *And longing to lie in its stead.*[94]

The fascinating meter and rhythm of the hymn reveal the dancing heart of the poet in the presence of the so-called master of terrors. In a long, two-part poem on the death of Grace Bowen, Charles wrote:

> *O let me on the image dwell,*
> *The soul-transporting spectacle*
> *On which even angels gaze!*
> *An hoary saint mature for God,*
> *And shaking off the earthly clod,*
> *To see His open face.*[95]

There are scores of such poems from the pen of Charles, all breathing the spirit of New Testament assurance and hope. One of the longest but most touching of these is "An Elegy on the Late Rev. George Whitefield, M.A.," which dwells on Whitefield's astonishing labors as an evangelist beyond compare, his incredible zeal and capacity for suffering "in the Saviour's cause," and his life and death—"His body, spirit, soul"—as a sacrifice to God. Far from qualifying as Wesley's finest poem, it nevertheless exudes brotherly affection and Christian confidence in the valley of the shadow.

> And is my Whitefield enter'd into rest,
> With sudden death, with sudden glory, blest?
>
> ✳ ✳ ✳
>
> Can I the memorable day forget,
> When first we by divine appointment met?
>
> ✳ ✳ ✳
>
> A stranger as my bosom-friend caress'd,
> And unawares received an angel-guest.
>
> ✳ ✳ ✳
>
> His one delightful work and steadfast aim
> To pluck poor souls as brands out of the flame,
> To scatter the good seed on every side,
> To spread the knowledge of the Crucified,
>
> ✳ ✳ ✳
>
> The man of God, whom God delights to' approve
> In his great labours of parental love,
> Love of the little ones,—for these he cares,
> The lambs, the orphans, in his bosom bears.[96]

On it goes through 536 lines. No outstanding facet of Whitefield's character or work is omitted, and in eulogizing Whitefield, the poet unintentionally reveals his own triumphant spirit and hope:

> He speaks—and dies! transported to resign
> His spotless soul into the hands divine!
> He sinks into his loving Lord's embrace,
> And sees his dear Redeemer face to face.[97]

However, Charles Wesley's hymns on death are at their best in the fellowship dimension. His own favorite has been the favorite with generations of Methodists and others since it was written, and wedded to the famed Handel tune called "David" is still high among the loved hymns.

> Rejoice for a brother deceased,
>   Our loss is his infinite gain;
> A soul out of prison released,
>   And free from its bodily chain;
> With songs let us follow his flight,
>   And mount with his spirit above,
> Escaped to the mansions of light,
>   And lodged in the Eden of love.
>
> Our brother the haven hath gained,
>   Outflying the tempest and wind;
> His rest he hath sooner obtain'd,
>   And left his companions behind,
> Still toss'd on a sea of distress,
>   Hard toiling to make the blest shore,
> Where all is assurance and peace,
>   And sorrow and sin are no more.
>
> There all the ship's company meet,
>   Who sailed with the Saviour beneath;
> With shouting each other they greet,
>   And triumph o'er trouble and death:
> The voyage of life's at an end,
>   The mortal affliction is past;
> The age that in heaven they spend,
>   Forever and ever shall last.[98]

That cannot be bettered for a singable hymn on Christian death. All of his life Charles Wesley felt, acted, and wrote like a transient on the earth. He had deep, strong yearnings for the "Jerusalem which is above . . . which is the mother of us all" (Gal. 4:26). This inspired rather than impeded him in his evangelism and pastoral work. He expressed this sense of impermanence here most remarkably under the figure of a person standing on the very tip of a promontory at Land's End with the vast Atlantic Ocean bashing on one side, and the Straits of Dover on the other, and he caught under the burden of eternity:

> Lo! on a narrow neck of land,
> 'Twixt two unbounded seas I stand
>   Secure, insensible:
> A point of life, a moment's space
> Removes me to that heavenly place,
>   Or shuts me up in hell.

O God, mine inmost soul convert,
And deeply on my thoughtful heart,
    Eternal things impress;
Give me to feel their solemn weight,
And tremble on the brink of fate,
    And wake to righteousness.

Be this my one great business here,
With serious industry, and fear,
    My future bliss to' insure.
Thine utmost counsel to fulfill,
And suffer all Thy righteous will,
    And to the end endure.

Then, Saviour, then my soul receive,
Transported from the vale, to live,
    And reign with Thee above,
Where faith is sweetly lost in sight,
And hope in full supreme delight,
    And everlasting love.[99]

Preparation for Death

In 1772 Wesley published a small collection of hymns titled "Preparation for Death." What I find notable in that collection is Wesley's constant emphasis on the death of Christ as the only hope of the world and certainly of the dying sinner:

Jesus, the just, the good,
    Remember Calvary,
And claim the purchase of Thy blood,
    Expended all for me:
My Saviour hitherto,
    A little longer save;
And pardon'd penitent renew,
    And hide me in the grave.

Giver of godly woe,
On me the grace bestow;
Stony into fleshly turn,
    By Thy last expiring cry;
Bid me look on Thee and mourn,
    Mourn, and with my Saviour die.

> *Thy bleeding love declare,*
> *Too strong for life to bear;*
> *Let it purge and break my heart,*
>   *Then my heart's desire I prove,*
> *Bowing on Thy cross depart,*
>   *Pay Thee back Thy bleeding love.*[100]

In this brief collection, hymn after hymn guides the soul to the cross of Christ, where, when the last word is said and the last breath expired, the soul's only true and secure resting place is found.

> *Away with my fears!*
> *The Redeemer appears*
> *Offer'd up in my stead,*
> *And for every offender inclining His head;*
> *He answer'd for me,*
> *When He bled on the tree,*
> *And my punishment took,*
> *By His Father aggrieved, by His Father forsook.*
>
> *'Tis finished, He cries;*
> *Our Deliverer dies,*
> *The Atonement is made,*
> *The ransom laid down, and the penalty paid.*
> *The all-conquering tomb*
> *Is by Jesus o'ercome,*
> *The terrible king*
> *Is disarmed of his dart, and despoiled of his sting.*
>
> *Triumphant I am*
> *Through the death of the Lamb,*
> *And redeem'd by His blood,*
> *I have nothing to fear from a pacified God.*
> *The favour divine,*
> *The image is mine,*
> *When His Son I receive,*
> *And united to Him I eternally live.*[101]

And at his own exodus, the precious blood of Jesus was still Wesley's only plea:

> *With humble faith his death I plead,*
>   *And cover'd with th' atoning blood,*
> *Calmly I sink among the dead,*
>   *The dead who ever live to God,*
> *Secure in that great day to rise*
> *And share Thy kingdom in the skies.*[102]

This is part of one of many hymns left in manuscript by Charles Wesley, about 20 of them in this collection alone.

Charles Wesley's faith on his deathbed reaches back to one of his earliest postconversion hymns:

> Bold I approach th' eternal throne
> And claim the crown, through Christ my own.[103]

The Return of Jesus Christ

Charles Wesley was convinced about the second advent of his Lord and not as quiet about it as some of his Methodist successors are and apparently wish he had been. At least, this seems evident when we consider how very sparse are his verses on this subject in modern hymnbooks.

Commenting on Mark 13:16, Charles wrote perhaps not one of his classics, but a good singable hymn:

> 'Tis all our blessed business here
> To wait till Jesus shall appear,
> Descending from His bright abode,
> The Son of man, th' Eternal God.
>
> He comes, He comes to fetch His bride!
> Even I shall see the heavens thrown wide,
> Discern Him on His cloudy car,
> And mount and meet Him in the air.
>
> And while He ready makes our place
> His Spirit in His members prays,
> "Appear to take Thine exiles home,
> Come quickly, Lord, to judgment come."[104]

From the same chapter of Scripture, Charles lifts the last words, "I say unto all, Watch," and he writes:

> Is there a saint who doth not need
>   To watch and pray, while stationed here?
> Doth grace the duty supersede,
>   Or love cast out the humble fear?
>
> Who bade the twelve, "Take heed and fear,"
>   Cautioning them, He cautions all:
> And those that watch with ceaseless care,
>   Can never sin, can never fall.[105]

Charles continues in the next number with

Jesus, inspire the watchful power,
And set me on Thy cross's tower,
Till life's sad moment's o'er:
Here may I still my station keep,
And never fold my arms to sleep,
And never slumber more.

O might I in Thy likeness wake,
Thy spotless purity partake
And fix my wistful eye,
Till coming in the clouds I see,
Thy mild triumphant majesty,
And to Thy bosom fly.[106]

Resurrection of Believers

Closely linked with the second advent of Jesus Christ, Charles Wesley felt the promise of the resurrection of believers. In a lovely hymn on the intercession of Christ above and Christian holiness below, there are these strikingly expressive verses:

He wills that I should holy be:
What can withstand His will?
The counsel of His grace in me
He surely can fulfill.

Jesus, I hang upon Thy word;
I steadfastly believe
Thou wilt return, and claim me, Lord,
And to Thyself receive.

Joyful in hope my spirit soars
To meet Thee from above,
Thy goodness thankfully adores,
And sure I taste Thy love.[107]

From a hymn that has been described as "great," "magnificent," and "majestic" comes this final verse:

Resting in this glorious hope
To be at last restored,
Yield we now our bodies up
To earthquake, plague, or sword;
Listening for the call Divine,
The latest trumpet of the seven,
Soon our soul and dust shall join,
And both fly up to heaven.[108]

Judgment

Despite all we have quoted, it can be safely claimed that the Wesley brothers themselves appealed little to the fear motive. It was certainly there in the background, and upon occasion they did employ it, but their preachers were much more inclined toward it than were the Wesleys. Hence we read in the *Minutes of Conference 1744:*

> Q: Do not some of our assistants preach too much of the wrath and too little of the love of God?
>
> A. We fear that they have leaned to that extreme.[109]

As we saw earlier, Charles Wesley presented the Last Things as persuasives, and very frequently even as declarative of the long-suffering and love of God. Death, for example, was not to be regarded as a horrible thing, but as something to be welcomed. Of natural disasters such as fire and famine, earthquake and war, Charles insists that even these declare the wonderful coming of Jesus.

> *Thy tokens we with joy confess,*
> *The war proclaims the Prince of Peace,*
> *The earthquake speaks Thy power,*
> *The famine all Thy fulness brings,*
> *The plague presents Thy healing wings,*
> *And nature's final hour.*[110]

Osborn, the editor of the *Poetical Works*, links the hymn of which the above is verse 4, on the one hand to Whitefield's "Short Address to Persons of All Denominations, Occasioned by the Alarm of an Invasion," and on the other hand to an American Fast-day sermon by Samuel Davies.

Beginning with a comforting verse, the hymn continues through all six verses to express the happiness and security of the believers who rest in Christ through any kind of crisis:

> *How happy are the little flock,*
> *Who safe beneath their guardian rock*
> *In all commotions rest!*
> *When wars and tumult's wares run high,*
> *Unmoved above the storm they lie,*
> *They lodge in Jesu's breast.*

> *Such happiness, O Lord, have we,*
> *By mercy gathered into Thee,*
> *Before the floods descend:*
> *And while the bursting flood comes down,*
> *We mark the vengeful day begun,*
> *And calmly wait the end.*

Whatever ill the world befall,
A pledge of endless good we call,
A sign of Jesus near:
His chariot will not long delay;
We hear the rumbling wheels, and pray,
Triumphant Lord, appear.

Appear with clouds on Sion's hill,
Thy word and mystery to fulfill,
Thy confessors to' approve:
Thy members on Thy throne to place,
And stamp Thy name on every face
In glorious heavenly love.[111]

Nevertheless God's judgment is real, and it will fall on nations and on individuals. In the context of a national fear of invasion he wrote:

Great God, whose wrath in ancient times
O'erflowed Thy sinful people's crimes;
Whose angry voice again I hear,
Which thundered in Ezekiel's ear;
Stir up Thy mercy with Thy power,
And arm us for the fiery hour.[112]

Charles then powerfully depicts the righteous people who intercede for the wicked as did Abram for Sodom, and as did the men whom Ezekiel desired to stand in the gap before God and pray for Israel. This hymn is Wesley's interpretation and application of Ezekiel 9, the slaughter of the guilty, and is in 12 parts, consisting of 65 stanzas.[113]

In Jesus Christ alone is refuge and salvation; in Him alone is deliverance from the wrath of a righteous God:

O happy, happy day
That calls thy exiles home!
The heavens shall pass away,
The earth receive its doom,
Earth we shall view and heaven destroyed,
And shout above the fiery void.

These eyes shall see them fall,
Mountains, and stars, and skies!
These eyes shall see them all
Out of their ashes rise!
These lips his praises shall release
Whose nod restores the universe!

> *Then let us wait the sound*
> *That shall our souls release,*
> *And labour to be found*
> *Of him in spotless peace;*
> *In perfect holiness renewed,*
> *Adorned with Christ, and meet for God!*[114]

This hymn was intended to be sung "At the parting of friends" and illustrates the joyful seriousness existent among the early Methodist societies.

Heaven and the Life Everlasting

Another of Charles Wesley's strong persuasives to draw sinners from their evil ways to God was to "describe heaven." Although he has to confess gaps in his knowledge of the geography and the life of that blessed place, such a place there is, and he uses what he knows of it to draw men to Jesus and to more fully and pictorially depict the Christian's destiny. Charles pokes satirical fun at people who look on earth's "real estate" as permanent. He sees this view of "reality" as illusion and folly:

> *How weak the thoughts and vain*
> *Of self-deluding men!*
> *Men, who fixed to earth alone*
> *Think their houses shall endure,*
> *Fondly call their lands their own,*
> *To their distant heirs secure!*[115]

But there is "an inheritance incorruptible, and undefiled, and that fadeth not away, reserved in heaven for you" (1 Pet. 1:4), and Charles explores all the adjectives in Greek and English to help us see what real estate is:

> *How happy then are we,*
> *Who build, O Lord, on thee!*
> *What can our foundation shock?*
> *Though the shattered earth remove,*
> *Stands our city on a rock,*
> *On the rock of heavenly love.*
>
> *A house we call our own,*
> *Which cannot be o'erthrown:*
> *In the general ruin sure,*
> *Storms and earthquakes it defies,*
> *Built immovably secure,*
> *Built eternal in the skies.*

> *Those amaranthine bowers,*
> *Unalienably ours,*
> *Bloom, our infinite reward,*
>   *Rise, our permanent abode,*
> *From the founded world prepared*
>   *Purchased by the blood of God!*[116]

Of this permanent abode, we have a taste now in our own spirits. This we noted earlier as part of the witness of the Holy Spirit to forgiveness and adoption, but to every soul "thirsty for God" Charles Wesley offers this persuasive to come to Christ:

> *Ye thirsty for God,*
>   *To Jesus give ear;*
> *And take through His blood*
>   *A power to draw near;*
> *His kind invitation*
>   *Ye sinners embrace,*
> *The sense of salvation*
>   *Accepting through grace.*
>
> *O Saviour of all,*
>   *Thy word we believe,*
> *And come at Thy call,*
>   *Thy grace to receive;*
> *The blessing is given*
>   *Wherever thou art;*
> *The earnest of heaven*
>   *Is love in the heart.*[117]

The inward heaven is part of the heaven of heavens, the "permanent abode" of the people of God!

> *Jesu, if still the same thou art,*
>   *If all thy promises are sure,*
> *Set up thy kingdom in my heart,*
>   *And make me rich, for I am poor;*
> *To me be all thy treasures given,*
> *The kingdom of an inward heaven.*

And again,

> *O shed it in my heart abroad,*
> *Fulness of love—of heaven—of God!*[118]

Finally, the Spirit of God himself will lead and direct every faithful soul to that "permanent abode," even if the way there is such a trackless wilderness as the Israelites traveled through on the way to

Canaan. Put Heb. 11:13-14 and 1 Pet. 2:11 down beside Exod. 13:20-22, and you have the background to a comforting and strengthening hymn that has been described as "the marching song of the pilgrim church."

> *Leader of faithful souls, and guide*
> *Of all that travel to the sky,*
> *Come, and with us, even us abide,*
> *Who would on thee alone rely*
> *On thee alone our spirits stay,*
> *While held on life's uneven way.*

> *Strangers and pilgrims here below,*
> *This earth, we know, is not our place,*
> *And hasten through the vale of woe,*
> *And restless to behold thy face,*
> *Swift to our heavenly country move,*
> *Our everlasting home above.*

> *We have no 'biding city here,*
> *But seek a city out of sight;*
> *Thither our steady course we steer,*
> *Aspiring to the plains of light,*
> *Jerusalem, the saints' abode,*
> *Whose founder is the living God.*

> *Patient th' appointed race to run*
> *This weary world we cast behind:*
> *From strength to strength we travel on*
> *The New Jerusalem to find;*
> *Our labour this, our only aim,*
> *To find the New Jerusalem.*

> *Through thee, who all our sins hast borne,*
> *Freely and graciously forgiven,*
> *With songs to Zion we return,*
> *Contending for our native heaven,*
> *The palace of our glorious king—*
> *We find it nearer while we sing.*

> *Raised by the breath of love divine,*
> *We urge our way with strength renewed;*
> *The church of the first-born to join,*
> *We travel to the mount of God;*
> *With joy upon our heads arise,*
> *And meet our Captain in the skies.*[119]

And it is all in Christ!

> *To me with Thy dear Name are given,*
> *Pardon and holiness, and heaven![120]*

Hell

There is but one hymn on hell in the 1780 hymnbook, but this is far from all that Charles Wesley has to say about the lost estate in eternity. He writes of "the burning pit":

> *O unexhausted grace!*
> *O love unsearchable!*
> *I am not gone to my own place,*
> *I am not yet in hell!*
> *Earth doth not open yet*
> *My soul to swallow up,*
> *And hanging o'er the burning pit,*
> *I still am forced to hope.*

And what is that hope but the hope of heaven, home, and the blessed face of the Savior himself?—

> *I hope at last to find*
> *The kingdom from above,*
> *The settled peace, the constant mind,*
> *The everlasting love:*
> *The sanctifying grace*
> *That makes me meet for home;*
> *I hope to see Thy glorious face*
> *Where sin can never come.[121]*

He writes also of "endless misery":

> *O Thou who wouldst not have*
> *One wretched sinner die,*
> *Who diedst thyself my soul to save,*
> *From endless misery.[122]*

He also pictures death and hell as pursuers of the soul:

> *To thee my last distress I bring!*
> *The heightened fear of death I find;*
> *The tyrant brandishing his sting,*
> *Appears, and hell is close behind.[123]*

Thus, there may be but one hymn devoted exclusively to the fear of hell, so far as the 1780 book is concerned; but Charles Wesley kept sinners and saints alike aware of the awful possibility of eternal damnation. To the saints he put a prayer in their hearts:

> *Help me to watch and pray,*
> *And on Thyself rely;*
> *Assured if I my trust betray,*
> *I shall forever die!*[124]

To sinners he balanced the sure possibility of hell with overwhelming promises of saving grace. They could all be "brands plucked from the burning" both of sin and evil in this life and the endless burnings beyond death. Nevertheless he did not allow men to lose sight of the fact of the terrible consequence of unbelief. There is One who

> *Consigns the men who will not know*
> *Their God, to everlasting woe,*
> *And makes damnation sure.*[125]

> *Alas, ye scorn the Lord to fear,*
> *To work out your salvation here,*
>   *Or all for Christ forego:*
> *His needy members ye despise,*
> *And shut against the light your eyes,*
>   *To lift them up—below!*[126]

Writing of the rich man in Luke 16, Charles Wesley asks,

> *Why is he doom'd to endless pain?*
> *Did he by fraud his wealth obtain?*

and he summarily answers,

> *No; but the blessings given*
> *On his rich neighbors he bestow'd,*
> *Enjoy'd himself instead of God,*
> *And sought no other heaven . . .*

> *And who from earth their joys receive,*
> *Their joys they soon, like him, shall leave*
> *For that eternal flame.*[127]

Even in this poem, however, Charles Wesley, ever the passionate evangelist, offers gospel hope. The final five verses expound the gospel of the New Testament, urging us to read and believe. Charles concludes with:

> *The sinner poor Thy Word believes,*
> *As full sufficient proof receives*
>   *What Thou art pleased to impart:*
> *But love alone can change the will,*
> *But only Gilead's balm can heal*
>   *The blindness of my heart.*[128]

=15
Sense and Sound

*I*T IS DIFFICULT FOR US TO UNDERSTAND WHY, after 1,700 years of hymn singing, hymn music for congregational song should have been so poor and dull, but we have ample witness that it was. The pedestrian plod did not merely predominate; it ruled at the keyboard and in the pew. Music for congregational singing was in very poor shape when the Wesley brothers arrived on the scene, and until the work of Isaac Watts, father of English hymnody, the poetry had been little better.

In Susanna Wesley's kitchen college in the Epworth parsonage, classes opened every morning with the singing of a psalm, and they closed at evening with the singing of another; but as far as we can tell, music was not in the curriculum.

The young Wesleys worshiped in the old Epworth church where their father was the rector, and there the praises of the people were expressed in lifeless and monotonous music led by "unawakened striplings," as John describes what was possibly a boy choir of sorts. The words were mostly, if not entirely, the psalms of David manipulated to rhyme in a manner later described by John as "scandalous doggerel." Tate and Brady had done their best, but it was not calculated to set either the pews or the Thames on fire. It seems not to have mattered too much which of the psalters was used—the music was still stilted and wingless. The old Sternhold and Hopkins version of 1562; the attempt at newness in the new version by Tate and Brady appearing in 1696, with a supplement in 1700; and Playford's attempted update of 1677—none of them injected vitality into English congregational praise. Isaac Watts's publication *Psalms and Spiritual Songs*, published when John Wesley was about four years old and in the year of Charles Wesley's birth, did improve the situation somewhat; but it took the Methodist Revival to set free the praises of the people of God in the 18th century. "The Methodist song," wrote Benson, "in its spiritual spontaneity, its fervor and its gladness, fulfilled to a remarkable degree the Apostolic ideal of Christian Song; and the injunctions of Wesley inevitably recall the figure of St. Paul, not so much to stimulate as to regulate the 'tongues,' and to deal prudently with their excesses and infelicities."[1]

For, strange as it may seem, although both John and Charles Wesley had strong musical instincts and natural gifts for music, it would seem that John was the dominant partner when it came to the singing of the congregations or Methodist societies.

The Holy Club at Oxford University, started by Charles but led by John, used to sing psalms, and it was at that time they discovered the *New Version of the Psalter*, by Tate and Brady. This book contained some new tunes that attracted the brothers, especially John, and some of those melodies he came to love and to use in later hymnbooks. Tunes such as those named "Hanover" and "St. Matthew" were included in John's first tune-book.

The Foundery Tune-Book, produced by John Wesley for the use of his congregation in his first chapel, was published in 1742. In it were tunes in more than a dozen meters with attention paid to the pitch of these tunes. It has been described as one of the worst hymnbooks ever published, and it scarcely suggests that John excelled as an editor of hymn tunes to the same standard as he did in the editing of Charles's words or the translating of Spanish and German hymns. Nevertheless, some tunes still being sung by English congregations were first used by Methodists at the old broken-down gun factory. "Easter Hymn," for example, must have been a thrilling sound as it broke out early Easter morning from the hearts and lips of the recently redeemed as they celebrated the resurrection victory of their new Master and Lord.

However, the Methodists were not confined to the use of hymn and chorale music from the older English or Moravian books. They broke new ground by gearing popular melodies to gospel truth. It is said that William Booth, the founder of the Salvation Army, grudged the devil any of the good tunes, by which presumably is meant those toe-tapping or nostalgic melodies that people inherit as folk songs or pick up from entertainers. The Wesleys soon discovered this source also.

More than once or twice during John Wesley's life, he discussed with the Conference both the melodies his people were singing and the manner in which they were being sung. Some of the counsel given by Wesley on those occasions indicate his desire for livelier congregational singing that would still retain reverence and a worshipful spirit. In *Sacred Melody*, the successor to the Foundery book of tunes, he included a relatively long list of suggestions concerning congregational singing:

That this part of Divine Worship may be the more acceptable to God, as well as the more profitable to yourself and others, be careful to observe the following directions.

I. Learn *these Tunes* before you learn any others; afterwards learn as many as you please.

II. Sing them exactly as they are printed here, without altering or mending them at all; and if you have learned to sing them otherwise, unlearn it as soon as you can.

III. Sing *All*. See that you join with the congregation as frequently as you can. Let not a slight degree of weakness or weariness hinder you. If it is a cross to you, take it up and you will find it a blessing.

IV. Sing *lustily* and with a good courage. Beware of singing as if you were half dead, or half asleep; but lift up your voice with strength. Be no more afraid of your voice now, nor more ashamed of its being heard, than when you sung the songs of *Satan*.

V. Sing *modestly*. Do not bawl, so as to be heard above or distinct from the rest of the congregation, that you may not destroy the harmony; but strive to unite your voices together, so as to make one clear melodious sound.

VI. Sing in *Time*. Whatever time is sung be sure to keep with it. Do not run before nor stay behind; but attend close to the leading voices, and move therewith as exactly as you can; and take care not to sing *too slow*. This drawling way naturally steals on all who are lazy; and it is high time to drive it out from among us, and sing all our tunes just as quick as we did at first.

VII. Above all sing *spiritually*. Have an eye to God in every word you sing. Aim at pleasing *Him* more than yourself, or any other creature. In order to do this attend strictly to the sense of what you sing, and see that your *Heart* is not carried away with the sound, but offered to God continually; so shall your singing be such as the *Lord* will approve of here, and reward when He cometh in the clouds of heaven.[2]

That seems to suggest that at least some Methodist societies were in danger of singing too enthusiastically. The "bawlers" and the "self-pleasers" seem to have numbered more than a few! Was John having a little difficulty keeping his "people" musically respectable?

Sacred Melody was really the first section of *Select Hymns with Tunes, Annex T*, which contained 133 hymns with a music section of 102 tunes following, and 12 pages of introduction headed "The Gamut, or Scale of Music," carrying the "tunes that are in common use" among the societies. Some of the tunes were plain going, but others rather demanding on any congregation, and a great proportion of them were in minor keys. Still others required some rather monotonous repetition of words to "use up" the tune. One tune named "Mourners" needed a repetition like

> Fix'd in my soul, I feel Thy dart;
> Groan—groan—groaning, I feel it night and day.[3]

Nevertheless, *Sacred Melody* must have been popular, for further editions of it were published in 1765 and 1770. John Wesley also published a pamphlet titled *The Grounds of Vocal Music,* which treated the basics of music as he saw them and gave seven "lessons for exercising the voice."

Despite the florid nature of one or two hymn tunes of Wesley's choice, he appears to have had quite a distaste for what he called "modern music" in which harmony was dominant:

> It is true, the modern music has been sometimes observed to have as powerful an effect as the ancient . . . But when was this? Generally, if not always, when a fine solo was sung; when "the sound has been an echo to the sense"; when the music has been extremely simple and inartificial, the composer having attended to melody, not harmony . . . It is this, it is counterpoint, it is harmony (so-called) which destroys the power of music. And if ever this should be banished from our composition, if ever we should return to the simplicity and melody of the ancients, then the effects of our music will be as surprising as any that were wrought by theirs; yea, perhaps they will be as much greater, as modern instruments are more excellent than those of the ancients.[4]

In Wesley's day, Conference after Conference took up discussions sometimes brief, at other times quite lengthy, on the matter of congregational praise. The societies were directed to "learn our own tunes first," not "to sing too slow," not to "learn new tunes till they are perfect in the old," to have "everyone in the congregation to sing, not one in ten only," to "pitch the tune properly."

They were to

> beware of formality in singing, as it will creep upon us unawares. Is it not creeping in already by those complex tunes which it is impossible to sing with devotion? Such is "Praise the Lord, ye blessed ones." Such the long quavering Hallelujah annexed to the Morning Song tune which I defy any living man to sing devoutly. The repeating the same word so often (but especially while another repeats different words—).[5]

One part of the cure of formality in singing was, according to John, "Do not suffer the people to sing too slow"; perhaps he had "suffered long" and desired to be kind! That would be quite difficult to bear if, as was sometimes the case with 18th-century Hallelujahs, they extended to around 30 bars of music!

Neither of the brothers was predisposed to tolerate congregational singing that savored of the vulgar or the flippant; as the excesses of exuberance arose in the revival gatherings or in the society meetings, steps were taken to harness and control it. John counseled his preachers that they should, if it seemed necessary, stop the singing and ask such questions as:

> Now do you know what you said last? Did it suit your case?
> Did you sing it as to God, with the spirit and understanding also?[6]

But as the Methodist societies became more established and less threatened, the dangers of formality began to appear, and gradually questions and answers in Conference reflected the tendency. For example, the above quotation is from the 1746 minutes; in 1765 it has become necessary for Wesley to warn his people about the tendency of slow and sluggish singing contributing to formality in worship. By 1768 the emergence of singing groups or "Singers" to lead the worship of the societies led in turn to a more florid kind of singing that drew Wesley's criticism. And the minutes of 1787, just a few years before John's death, brought forth a ban on anthem singing as not conducive to fellowship in praise. For years, John had tried to steer his people clear of these particular dangers. His most caustic criticism of flowery religious music was made in Scotland in 1779, when he wrote a tract titled *Thoughts on the Power of Music.*[7]

It was not until after the death of both brothers that the Methodists began to make concessions to the principle of anthem singing in their chapel. The first such concession was made in 1796; and by 1800, less than 10 years after John's death, professional theatrical singers (we call them "stars") had been introduced into chapels to sing the more elaborate and florid parts, solos, and leads in the oratories. This is a custom now generally accepted and practiced much more widely than by Methodists.

On the other hand, while we know that Charles was fairly well skilled on the flute, he was not otherwise any more of a musician than John, and he certainly said a lot less in criticism of contemporary music. He did, however, cultivate friendship with musicians. As we saw earlier, he did this at one point to aid the music education of his two sons as they captured the ears of London society by their Marylebone recitals. And it is evident that Charles enjoyed much of the music that apparently John disliked.

Charles's astonishing variety of meters in his poetry indicates that he would not meekly submit to John's tastes in music, and it appears that some at least of those meters were related to the meters of the German chorales and to German hymnody. John found in the words of the German poets ample scope for his power as a translator, but it was the German composers rather than the poets who helped empower Charles's hymns.

Outstanding among the composers whose names appear on some of Charles Wesley's hymns are George Frideric Handel and Johann Friedrich Lampe. Haydn, too, can be associated with the Wesley hymns, but his contribution was not forthcoming until shortly after John Wesley's death.

According to Samuel Wesley, the son of Charles, G. F. Handel composed at least three tunes specifically for use with particular hymns written by Charles. The hymns that appealed to Handel were

"The Invitation"

Sinners, obey the gospel word,
Haste to the supper of my Lord;
Be wise to know your gracious day,
All things are ready; come away![8]

"Desiring to Love"

O Love Divine, how sweet Thou art!
When shall I find my longing heart
　　All taken up by Thee?
I thirst, I faint, I die to prove
The greatness of redeeming love,
　　The love of Christ to me.[9]

"On the Resurrection"

Rejoice, the Lord is King;
　　Your Lord and King adore!
Rejoice, give thanks, and sing,
　　And triumph evermore.
Lift up your heart; Lift up your voice!
Rejoice; again I say: "Rejoice!"[10]

These Wesley-Handel combinations were discovered by Samuel Wesley, Jr., and published by him in 1826 after "a lapse of seventy to eighty years," which is indeed "a circumstance of no common curiosity."[11] It is also remarkable that none of these combinations survived the pen of the editors of the Methodist Hymnal, 1964, 1966. In two instances Wesley's words were spared, but Handel's tunes were divorced from all three!

The connecting link between the Wesley brothers and these celebrated musicians was a certain Mrs. Rich, an actress and wife of the leasee of the opera house at Covent Garden. She had been converted under Charles Wesley's preaching and left the acting profession, to the annoyance of her husband.

Charles Wesley's friendship with Lampe was quite close. The musician-composer had been a deist for many years, but under the impact of John Wesley's *Earnest Appeal* had become a Christian. The two men, Charles and Johann, formed quite a close relationship, and in appreciation of the Wesleys, Lampe wrote quite a large number of tunes for Wesley's hymns. In 1746 Lampe published at his own expense a collection of 24 tunes for Wesley's *Festival Hymns*. These tunes appeared in 10 editions of Wesley's *Redemption Hymns* and in at least 2 other Wesley collections.

Brother John obviously had been impressed by Lampe's tunes also and actually wished that he had known more about him earlier than he had. Although some of the tunes were rather "classically florid," most of them were enjoyably singable and have survived fairly well, such as those called "Invitation," "Crucifixion," "Derby," "Funeral," and "Chapel" (or "Chappel").

When Lampe died, it seemed to Charles Wesley that he had been transferred to higher service as music director in heaven!

> 'Tis done! the Sovereign's will's obey'd,
> The soul, by angel-guards convey'd
>   Has took its seat on high;
> The brother of my choice has gone
> To music sweeter than his own,
>   And concerts in the sky.
>
> Our number and our bliss complete,
> And summon all the choir to meet
>   Thy glorious throne around;
> The whole musician-band bring in,
> And give the signal to begin,
>   And let the trumpet sound.[12]

Charles Wesley, then, was not a musician, but his interest and pleasure in serious music went very far beyond its surface. Lightwood reminds us of a couple of Charles's poetical quips that reveal a little of his opinions. On a copy on Handel's *Lessons* used by his sons, he scribbled:

> Here all the mystic powers of sound,
> The soul of Harmony is found.
> Its perfect chapter receives,
> And Handel <u>dead</u> for ever lives![13]

Joseph Kelway, young Samuel's music master, was a disciple and friend of Handel. On the script for one of Kelway's sonatas being studied by Samuel, Charles wrote:

> Kelway's sonatas who can hear,
> They want both harmony and air,
> Heavy they make the player's hand,
> And who their tricks can understand?
> Kelway to the profound G [Giardini],
> Or B [Boyce] compared, is but a ninny,
> A dotard old (The moderns tell ye)
> Mad after Handel and Corelli,
> Spoilt by the original disaster,
> For Geminiani was his Master,
> And taught him, in his nature's ground,
> To gape for sense as well as sound.
> 'Tis thus the leaders of our nation,
> Smit with the music most in fashion,
> Thus absolute decisions deal,
> As from the chair infallible,
> And praise the fine Italian taste,
> Too fine—too exquisite to last![14]

Giardini was a violinist very popular around the 1760s but remembered hymnwise only by his hymn tune "Moscow," to which we now sing "Thou Whose Almighty Word." Another version of the tune, "Italian Hymn," is better known in the United States. It is the tune to which "Come, Thou Almighty King" is sung. Kelway was an outstanding organist controlling music at St. Martins-in-the-field, Trafalgar Square. Boyce was a close friend to Charles Wesley and his family. On the death of Boyce, Charles Wesley wrote a funeral hymn coupling Boyce with the then departed and, according to Wesley, glorified Handel:

> Father of harmony, farewell!
> Farewell for a few fleeting years!
> Translated from the mournful vale,
> Jehovah's flowing ministers
> Have borne thee to thy place above,
> Where all is harmony and love.

Handel, and all the tuneful train,
  Who well employed their art divine
To' announce the great Messiah's reign,
  In joyous acclamations join,
And, springing from their azure seat,
With shouts their new-born brother greet.[15]

Hymns Sung to Popular Melodies

It is difficult to say with any real sense of finality just how many hymns Charles Wesley wrote to be sung to popular song tunes or folk music, but it is certain that he did write some. He was naturally gifted with a facility of expression that enabled him to express poetically what he saw going on around him. John Kirk wrote concerning him:

> During his student-life at Oxford, his brother John often dreaded to see him enter his study. Mentally absorbed in the manufacture of his glowing lines, and the "fine phrenzy" rolling at its flood, he sometimes upset the table and scattered its contents on the floor. Anon he would ask half-a-dozen questions without waiting for a single reply, repeat a few lines which he had just made, and finally hurry away to write down what he had composed during these eccentric moments, leaving the study in a state of great confusion. The same impulse was upon him during the heyday of life, and gave birth to appropriate hymns in the suddenest emergency.[16]

It is said that one of these sudden emergencies occurred while Charles was preaching in a southern seaport. Intent upon breaking up the service, a group of sailors who had had too much alcohol burst in on the singing with one of their own popular but lewd songs called "Nancy Dawson." Charles quickly caught the tune and measure of the ditty and was prepared for the next interruption. It came at the next service, and he quickly gave out his words to the "Nancy Dawson" tune. Seven verses he gave out, and that seems to have been enough, and the sea salts, taken in their own net, gave up the fight and allowed the meeting to proceed. Here are some of the lines:

Listed into the cause of sin,
  Why should a good be evil?
Music, alas! too long has been,
  Prest to obey the devil.
Drunken, or lewd, or light the lay,
  Flowed to the soul's undoing.
Widen'd, and strewed with flowers the way
  Down to eternal ruin.

> *Come, let us try if Jesu's love*
>   *Will not as well inspire us;*
> *This is the theme of those above,*
>   *This upon earth shall fire us.*
> *Say, if your hearts are tuned to sing,*
>   *Is there a subject greater?*
> *Harmony all its strains may bring,*
>   *Jesus's name is sweeter.*[17]

In his "Directions for Singing," John Wesley had been pretty firm in his insistence that his people "strictly attend to the sense of what" they sang. He commanded them to pay heed to the words and their meaning as having preeminence and superiority to the music to which the words were set. It was a sentiment of which Charles heartily approved. In a poem that is titled "Another" to that quoted above, he wrote:

> *Still let us on our guard be found,*
> *And watch against the power of sound,*
>   *With sacred jealousy;*
> *Lest haply sense should damp our zeal*
> *And music's charms bewitch and steal*
>   *Our hearts away from Thee.*[18]

Thus, whatever may be said of Charles Wesley's enlistment of popular melodies, he would certainly avoid all music that he considered not conducive to the greater glory of God.

> *That hurrying strife far off remove,*
> *That noisy burst of selfish love,*
> *Which swells the formal song . . .*
>
> *Jesus, Thyself in us reveal,*
> *And all our faculties shall feel*
> *Thine harmonizing name.*
>
> *With calmly reverential joy*
> *We then shall all our lives employ*
> *In setting forth Thy love . . .*[19]

Just as some of Charles's hymns and poems were rooted in ideas, and sometimes the very expressions that were used in classical and contemporary literature,[20] so some of the hymns were written not only to express faith or Christian experience but also because Charles sensed a higher use for a fine melody of composition.

The relationship of "sound and sense" in the Wesley hymns is really quite remarkable. Charles Wesley's verses were written in at least

20 different meters; thus, save for those hymns written to a particular tune, whether popular or classical, Lampe or whoever had a very wide and varied field in which to work their genius. In addition, the Revival called for tunes of many kinds. There had to be tunes that suited the hymns for the repentant sinner turning from the error of his ways, and tunes for the saint of many years as he praised the Lord in personal devotion, and others for worship, fellowship, and evangelism.

> Depth of mercy! Can there be
> Mercy still reserved for me?
> Can my God His wrath forbear?
> Me, the chief of sinners spare?[21]

Those verses called for music that breathed penitence and conviction. But the words

> He hath ransomed our race,
> O how shall we praise
> Or worthily sing Thy unspeakable grace?[22]

cried out for a toe-tapping and joyful tune. It was really John Wesley's insights that made many of the weddings of sense and sound, which partly explains his preface to the 1761 collection, Sacred Melody, which carried 140 tunes that met all the requirements of all the meters used by Charles:

> I want the people called Methodists to sing true the tunes which are in common use among them. At the same time I want them to have in one volume the best hymns which we have printed: and that, in a small and portable volume, and one of an easy price. I have been endeavouring for more than twenty years to procure such a book as this. But in vain: Masters of music were above following any direction but their own. And I was determined, whoever compiled this, should follow my direction: Not mending our tunes, but setting down, neither better nor worse than they were. At length I have prevailed. The following collection contains all the tunes which are in common use among us. They are pricked true, exactly as I desire all our congregations may sing them: And here is the prefixt to them a collection of those hymns which are (I think) some of the best we have published. The volume likewise is small as well as the price. This, therefore, I recommend preferable to all others.[23]

One 18th-century divine, probably somewhat alarmed by the attractive powers of Methodism over the populace, said, "For one who has been drawn away by doctrine, 10 have been induced by music."[24] It was an understatement, for in the persuasive powers of Charles Wesley it was both: here was sense wedded to sound.[25]

EPILOGUE

The Passing of the Man with the Dancing Heart

Born December 18, 1707, Charles Wesley joined "all the ship's company" March 29, 1788, being 80 years and three months of age.

"I visited him several times in his last sickness, and his body was indeed reduced to the most extreme state of weakness. He possessed that state of mind which he had been always pleased to see in others—unaffected humility, and holy resignation to the will of God. He had no transports of joy, but solid hope and unshaken confidence in Christ, which kept his mind in perfect peace. A few days before his death he composed the following lines. Having been silent and quiet for some time, he called Mrs. Wesley to him, and bid her write as he dictated." Mrs. Wesley herself headed the copy in her hymnbook thus, "The following lines I wrote from Mr. Charles Wesley's repeating, a few days before he departed ys. [this] Life."[1]

Extremely weak, and unable to hold a pen, Charles, with "a mind as calm as a summer evening," dictated the following verses to his long-loved and ever-beloved Sally:

> In age and feebleness extream,
> Who shall a helpless worm redeem?
> Jesus, my only Hope thou art,
> Strength of my failing flesh and heart,
> O could I catch a smile from Thee,
> And drop into eternity![2]

Charles Wesley died the death of the righteous: "the end of that man" was "peace" (Ps. 37:37). He had so often prayed that his passing would be calm and confident, and when his hour came, it seemed like a positive answer to the desire expressed by a fellow poet:

> So be my passing!
> My task accomplished and the long day done,
> My wages taken, and in my heart
> Some late lark singing:
> May I be gathered to the west,
> The sundown splendid and serene—Death![3]

Just a few years before he died, the man with the dancing heart
had written

> Soft! attend that awful Sound!
>   Earth receives her borrowed clay,
> BUT—the sky-born Soul is found
>   In mansions of eternal day:
> Borne thro' the Open Fount of Jesus' blood,
> He springs! He flies! He 'scapes into the arms of God! . . .
>
> There the pure inraptured Spirit
> Doth his Lord's delight inherit,
>   Doth the Father's glory see!
> There in hymns or silent praises
> Blest on our Redeemer gazes,
>   Blest thro' all Eternity.[4]

And so, singing to the last, and Anglican to the end, his corpse
was borne to Marylebone churchyard, because he did not desire to be
laid in unconsecrated ground, and buried there. What matters it now
to Brother Charles that Marylebone graveyard had never been consecrated? Whitehead wrote:

> On his tombstone were the following lines, written by himself
> on the death of one of his friends: they could not be more aptly ap-
> plied to any person, than to Mr. Charles Wesley:
>
> > With poverty of spirit bless'd,
> > Rest, happy Saint, in Jesus rest;
> > A Sinner sav'd, through grace forgiv'n,
> > Redeem'd from earth to reign in heav'n!
> > Thy labours of unwearied love,
> > By thee forgot, are crown'd above;
> > Crown'd, through the mercy of thy Lord,
> > With a free, full, immense reward![5]

NOTES

Introduction

1. Frank Baker, *Charles Wesley as Revealed by His Letters* (London: Epworth Press, 1948), 1.

2. Maldwyn Edwards, *Sons to Samuel* (London: Epworth Press, 1961), 82.

3. F. Luke Wiseman, "All Saints Day: Suitable Hymns," *Methodist Recorder*, October 22, 1936, 17.

Chapter 1

1. Hymn 22 in *A Collection of Hymns for the Use of the People Called Methodists*, ed. Franz Hildebrandt and Oliver Beckerlegge, vol. 7 of *The Works of John Wesley* (Oxford: Clarendon Press, 1983). See also Hymn 428 in *The Methodist Hymnal* (Nashville: Methodist Publishing House, 1964).

2. *The Letters of the Rev. John Wesley, M.A.*, ed. John Telford (London: Epworth Press, 1931), 1:286. This source is referred to in subsequent endnotes as *The Letters of John Wesley*.

3. *The Poetical Works of John and Charles Wesley*, ed. G. Osborn (London: Wesleyan Methodist Conference Office, 1868-72), 3:72.

4. George J. Stevenson, *Memorials of the Wesley Family* (London: S. W. Partridge Co., 1876), 106-9, 193.

5. Hymns 218 and 210 in *A Collection of Hymns for the Use of the People Called Methodists*.

6. George J. Stevenson, *Memorials of the Wesley Family*, 110.

7. Ibid., 198.

8. Ibid., 199.

9. Ibid., 263.

10. Arthur Quiller-Couch, *Hetty Wesley* (London: Dent, 1903), 244.

11. George J. Stevenson, *Memorials of the Wesley Family*, 231.

12. Letter to Dr. Candler, April 28, 1785. See also Maldwyn Edwards, *Family Circle* (London: Epworth Press, 1949), 101.

13. Maximin Piette, *John Wesley in the Evolution of Protestantism* (London: Sheed and Ward, 1938), 226.

14. Baker, *Charles Wesley as Revealed by His Letters*, 6.

Chapter 2

1. Baker, *Charles Wesley as Revealed by His Letters*, 8-9.

2. Ibid., 11.

3. *The Works of John Wesley*, ed. Thomas Jackson (London: 1825-31), 6:447. All subsequent citations of this title refer to this edition unless otherwise noted.

4. Baker, *Charles Wesley as Revealed by His Letters*, 16.

5. Ibid., 12.

6. Ibid.

7. Ibid., 13.

8. Ibid., 14.

9. Ibid., 15-16.

10. Ibid.

11. Ibid., 16.

12. Ibid.

13. Ibid.

14. Ibid., 18.

15. Ibid., 17.

16. *The Journal of the Rev. John Wesley, M.A.*, ed. Nehemiah Curnock (London: Epworth Press, 1938), 8:266-68. This source is referred to in subsequent endnotes as *The Journal of John Wesley*.

17. Ibid., 266-67.

18. *George Whitefield's Journal* (London: Banner of Truth Trust, 1960), 45-46.

19. Ibid., 50-51.

20. Quoted by Rev. John Gillies, comp., in *Memoirs of the Life of the Rev. George Whitefield, M.A.*, first edition (London: printed for Edward and Charles Dilley, 1772), 2.

21. Ibid., 2-3.

22. Ibid., 6-7.

23. *George Whitefield's Journal*, 45-46.

24. Ibid., 47.

25. *The Works of John Wesley*, 11:367.

26. A. K. Walker, *William Law, His Life and Work* (London: SPCK [Society for Promoting Christian Knowledge], 1973), 96.

27. Ibid., 96-97.

28. Charles Wesley, *Wesley's Hymns* (London: John Mason, 1849), No. 529, v. 4.

29. Ibid., v. 1.

30. *The Letters of John Wesley*, 6:66.

31. Baker, *Charles Wesley as Revealed by His Letters*, 18-19; and Frederick C. Gill, *Charles Wesley: The First Methodist* (London: Lutterworth Press, 1964), 42-43.

32. Baker, *Charles Wesley as Revealed by His Letters*, 19.

33. Thomas Jackson, *The Life of the Rev. Charles Wesley, M.A.* (London: John Mason, 1841), 1:34.

34. Baker, *Charles Wesley as Revealed by His Letters*, 19.

35. *Memoirs of the Rev. Charles Wesley, M.A.*, ed. Thomas Jackson (London: John Mason, 1848), 19.

36. *The Letters of John Wesley*, 2:134.

Chapter 3

1. Baker, *Charles Wesley as Revealed by His Letters*, 22.

2. *The Poetical Works of John and Charles Wesley*, 4:316.

3. Baker, *Charles Wesley as Revealed by His Letters*, 22.

4. William B. Peabody, "Life of James Oglethorpe: The Founder of Georgia," in *Makers of American History* (New York: University Society, 1905), 2:92.

5. Samuel Wesley, Jr., *Poems on Several Occasions* (Cambridge, England: Cambridge University Press, 1743), 142.

6. Leslie F. Church, *Oglethorpe: A Study of Philanthropy in England and Georgia* (London: Epworth Press, 1932), 2.

7. Peabody, "Life of James Oglethorpe: The Founder of Georgia," in *Makers of American History*, 92.

8. Martin Schmidt, *The Young Wesley* (London: Epworth Press, 1961), 35-36.

9. Piette, *John Wesley in the Evolution of Protestantism*, 299.

10. Edwards, *Sons to Samuel*, 36-37.

11. Luke Tyerman, *The Life and Times of the Rev. John Wesley, M.A.* (New York: Harper and Brothers, 1872), 1:121.

12. It is accurately and wittily told by Willie Snow Etheridge in *Strange Fire* (New York: Vanguard Press, 1971), 100-110.

13. Baker, *Charles Wesley as Revealed by His Letters*, 22.

14. Ibid., 23.

15. *The Journal of the Rev. Charles Wesley, M.A.* (Kansas City: Beacon Hill Press of Kansas City, 1980), 1:1. This source is referred to in subsequent endnotes as *The Journal of Charles Wesley*.

16. Ibid., 4.
17. Ibid., 5.
18. Ibid., 12.
19. Ibid., 6.
20. Jackson, *Memoirs of the Rev. Charles Wesley, M.A.*, 34-35.
21. *The Journal of Charles Wesley*, 1:15.
22. Ibid., 21-22.
23. Ibid., 35.
24. Ibid.
25. Ibid., 36.
26. Baker, *Charles Wesley as Revealed by His Letters*, 26.
27. John Whitehead, *The Life of the Rev. John Wesley, M.A., and the Life of the Rev. Charles Wesley, M.A.*, two volumes in one (London: Stephen Cauchman, 1796), 95-96.
28. Ibid.
29. Ibid., 90.
30. *The Journal of Charles Wesley*, 1:55-56.

Chapter 4

1. Baker, *Charles Wesley as Revealed by His Letters*, 29.
2. *The Journal of John Wesley*, 1:475-76.
3. *The Poetical Works of John and Charles Wesley*, 1:300. Verse 7 in this hymn also begins the popular hymn "O for a Thousand Tongues."
4. Ibid., 1:299.
5. *The Journal of John Wesley*, 1:436-37.
6. Ibid., 460.
7. V. H. H. Green, *The Young Mr. Wesley* (London: Edwin Arnold, 1961), 281.
8. *The Journal of Charles Wesley*, 1:82.
9. Ibid., 86.
10. Ibid., 88.
11. See *The Journal of John Wesley*.
12. *The Journal of Charles Wesley*, 1:88.
13. Ibid., 89.
14. Ibid., 90.
15. *The Journal of John Wesley*, 1:463.
16. *The Poetical Works of John and Charles Wesley*, 1:105-6.
17. Ibid., 5:403.
18. *The Journal of Charles Wesley*, 1:90-93.
19. *The Journal of John Wesley*, 1:463-64.
20. Ibid., 464-65.
21. Edwards, *Sons to Samuel*, 57-58.
22. *The Journal of Charles Wesley*, 1:95.
23. *The Poetical Works of John and Charles Wesley*, 1:83.
24. *The Journal of Charles Wesley*, 1:94.

Chapter 5

1. *The Poetical Works of John and Charles Wesley*, 5:111-13.
2. Whitehead, *The Life of the Rev. John Wesley, M.A., and the Life of the Rev. Charles Wesley, M.A.*, 106. Cf. *The Journal of Charles Wesley*, 1:100-118.
3. Baker, *Charles Wesley as Revealed by His Letters*, 33.
4. *The Journal of Charles Wesley*, 1:98.
5. Ibid., 99.
6. Ibid., 109-10.
7. See Charles Colson, *Life Sentence* (Lincoln, Va.: Chosen Books, 1979).
8. *The Journal of Charles Wesley*, 1:117.
9. Ibid., 120.
10. Ibid.

11. Ibid.
12. Ibid., 121.
13. Ibid., 122.
14. Ibid., 122-23.
15. Ibid., 123.
16. Ibid., 130.
17. Ibid., 133.
18. Whitehead, *The Life of the Rev. John Wesley, M.A., and the Life of the Rev. Charles Wesley, M.A.,* 115-16.
19. Ibid., 116.
20. *The Journal of Charles Wesley,* 1:148.
21. Ibid., 154.
22. Ibid., 155.
23. Ibid., 155-56.
24. Ibid., 146.
25. *The Journal of John Wesley,* 2:159.
26. Ibid., 157.
27. Ibid., 158.
28. *The Journal of Charles Wesley,* 1:164-65.
29. Ibid., 166.
30. Ibid., 166-67.
31. Norman Sykes, *From Sheldon to Secker: Aspects of England Church History* (Cambridge, England: Cambridge University Press, 1974), 92.
32. Quoted by Anthony Armstrong, *The Church of England, the Methodist and Society* (London: University of London Press, 1973), 9-10.
33. *The Letters of John Wesley,* 3:224.
34. Frank Baker, *John Wesley and the Church of England* (London: Epworth Press, 1970), 164-66.

Chapter 6

1. Title of chap. 4 of Edwards, *Sons to Samuel,* 62-84.
2. *Standard Sermons of John Wesley,* ed. Edward H. Sugden (London: Epworth Press, 1921), 1:68 ff.
3. *The Poetical Works of John and Charles Wesley,* 105-6. This is part of Hymn 12: "For a Preacher of the Gospel."
4. *The Letters of John Wesley,* 5:15.
5. *The Journal of Charles Wesley,* 1:444.
6. Ibid., 443.
7. Ibid., 447.
8. Ibid., 319.
9. Ibid., 337.
10. Ibid., 337-38.
11. *The Journal of John Wesley,* 1:98-104.
12. *The Journal of Charles Wesley,* 1:338-39.
13. Ibid., 339.
14. Ibid., 340.
15. Ibid.
16. *The Poetical Works of John and Charles Wesley,* 5:366, 467.
17. *The Journal of John Wesley,* 2:227.
18. *The Poetical Works of John and Charles Wesley,* 4:371-72.

Chapter 7

1. *The Journal of John Wesley,* 3:22 ff.
2. Adam Clarke, *The Holy Bible: Old and New Testaments, with Comments and Critical Notes* (Nashville: Abingdon Cokesbury Press, 1831), commentary on Prov. 31:10. See al-

so Clarke's remarks on Susanna Wesley as comparable to the virtuous woman of Prov. 31:10-31 in his *Memoirs of the Wesley Family* (New York: Lane and Scott, 1851), 318-420.

3. *The Journal of John Wesley*, 3:29-30.

4. *The Journal of Charles Wesley*, 1:455.

5. Ibid., 2:11.

6. Ibid., 11-12.

7. Thomas Jackson, *The Life of the Rev. Charles Wesley, M.A.* (London: John Mason, 1841), 1:520. See also 1:516-17.

8. *The Journal of Charles Wesley*, 2:54.

9. Ibid., 55.

10. Ibid., 55-56.

11. Baker, *Charles Wesley as Revealed by His Letters*, 67.

12. Ibid., 68.

13. *The Journal of Charles Wesley*, 2:64-65.

14. Jackson, *The Life of the Rev. Charles Wesley, M.A.*, 2:236-37.

15. D. M. Jones, *Charles Wesley: A Study* (London: Epworth Press, n.d.), 56.

16. *The Journal of John Wesley*, 3:440.

17. Cf. *The Letters of John Wesley*, 3:15 ff.

18. *The Journal of Charles Wesley*, 2:78.

19. Jackson, *The Life of the Rev. Charles Wesley, M.A.*, 1:566 ff.

20. Ibid., 685.

21. Ibid., 571.

Chapter 8

1. John Telford, *The Life of Rev. Charles Wesley* (London: R.T.S. [Religious Tract Society], c. 1912-13), 193.

2. Gill, *Charles Wesley: The First Methodist*, 166.

3. Frank Baker has given us a fine profile and assessment of Charles Wesley in his *Charles Wesley as Revealed by His Letters*. In the following text, selected letters are numbered as in Charles Wesley's journal and presented with the editor's footnotes.

4. *The Journal of Charles Wesley*, 2:181-84, 188-89, 195, 208, 239.

5. During the research preceding the restoration of the Holborn Cemetery following World War II, it was discovered that the ground had in fact never been "consecrated"! The remains of many a saint was sufficient "consecration," but how fitting if the Wesley brothers had been laid to rest together in the City Road Chapel burial ground, or even across the street beside Susanna in Bunhill Fields.

6. F. Luke Wiseman, *Charles Wesley* (London: Epworth Press, 1932), 229-31. See also Thomas R. Albin, *Charles Wesley: Poet and Theologian* (Nashville: Abingdon Press, 1992), 85-95.

7. Baker, *Charles Wesley as Revealed by His Letters*, 116. For six interesting letters from father to daughter, see *The Journal of Charles Wesley*, 2:275-83.

8. Robert M. Stevenson, *Patterns of Protestant Church Music* (Durham, N.C.: Duke University Press, 1953), 131.

9. James T. Lightwood, *Samuel Wesley, Musician: The Story of His Life* (London: Epworth Press, 1937), 21.

10. *Oxford History of Music* (London: Oxford University Press, 1905), 6:289.

11. Ibid.

12. *The Journal of Charles Wesley*, 2:153-54, 157-58.

13. Ibid., 158.

14 *The Letters of John Wesley*, 7:216-17.

15. Jackson, *The Life of the Rev. Charles Wesley, M.A.*, 2:360 ff.

16. Ibid., 361.

17. Ibid., 361 ff.

18. *The Journal of Charles Wesley*, 2:140-41.

19. Jackson, *The Life of the Rev. Charles Wesley, M.A.*, 2:396 ff.

20. Ibid., 2:353.

21. Ibid., 352.

22. Baker, *Charles Wesley as Revealed by His Letters*, 111.

23. From *The Journal of John Wesley*, 6:303: "I spent an agreeable hour at a concert of my nephew. But I was a little out of my element among lords and ladies. I love plain music and plain company best." Nevertheless, John attended two more concerts.

24. *The Letters of John Wesley*, 7:324.

25. Apparently for tuition and instruments.

26. Baker, *Charles Wesley as Revealed by His Letters*, 113.

27. Quoted by James T. Lightwood in *The Music of the Methodist Hymnbook* (London: Epworth Press, 1935), 14-15.

28. George J. Stevenson, *Memorials of the Wesley Family*, 471.

29. Ibid., 472.

30. Ibid., 475.

31. Ibid., 477.

32. *The Journal of Charles Wesley*, 2:276-77.

33. George J. Stevenson, *Memorials of the Wesley Family*, 475-76.

34. Ibid., 474, in his letter to Adam Clarke.

35. Ibid., in the same letter.

36. Ibid., in the same letter.

37. Ibid., in the same letter.

38. Mrs. Richard Smith, *The Life of Rev. Henry Moore* (New York, n.p., 1845), 305-7.

39. George J. Stevenson, *Memorials of the Wesley Family*, 486-87.

40. *The Poetical Works of John and Charles Wesley*, 2:317-19. These words are repeated eight times in these lines by Charles Wesley.

Chapter 9

1. Hymn 30 in *A Collection of Hymns for the Use of the People Called Methodists*.

2. Ibid., Hymn 1.

3. *The Poetical Works of John and Charles Wesley*, 1:99-100.

4. Frank Baker, *Representative Verse of Charles Wesley* (Nashville: Abingdon Press, 1962), xiv. See also *Charles Wesley's Verse* (London: Epworth Press, 1964), 13. This work is Baker's revised edition of his *Introduction to Representative Verse*.

5. *The Poetical Works of John and Charles Wesley*, 8:102.

6. Ibid., 1:333-34.

7. John Bunyan, *Pilgrim's Progress* (Westwood, N.J.: Barbour and Co., 1989), 36.

8. *The Poetical Works of John and Charles Wesley*, 5:24.

9. *The Journal of Charles Wesley*, 1:95.

10. *The Poetical Works of John and Charles Wesley*, 1:91-92.

11. Ibid., 91.

12. Ibid., 92.

13. Ibid., 105-6 (emphasis added by underlining in this and various other subsequent hymn and poetry quotes).

14. Ibid., 371-72.

15. S. G. Dimond, *The Psychology of the Methodist Revival* (London: Oxford University Press, 1926), 101 ff.

16. Ibid., 103.

Chapter 10

1. *The Poetical Works of John and Charles Wesley*, 4:175.

2. Ibid., 9:58.

3. *The Poetical Works of John and Charles Wesley*, 7:248.

4. Ibid., 4:199.

5. Ibid., 198.

6. Ibid., 203.

7. Roy H. Short, *My Great Redeemer's Praise* (Nashville: Tidings, n.d.), 3.

8. John Kirk, *Charles Wesley, the Poet of Methodism: A Lecture* (London: Hamilton Adams Co., 1860), 22.

9. *The Poetical Works of John and Charles Wesley*, 4:191.

10. Ibid.

11. Henry Bett, *The Hymns of Methodism* (London: Epworth Press, 1945), 71.

12. J. Ernest Rattenbury, *Wesley's Legacy to the World* (London: Epworth Press, 1928), 254. This is but one of many such examples.

13. *The Journal of Charles Wesley*, 1:312.

14. *The Poetical Works of John and Charles Wesley*, 9:94-95.

15. Eric Waterhouse, *The Bible in Charles Wesley's Hymns*, Fellowship Manual No. 5 (London: Epworth Press, c. 1954), no page.

16. *The Poetical Works of John and Charles Wesley*, 1:238.

17. Ibid.

18. *Sermons 1-33*, ed. Albert C. Outler, vol. 1 of *The Works of John Wesley* (Nashville: Abingdon Press, 1984), 1:104-5.

19. *The Poetical Works of John and Charles Wesley*, 1:238.

20. Ibid., 238-39.

21. Ibid., 4:196.

22. John Wesley's notes on Eph. 2:8 in *Wesley's Notes upon the New Testament* (Kansas City: Beacon Hill Press of Kansas City, 1981). Pages in this book are not numbered.

23. G. Croft Cell, *The Rediscovery of John Wesley* (New York: Henry Holt and Co., 1935), 301. This work was reprinted with identical pagination in 1983 by the University of New York Press.

24. *The Works of John Wesley*, 6:394 ff.

25. *The Poetical Works of John and Charles Wesley*, 4:196.

26. Ibid., 196-97.

27. Ibid., 199-200.

28. Ibid., 201.

29. Ibid., 169.

30. Ibid., 5:364.

31. Introduction from sermon XXIX in *Standard Sermons of John Wesley*, 1:226-27.

32. *The Poetical Works of John and Charles Wesley*, 1:99.

33. *The Works of John Wesley*, 11:240.

Chapter 11

1. See Robert E. Chiles, *Theological Transition in American Methodism: 1790-1935* (Nashville: Abingdon Press, 1965), 38.

2. *The Journal of John Wesley*, 1:38 ff.

3. Quoted by Robert Stevenson in *Patterns of Protestant Church Music*, 716.

4. Frank Whaling, ed., *John and Charles Wesley: Selected Prayers, Hymns, Journal Notes, Sermons, Letters, and Treatises* (New York: Paulist Press, 1981), xiv-xv.

5. J. Ernest Rattenbury, *The Evangelical Doctrines of Charles Wesley's Hymns* (London: Epworth Press, 1941), 60.

6. *A Collection of Hymns for the Use of the People Called Methodists.*

7. Bernard L. Manning, *The Hymns of Wesley and Watts: Five Informal Papers* (London: Epworth Press, 1954), 14.

8. John M. Todd, *John Wesley and the Catholic Church* (London: Hodder and Stoughton, 1958), 26.

9. *The Works of Rev. Richard Watson* (London: John Mason, 1858), 7:430-32.

10. John Kirk, *The Mother of the Wesleys* (London: Charles H. Kelly, 1864).

11. Kirk, *Charles Wesley, the Poet of Methodism: A Lecture*, 8.

12. Ibid., 51.

13. Norman P. Goldhawk, *On Hymns and Hymnbooks* (London: Epworth Press, 1979), 42 ff.

14. *The Poetical Works of John and Charles Wesley*, 4:163-204. This work (*Hymns of Petition and Thanksgiving for the Promise of the Father*) was reprinted in popular form, with commentary by Timothy L. Smith, by Beacon Hill Press of Kansas City in 1982.

15. Maldwyn Edwards, "Prophet for All Time," *Methodist Recorder*, December —, 1957, no page, exact date not known.

16. Handley Moule, *Studies in Colossians* (London: Hodder and Stoughton, n.d.), 226-27.

17. Thomas S. Gregory, *Praises with Understanding* (London: Epworth Press, 1936), 9.

18. John Richard Green, *A Short History of the English People* (London: McMillan and Company, 1882), 718.

19. Preface to *A Collection of Hymns for the Use of the People Called Methodists*, in *The Works of John Wesley*, 14:252 ff.

20. Quoted from preface to *A Collection of Hymns for the Use of the People Called Methodists*.

21. Ibid.

22. *The Poetical Works of John and Charles Wesley*, 5:403.

23. *Standard Sermons of John Wesley*, 1:31-32.

24. *The Poetical Works of John and Charles Wesley*, 13:221.

25. *The Journal of Charles Wesley*, 1:417. See also *The Poetical Works of John and Charles Wesley*, 5:112; and *The Journal of John Wesley*, 2:202.

26. *The Poetical Works of John and Charles Wesley*, 1:92.

27. Albert D. Belden, *George Whitefield, the Awakener* (London: Banner of Truth Trust, 1970), 1:132.

28. *The Poetical Works of John and Charles Wesley*, 4:230-31.

29. Ibid., 3:3-5.

30. Ibid., 5:120-21.

31. Ibid., 9:446.

32. Gordon E. Rupp, *Principalities and Powers* (Cambridge, England: Cambridge University Press, 1952), 77-78.

33. *The Poetical Works of John and Charles Wesley*, 3:173-76.

34. *The Hymns of Wesley and Watts: Five Informal Papers*, 78; and *Representative Verse of Charles Wesley*, 37.

35. Quoted by John Telford, *The New Methodist Hymnbook Illustrated* (London: Epworth Press, 1934), 180 ff. See also the footnote in *The Poetical Works of John and Charles Wesley*, 2:173, and Jackson, *The Life of the Rev. Charles Wesley, M.A.*, 2:456-92.

36. Mary Champness, *Half-Hours with the Methodist Hymnbook* (London: Charles H. Kelly, n.d.), 18.

37. *The Poetical Works of John and Charles Wesley*, 3:71-73, emphasis added.

38. Ibid., 3-7, emphasis added.

39. Ibid., 21-23.

40. Ibid., 4.

41. Ibid., 4:372.

42. Ibid., 3:23, emphasis added.

43. Ibid., 4:275.

44. Ibid., 3:23.

45. Ibid., 1:301.

46. Ibid., 300.

47. Ibid., 3:87.

48. Ibid., 1:206.

49. *The Journal of Charles Wesley*, 1:87.

50. Ibid.

51. Ibid.

52. *The Poetical Works of John and Charles Wesley*, 4:205.

53. Ibid., 315-16.

54. Ibid., 1:6.
55. Ibid., 4:302-3.
56. *The Journal of Charles Wesley*, 1:324-25.
57. *The Poetical Works of John and Charles Wesley*, 4:237-38.
58. Ibid., 1:287-88.
59. Ibid., 4:371.
60. Ibid., 274-77.
61. Ibid., 212-14.
62. Ibid., 1:202-9.
63. Erik Routley, *Hymns and Human Life* (London: John Murray, 1952), 69.

Chapter 12

1. *The Journal of John Wesley*, 4:536.
2. *The Poetical Works of John and Charles Wesley*, 9:59.
3. Ibid., 2:243-44.
4. Ibid., 5:310-11.
5. Ibid., 11:45.
6. *The Letters of John Wesley*, 5:19-20.
7. *The Works of John Wesley*, 8:328-29.
8. *The Poetical Works of John and Charles Wesley*, 5:308-9.
9. Ibid., 309.
10. Ibid., 310.
11. Ibid., 5:313-14.
12. Ibid., 336.
13. John Wesley, *A Plain Account of Christian Perfection* (Kansas City: Beacon Hill Press of Kansas City, 1966), 47-50.
14. Ibid., 47.
15. Rattenbury, *The Evangelical Doctrines of Charles Wesley's Hymns*, 84.
16. *The Poetical Works of John and Charles Wesley*, 4:341-42.
17. Ibid., 8:371.
18. Ibid., 386.
19. Ibid., 2:74-75.
20. John Wesley, *A Plain Account of Christian Perfection*, 51.
21. A summation of John Wesley's equation of entire sanctification as perfect love. See *The Works of John Wesley*, 2:368.
22. Quoted in *The Poetical Works of John and Charles Wesley*, 9:vii.
23. Ibid.
24. Ibid., 409.

Chapter 13

1. Robert J. Paul, *The Atonement and the Sacraments* (London: Hodder and Stoughton, 1961), 359.
2. *The Poetical Works of John and Charles Wesley*, 225.
3. Hymn 623 in *A Collection of Hymns for the Use of the People Called Methodists*.
4. *The Poetical Works of John and Charles Wesley*, 3:216.
5. *The Journal of John Wesley*, 1:61; 3:434.
6. George J. Stevenson, *Memorials of the Wesley Family*, 167.
7. John R. Parris, *John Wesley's Doctrine of the Sacraments* (London: Epworth Press, 1963), 32-33.
8. Printed in full in W. E. Dutton's *The Eucharistic Manuals of John and Charles Wesley* (London, 1871) and J. Ernest Rattenbury's *The Eucharistic Hymns of John and Charles Wesley* (London: Epworth Press, 1941).
9. Dutton, *The Eucharistic Manuals of John and Charles Wesley*, 97.
10. Ibid., 114.
11. Ibid., 102.
12. Ibid.

13. Ibid., 220.
14. Ibid., 247.
15. Ibid., 137.
16. Ibid., 172.
17. Ibid., 125.
18. *The Works of John Wesley*, 10:121.
19. Ibid.
20. *The Poetical Works of John and Charles Wesley*, 3:338.
21. Ibid., 338-39.
22. *The Poetical Works of John and Charles Wesley*, 6:215.
23. *The Letters of John Wesley*, 4:272.
24. *The Works of John Wesley*, 2:335-36. See also Baker, *John Wesley and the Church of England*, 326-29.
25. Parris, *John Wesley's Doctrine of the Sacraments*, 80.
26. Edwards, *Sons to Samuel*, 79-80.
27. A. W. Harrison, *The Separation of Methodism from the Church of England* (London: Epworth Press, 1945), 12.
28. Ole E. Borgen, *John Wesley and the Sacraments* (Zurich, Switzerland, 1972). Assigned to author: Francis Asbury Press (Grand Rapids: Zondervan Publishing House, 1985), 152.
29. *The Works of John Wesley*, 13:476.
30. *The Letters of John Wesley*, 4:38-39.
31. *Standard Sermons of John Wesley*, 2:237.
32. *The Works of John Wesley*, 10:191.
33. *The Journal of Charles Wesley*, 1:192-93.
34. Ibid., 234.
35. Ibid., 414.
36. Ibid., 415.
37. Ibid., 2:16.
38. Ibid., 59.
39. Ibid.
40. Ibid., 71.
41. Ibid., 73.
42. Ibid., 81.
43. *The Poetical Works of John and Charles Wesley*, 10:322.
44. Ibid., 9:31.
45. Hymn 742 in *A Collection of Hymns for the Use of the People Called Methodists*. See also *The Poetical Works of John and Charles Wesley*, 11:119-20.
46. *The Poetical Works of John and Charles Wesley*, 10:445.
47. Ibid., 9:193.
48. Ibid., 1:283.
49. Ibid., 10:445-46.
50. Ibid., 5:40-44.

Chapter 14

1. Rattenbury, *The Evangelical Doctrines of Charles Wesley's Hymns*, 137.
2. *The Poetical Works of John and Charles Wesley*, 4:254-55.
3. William Ragsdale Cannon, *The Theology of John Wesley* (Nashville: Abingdon Press, 1946), 15.
4. Ibid., 53.
5. *The Journal of John Wesley*, 2:278.
6. Ibid., 347.
7. *The Poetical Works of John and Charles Wesley*, 7:204.
8. Ibid., 206.
9. Ibid., 208.
10. Ibid., 209.

11. Ibid., 7:210-11.

12. Ibid., 211.

13. Ibid., 214.

14. Ibid., 215-16.

15. Ibid., 218.

16. *The Poetical Works of John and Charles Wesley*, 1:183-84.

17. Ibid.

18. From *Whitefield's Hymn Book of 1737*. See Baker, *Representative Verse of Charles Wesley*, 12-14.

19. *The Poetical Works of John and Charles Wesley*, 4:107.

20. Ibid., 108-9.

21. Ibid., 109-10.

22. Ibid., 113-14.

23. Ibid., 116.

24. Ibid., 122-23.

25. Ibid., 125-26.

26. Gustav Aulen, *Christus Victor* (London: SPCK [Society for Promoting Christian Knowledge], 1931), 70-71.

27. *The Poetical Works of John and Charles Wesley*, 143-44.

28. I. H. Marshall, *The Work of Christ* (Exeter, England: Paternoster Press, 1981), 101.

29. Quoted by Thomas J. Crawford, *Doctrine of Scripture Respecting Atonement* (Edinburgh, Scotland: Blackwood, 1871), 127.

30. Colin W. Williams, *John Wesley's Theology Today* (London: Epworth Press, 1960), 87.

31. *The Works of John Wesley*, 10:81.

32. *The Poetical Works of John and Charles Wesley*, 5:30-32.

33. Ibid., 1:301.

34. Ibid., 13:252.

35. In his poetry and hymns, Charles Wesley often used "Jesus," "Jesu's," and "Jesus's" to fit the rhythm. The latter two are possessives. If he needed two syllables, he used "Jesu's." If he needed three, he used "Jesus's."

36. Ibid., 4:228.

37. Ibid., 1:278.

38. Ibid., 4:140-41.

39. Ibid., 140.

40. Ibid., 1:185-86.

41. Ibid., 3:228-29.

42. Ibid., 2:323-24.

43. Ibid., 8:110-11.

44. Ibid., 48-49.

45. Ibid., 13:126.

46. Ibid., 4:203-4.

47. Ibid., 165-66.

48. Rattenbury, *The Evangelical Doctrines of Charles Wesley's Hymns*, 180.

49. *The Poetical Works of John and Charles Wesley*, 7:248-49.

50. Ibid., 4:219-20.

51. Bett, *The Hymns of Methodism*, 126.

52. John Lawson in *The Wesley Hymns: A Guide to Scriptural Teaching* (Grand Rapids: Francis Asbury Press of Zondervan Publishing House, 1987) lists 43 scriptures.

53. *The Poetical Works of John and Charles Wesley*, 4:307.

54. Ibid., 196-97.

55. Ibid., 3:85.

56. Ibid., 86.

57. Ibid., 84.

58. Ibid., 84-85.

59. Ibid., 85.

60. Ibid., 88-89.

61. *The Journal of Charles Wesley*, 1:85.
62. Ibid.
63. Ibid.
64. *The Poetical Works of John and Charles Wesley*, 1:91.
65. Ibid., 5:24.
66. Ibid., 4:408.
67. G. Eayrs, W. J. Townsend, and H. B. Workman, eds., *A New History of Methodism* (London: Hodder and Stoughton, 1909), 1:305-6.
68. *Standard Sermons of John Wesley*, 203.
69. *The Journal of John Wesley*, 1:476.
70. Leslie F. Church, *The Early Methodist People* (London: Epworth Press, 1948), 19.
71. *The Poetical Works of John and Charles Wesley*, 1:106.
72. Ibid., 5:363.
73. Ibid., 365.
74. Ibid., 368.
75. Ibid., 363.
76. Ibid.
77. Ibid.
78. Ibid., 364.
79. Ibid.
80. Ibid.
81. Ibid., 364-65.
82. *The Poetical Works of John and Charles Wesley*, 13:66.
83. Ibid., 7:46-47.
84. Quoted in Telford, *New Methodist Hymnbook Illustrated*, 293.
85. Rattenbury, *The Evangelical Doctrines of Charles Wesley's Hymns*, 162.
86. *The Poetical Works of John and Charles Wesley*, 1:172.
87. Ibid., 2:277.
88. Ibid., 141.
89. *A Collection of Hymns for the Use of the People Called Methodists*, contents page.
90. *The Poetical Works of John and Charles Wesley*, 2:191.
91. Ibid., 6:143.
92. *The Journal of Charles Wesley*, 1:271.
93. Ibid.
94. *The Poetical Works of John and Charles Wesley*, 6:193.
95. *The Journal of Charles Wesley*, 2:325.
96. Ibid., 418-19, 423.
97. Ibid., 430.
98. *The Poetical Works of John and Charles Wesley*, 6:189-90.
99. Ibid., 4:316-17.
100. Ibid., 7:361-62.
101. Ibid., 369-70.
102. Ibid., 396.
103. *The Poetical Works of John and Charles Wesley*, 1:106.
104. Ibid., 11:65.
105. Ibid., 68.
106. Ibid., 68-69.
107. Ibid., 2:243-44.
108. Ibid., 6:94-95.
109. *The Journal of John Wesley*, 3:143-44.
110. *The Poetical Works of John and Charles Wesley*, 6:95.
111. Ibid.
112. Ibid., 79-80.
113. Ibid., 79.
114. Ibid., 4:272-73.
115. Ibid., 6:43.

116. Ibid., 44.
117. Ibid., 11:407-8.
118. Ibid., 1:258.
119. Ibid., 4:262-63.
120. Ibid., 5:50.
121. Ibid., 448-49.
122. Ibid., 6:427-28.
123. Ibid., 13:130.
124. Ibid., 9:60-61.
125. Ibid., 11:243.
126. Ibid.
127. Ibid., 245.
128. Ibid., 248.

Chapter 15

1. Louis F. Benson, *The English Hymn* (Richmond, Va.: John Knox Press, 1962), 241-42.
2. *The Journal of John Wesley*, 2:78-79.
3. From one of the Methodist hymn books of the early 19th century (exact source unknown).
4. From the preface to *Sacred Melody*, published in 1761. See *The Methodist Hymnal* (Nashville: Methodist Publishing House, 1964), viii.
5. *The Journal of John Wesley*, 5:281, 290; 6:307.
6. From the minutes of the 1746 Methodist conference.
7. *A Collection of Hymns for the Use of the People Called Methodists*, 7:766-69.
8. *The Poetical Works of John and Charles Wesley*, 5:63-64.
9. Ibid., 341-42.
10. Ibid., 9:140-41.
11. Erik Routley, Appendix II of *The Musical Wesleys* (Westport, Conn.: Greenwood Press, 1976), 250-53.
12. *The Journal of Charles Wesley*, 2:408-9.
13. Quoted by Lightwood, *Samuel Wesley, Musician: The Story of His Life*, 15.
14. Ibid., 15-16.
15. *The Journal of Charles Wesley*, 2:410.
16. Kirk, *Charles Wesley, the Poet of Methodism: A Lecture*, 43-44.
17. Ibid., 45-46.
18. *The Poetical Works of John and Charles Wesley*, 5:400.
19. Ibid.
20. For this, consult such works as Bett, *The Hymns of Methodism*, and Frederic C. Gill, *The Romantic Movement and Methodism* (London: Epworth Press, 1937).
21. *The Poetical Works of John and Charles Wesley*, 1:271.
22. Ibid.
23. From John Wesley's preface to *Sacred Melody*.
24. Eayrs, Townsend, and Workman, eds., *A New History of Methodism*, 1:557.
25. See *A New History of Methodism*, 557-62.

Epilogue

1. Whitehead, *The Life of the Rev. John Wesley, M.A., and The Life of the Rev. Charles Wesley, M.A.*, 227.
2. *The Poetical Works of John and Charles Wesley*, 8:432.
3. W. E. Henley, "Echoes," no. 35 of "In Memoriam Margaritae Sorori," in Arthur Quiller-Couch's *The Oxford Book of English Verse* (Oxford: Clarendon Press, 1939), 1028.
4. Baker, *Charles Wesley as Revealed by His Letters*, 377-78.
5. Whitehead, *The Life of the Rev. John Wesley, M.A., and The Life of the Rev. Charles Wesley, M.A.*, 227.

WORKS CITED

BOOKS

Albin, Thomas R. *Charles Wesley: Poet and Theologian*. Nashville: Abingdon Press, 1992.

Armstrong, Anthony. *The Church of England, the Methodist and Society*. London: University of London Press, 1973.

Aulen, Gustav. *Christus Victor*. London: SPCK (Society for Promoting Christian Knowledge), 1931.

Baker, Frank. *Charles Wesley as Revealed by His Letters*. London: Epworth Press, 1948.

———. *Charles Wesley's Verse*. London: Epworth Press, 1964.

———. *John Wesley and the Church of England*. London: Epworth Press, 1970.

———. *Representative Verse of Charles Wesley*. Nashville: Abingdon Press, 1962.

Belden, Albert D. *George Whitefield, the Awakener*. London: Banner of Truth Trust, 1970.

Benson, Louis F. *The English Hymn*. Richmond, Va.: John Knox Press, 1962.

Bett, Henry. *The Hymns of Methodism*. London: Epworth Press, 1945.

Borgen, Ole E. *John Wesley and the Sacraments*. Zurich, Switzerland, 1972. Assigned to author: Francis Asbury Press (Grand Rapids: Zondervan Publishing House, 1985).

Bunyan, John. *Pilgrim's Progress*. Westwood, N.J.: Barbour and Co., 1989.

Cannon, William Ragsdale. *The Theology of John Wesley*. Nashville: Abingdon Press, 1946.

Cell, G. Croft. *The Rediscovery of John Wesley*. New York: Henry Holt and Co., 1935.

Champness, Mary. *Half-Hours with the Methodist Hymnbook*. London: Charles H. Kelly, n.d.

Chiles, Robert E. *Theological Transition in American Methodism: 1790-1935*. Nashville: Abingdon Press, 1965.

Church, Leslie F. *The Early Methodist People*. London: Epworth Press, 1948.

———. *Oglethorpe: A Study of Philanthropy in England and Georgia*. London: Epworth Press, 1932.

Clarke, Adam. *The Holy Bible: Old and New Testaments, with Comments and Critical Notes*. Nashville: Abingdon Cokesbury Press, 1831.

———. *Memoirs of the Wesley Family*. New York: Lane and Scott, 1851.

Colson, Charles. *Life Sentence*. Lincoln, Va.: Chosen Books, 1979.

Crawford, Thomas J. *Doctrine of Scripture Respecting Atonement*. Edinburgh, Scotland: Blackwood, 1871.

Dimond, S. G. *The Psychology of the Methodist Revival*. London: Oxford University Press, 1926.

Dutton, W. E., ed. *The Eucharistic Manuals of John and Charles Wesley*. London, 1871.

Eayrs, G.; W. J. Townsend; and H. B. Workman, eds. *A New History of Methodism*. London: Hodder and Stoughton, 1909.

Edwards, Maldwyn. *Family Circle*. London: Epworth Press, 1949.

———. *Sons to Samuel*. London: Epworth Press, 1961.

Etheridge, Willie Snow. *Strange Fire*. New York: Vanguard Press, 1971.

Gill, Frederick C. *Charles Wesley: The First Methodist*. London: Lutterworth Press, 1964.

———. *The Romantic Movement and Methodism*. London: Epworth Press, 1937.

Gillies, Rev. John, comp. *Memoirs of the Life of the Rev. George Whitefield, M.A.* First edition. London: printed for Edward and Charles Dilley, 1772.

Goldhawk, Norman P. *On Hymns and Hymnbooks*. London: Epworth Press, 1979.

Green, John Richard. *A Short History of the English People*. London: McMillan and Co., 1882.

Green, V. H. H. *The Young Mr. Wesley*. London: Edwin Arnold, 1961.

Gregory, Thomas S. *Praises with Understanding*. London: Epworth Press, 1936.

Harrison, A. W. *The Separation of Methodism from the Church of England*. London: Epworth Press, 1945.

Hildebrandt, Franz; and Oliver Beckerlegge, eds. *A Collection of Hymns for the Use of the People Called Methodists*. Vol. 7 of *The Works of John Wesley*. Oxford: Clarendon Press, 1983.

Jackson, Thomas. *The Life of the Rev. Charles Wesley, M.A.* London: John Mason, 1841.

———, ed. *Memoirs of the Rev. Charles Wesley, M.A.* London: John Mason, 1848.

Jones, D. M. *Charles Wesley: A Study*. London: Epworth Press, n.d.

Kirk, John. *Charles Wesley, the Poet of Methodism: A Lecture*. London: Hamilton Adams Co., 1860.

———. *The Mother of the Wesleys*. London: Charles H. Kelly, 1864.

Lawson, John. *The Wesley Hymns: A Guide to Scriptural Teaching*. Grand Rapids: Francis Asbury Press of Zondervan Publishing House, 1987.

Lightwood, James T. *The Music of the Methodist Hymnbook*. London: Epworth Press, 1935.

———. *Samuel Wesley, Musician: The Story of His Life*. London: Epworth Press, 1937.

Manning, Bernard L. *The Hymns of Wesley and Watts: Five Informal Papers*. London: Epworth Press, 1954.

Marshall, I. H. *The Work of Christ*. Exeter, England: Paternoster Press, 1981.

Moule, Handley. *Studies in Colossians*. London: Hodder and Stoughton, n.d.

Oxford History of Music. London: Oxford University Press, 1905.

Paul, Robert J. *The Atonement and the Sacraments*. London: Hodder and Stoughton, 1961.

Peabody, William B. *Makers of American History*. New York: University Society, 1905.

Quiller-Couch, Arthur. *Hetty Wesley*. London: Dent, 1903.

———, ed. *The Oxford Book of English Verse*. Oxford: Clarendon Press, 1939.

Rattenbury, J. Ernest. *The Eucharistic Hymns of John and Charles Wesley*. London: Epworth Press, 1941.

———. *The Evangelical Doctrines of Charles Wesley's Hymns*. London: Epworth Press, 1941.

———. *Wesley's Legacy to the World*. London: Epworth Press, 1928.

Routley, Erik. *Hymns and Human Life*. London: John Murray, 1952.

———. *The Musical Wesleys*. Westport, Conn.: Greenwood Press, 1976.

Rupp, Gordon E. *Principalities and Powers*. Cambridge, England: Cambridge University Press, 1952.

Schmidt, Martin. *The Young Wesley*. London: Epworth Press, 1961.

Short, Roy H. *My Great Redeemer's Praise*. Nashville: Tidings, n.d.

Smith, Mrs. Richard. *The Life of Rev. Henry Moore*. New York, n.p., 1845.

Stevenson, George J. *Memorials of the Wesley Family*. London: S. W. Partridge Co., 1876.

Stevenson, Robert. *Patterns of Protestant Church Music*. Durham, N.C.: Duke University Press, 1953.

Sykes, Norman. *From Sheldon to Secker: Aspects of England Church History.* Cambridge, England: Cambridge University Press, 1974.

Telford, John. *The Life of Rev. Charles Wesley.* London: R.T.S. (Religious Tract Society), c. 1912-13.

———. *The New Methodist Hymnbook Illustrated.* London: Epworth Press, 1934.

Todd, John M. *John Wesley and the Catholic Church.* London: Hodder and Stoughton, 1958.

Tyerman, Luke. *The Life and Times of the Rev. John Wesley, M.A.* New York: Harper and Brothers, 1872.

Walker, A. K. *William Law, His Life and Work.* London: SPCK (Society for Promoting Christian Knowledge), 1973.

Waterhouse, Eric. *The Bible in Charles Wesley's Hymns.* Fellowship Manual No. 5. London: Epworth Press, c. 1954.

Watson, Richard. *The Works of Rev. Richard Watson.* London: John Mason, 1858.

Wesley, Charles. *The Journal of the Rev. Charles Wesley, M.A.* Kansas City: Beacon Hill Press of Kansas City, 1980.

———. *Wesley's Hymns.* London: John Mason, 1849.

Wesley, John. *The Journal of the Rev. John Wesley, M.A.* Ed. Nehemiah Curnock. London: Epworth Press, 1938.

———. *The Letters of John Wesley.* Ed. John Telford. London: Epworth Press, 1931.

———. *A Plain Account of Christian Perfection.* Kansas City: Beacon Hill Press of Kansas City, 1966.

———. *Sermons, 1-33.* Ed. Albert C. Outler. Vol. 1 of *The Works of John Wesley.* Nashville: Abingdon Press, 1984.

———. *Standard Sermons of John Wesley.* Ed. Edward H. Sugden. London: Epworth Press, 1921.

———. *Wesley's Notes upon the New Testament.* Kansas City: Beacon Hill Press of Kansas City, 1981.

———. *The Works of John Wesley.* Ed. Thomas Jackson. London, 1825-31.

Wesley, John and Charles. *The Poetical Works of John and Charles Wesley.* London: Wesleyan Methodist Conference Office, 1868-72.

Wesley, Samuel, Jr. *Poems on Several Occasions.* Cambridge, England: Cambridge University Press, 1743.

Whaling, Frank, ed. *John and Charles Wesley: Selected Prayers, Hymns, Journal Notes, Sermons, Letters, and Treatises.* New York: Paulist Press, 1981.

Whitefield, George. *George Whitefield's Journal.* London: Banner of Truth Trust, 1960.

Whitehead, John. *The Life of the Rev. John Wesley, M.A., and the Life of the Rev. Charles Wesley, M.A.* Two volumes in one. London: Stephen Cauchman, 1796.

Williams, Colin W. *John Wesley's Theology Today.* London: Epworth Press, 1960.

Wiseman, F. Luke. *Charles Wesley.* London: Epworth Press, 1932.

ARTICLES

Edwards, Maldwyn. "Prophet for All Time." *Methodist Recorder,* December —, 1957. Page number and exact date not known.

Wiseman, F. Luke. "All Saints Day: Suitable Hymns." *Methodist Recorder,* October 22, 1936.

HYMNBOOK

The Methodist Hymnal. Nashville: Methodist Publishing House, 1964.

INDEX OF PERSONS/SUBJECTS

VERSE INDEX
FIRST LINES/KEY LINES